HITTING
Military History Trail

VFW'S TRAVEL GUIDE TO BATTLEFIELDS, MUSEUMS & HISTORIC SITES

SO-ALM-282

MILITARY HISTORY TRAIL

By Shannon L.W. Hanson

PUBLISHED BY VETERANS OF FOREIGN WARS

Author and Editor: Shannon L.W. Hanson

Book Designer: Joseph C. Moran

Executive Editor: Richard K. Kolb

VFW Publications Department

406 West 34th Street, Suite 523

Kansas City, MO 64111

Phone: (816) 756-3390

Fax: 816-968-1169

E-Mail: shanson@vfw.org

Library of Congress Control Number: 2007931227

ISBN 978-0-9743643-3-9 9.95

ALSO PRODUCED BY VFW PUBLICATIONS:

Combat Action: Cambodia to the Balkans, 1975-1999 (2005)

Cold War Clashes: Confronting Communism, 1945-1991 (2004)

Battles of the Korean War: Americans Engage in Deadly Combat, 1950-1953 (2003)

Blaze in the Boondocks: Fighting on America's Imperial Frontier in the Philippines, 1899-1913 (2002)

Combat: America at War in the 20th Century (2001)

VFW: Our First Century, 1899-1999 (1999)

Faces of Victory: Europe—Liberating a Continent (1995)

Faces of Victory: Pacific—The Fall of the Rising Sun (1995)

SET COURSE

TABLE OF CONTENTS

The John Smith Statue and church tower at Historic Jamestowne, Jamestown, Va.

GET MOVING

Navigate 400 Years of Military History ...

When Richard Kolb, the editor of *VFW* magazine, decided to run a series of articles highlighting sites of military interest across the country, he didn't know what he was getting himself into.

After years of planning trips to military history sites, he thought it would be nice to have a single source—a travel "bible" for military history buffs—to consult when taking a vacation. His idea was reinforced after he actually visited sites and was disappointed, or pleasantly surprised, at what there was to see.

The 15-part series ran in the magazine about every other month from August 2003 through March 2006. It received such a positive response from VFW readers that we decided to publish the series in book form.

Now, after four years and hundreds of hours of research, phone calls and updates, the articles have been reformatted, updated and expanded. We've added a multitude of brilliant color photos, locator maps with numbered sites, profiles of famous veterans with their native states, "Did You Know?" fun facts, a recommended reading list and a helpful alphabetical index of the more than 900 sites the country has to offer.

Profiled are national parks and memorials, historic forts, Indian-settler conflict sites, military museums, homes of famous veterans and more.

We've done our best to indicate the historical significance of sites and battlefields, and what there is to see and do at each one. Museum listings include U.S. military, state and private museums, plus other institutions with significant military-themed exhibits. All sites, with one or two exceptions, also list the city in which they are located and a contact phone number.

This is the most up-to-date guidebook on the market, bar none. We have been perfecting the information through four years of natural disasters, relocations and restorations. We've tried to keep up with upcoming or current site renovations or closures, and expected reopening dates. But be sure to call the sites you're planning to visit and make sure they will be open.

The actions and events covered in this book span 400 years of history from the first fighting at Jamestown, Va., in May 1607, where our military traditions originated. Get ready to travel not only across the country, but back in time into our nation's history.

ALABAMA

Alabama hosted much of the fighting of the Creek War (1813-1814), which began as a civil war between the Creek Indian nation but soon engaged U.S. troops as well. The final battle of this conflict is now interpreted at Horseshoe Bend National Military Park. The Yellowhammer State also has a wealth of Civil War history, with four battle sites and three museums exhibiting information on the war.

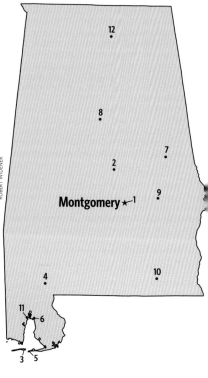

U.S. Army Aviation Museum, Fort Rucker (Daleville)

1. ALABAMA DEPARTMENT OF ARCHIVES & HISTORY MUSEUM
Montgomery, (334) 242-4363
Military gallery covers state military activities from 1702 to the present, with strong collections on Civil War and WWI.

2. CONFEDERATE MEMORIAL PARK
Marbury, (205) 755-1990
Site of Alabama's only Old Soldiers Home for Confederate Veterans, 1902-1939. Museum with exhibits on Civil War and history of the home.

3. FORT GAINES HISTORIC SITE
Dauphin Island
(251) 861-6992
1861 fort involved in Battle of Mobile Bay. Self-guided tours of 5-sided brick rampart with bastions, battlements and living quarters. Small museum contains Civil War artifacts.

4. FORT MIMS
Tensaw, (251) 937-9464
Site of August 1813 Creek Indian massacre of 247 militiamen and settlers that was the chief cause of the Creek War. Interpretive walkway with historical markers.

5. FORT MORGAN STATE HISTORIC SITE
Fort Morgan, (251) 540-5257
Constructed 1819-34. Surrendered after 1864 Battle of Mobile Bay and recommissioned for later wars. Historic brick fort remains in excellent condition and features self-guided walking tours, concrete gun batteries, officers housing and museum.

6. HISTORIC BLAKELY STATE PARK
Spanish Fort, (251) 626-0798
Site of last major battle of the Civil War, April 1865. 5 miles of pristine breastworks and Civil War fortifications can be seen along 8 miles of trails.

USS Alabama Battleship Memorial Park, Mobile

7. HORSESHOE BEND NATIONAL MILITARY PARK

Daviston, (256) 234-7111

Site of last battle of the Creek War of 1813-14 (War of 1812), March 1814. Visitor center, museum, 22-minute film on the battle, 3-mile loop road with interpretive markers and a 2.8-mile nature trail through battlefield.

8. SOUTHERN MUSEUM OF FLIGHT

Birmingham, (205) 833-8226

Military displays include Korea, Vietnam, Tuskegee Airmen, Birmingham airfields, Alabama Air National Guard, Medal of Honor recipients and outdoor aircraft.

9. TUSKEGEE AIRMEN NATIONAL HISTORIC SITE

Tuskegee, (334) 724-0922

Temporary visitor center houses exhibits and shows 5 historical films on Tuskegee Airmen (black pilots of WWII).

Horseshoe Bend National Military Park, Daviston

10. U.S. ARMY AVIATION MUSEUM

Fort Rucker (Daleville) (334) 255-2893

More than 160 military aircraft displayed in 70,000 square feet of exhibit space, including one of the largest collections of military helicopters in the world. Covers Army's involvement in aviation from the days of the Wright brothers to the present, with major exhibits on Korea, Vietnam and Persian Gulf War. Includes interactive exhibits and re-created scenes. Memorial for Vietnam War Army aviators.

11. USS ALABAMA BATTLESHIP MEMORIAL PARK

Mobile, (251) 433-2703

155-acre park features the *Alabama* and the submarine *USS Drum* (both open for tours), plus 24 historic aircraft and memorials to the Korean and Vietnam wars.

12. VETERANS MEMORIAL MUSEUM

Huntsville, (256) 883-3737

Displays include more than 30 historical military vehicles from WWI to the present, plus dioramas, artifacts and memorabilia dating back to the Revolutionary War.

DID YOU KNOW?

The famous command "Damn the torpedoes, full speed ahead" was made by Adm. David Farragut during the Battle of Mobile Bay, Aug. 5, 1864. (Fort Morgan)

ALASKA

Unbeknownst to many Americans, the Last Frontier was a site of fighting during WWII. The Japanese raided Dutch Harbor in Unalaska, June 2-4, 1942, sparking the Aleutian Campaign (including the Battle of Attu), which is interpreted at several sites in the state, including a national historic area.

> ❋   ❋   ❋
> **DID YOU KNOW?**
> In 1943, 152,000 of Alaska's 233,000 residents were members of the military stationed there during WWII.

₁**Juneau**

3

4

2

NATIONAL PARK SERVICE

Aleutian World War II National Historic Area, Unalaska

1. ALASKA STATE MUSEUM
Juneau, (907) 465-4826
Military artifacts relating to Alaska history after U.S. purchase in 1867. American and Japanese WWII military objects from the 1943 Aleutian campaign.

2. ALEUTIAN WORLD WAR II NATIONAL HISTORIC AREA
Unalaska, (907) 581-9944
Site of Japanese raid on Dutch Harbor, June 2-4, 1942, and center for history of WWII Aleutian campaign. Visitor center, memorial park, bunkers.

3. FORT ABERCROMBIE STATE HISTORICAL PARK
Kodiak, (907) 486-6339
Remnants of WWII military installations within 186-acre wooded park, including coastal defense guns and bunkers. Miller Point bunker houses **KODIAK MILITARY HISTORY MUSEUM.**

4. SITKA NATIONAL HISTORICAL PARK
Sitka, (907) 747-6281
Site of 1804 battle between Russians and Tlingit natives. Visitor center, Russian Bishop's House and tour trail.

ARIZONA

Much of the Grand Canyon State's military history revolves around Indian campaigns, especially those against the Apaches in the mid-to-late 1800s. Several sites capture these times through fort ruins and museums. The state also hosts the Pima Air and Space Museum, and the "airplane graveyard" — sites not to be missed by any fan of aviation.

NATIONAL PARK SERVICE

Fort Bowie National Historic Site, Bowie

1. ARIZONA MILITARY MUSEUM
Phoenix, (602) 267-2676
More than 25 displays covering arrival of Spanish Conquistadors through Persian Gulf War. Includes Arizona National Guard from 1865 to present, POWs/MIAs and research library.

2. ARIZONA WING OF THE COMMEMORATIVE AIR FORCE
Mesa, (480) 924-1940
Focuses primarily on WWII aviation, with aircraft, onboard equipment, weapons and ammunition, and crew survival equipment.

3. CANYON DE CHELLY NATIONAL MONUMENT
Chinle, (928) 674-5500
Site of Col. Kit Carson's controversial 1863-64 campaign against Navajos. Visitor center, museum focus on Southwestern Indian history.

4. FORT APACHE HISTORIC PARK
Fort Apache, (928) 338-1392
Closely involved with Apache campaigns from founding in 1870 until 1886 (attacked July 17, 1882). 288-acre site with more than 20 buildings dating from 1870s through 1930s. Guided or self-guided tours, prehistoric ruins, Apache Culture Center, re-created Apache village.

5. FORT BOWIE NATIONAL HISTORIC SITE
Bowie, (520) 847-2500
Site of July 1862 Battle of Apache Pass between Chiricahua Apaches (led by Cochise) and California Volunteers. Fort established to protect the pass and Apache Spring (vital way-station on Butterfield Overland Trail between St. Louis and San Francisco) from 1862 to 1894, 8 years after Apache leader Geronimo surrendered. 1.5-mile foot trail to adobe ruins, visitor center.

Titan Missile Museum,
Green Valley

Kinishba Ruins at Fort Apache Historic Park, Fort Apache

6. FORT HUACHUCA HISTORICAL MUSEUM

Fort Huachuca (Huachuca City), (520) 533-5736

Tells story of U.S. Army on Southwestern frontier. Displays cover Indian campaigns through WWII and more.

7. FORT LOWELL MUSEUM

Tucson, (520) 770-1473

Exhibits focus on mid-to-late-1800s Army life in the Southwest, with emphasis on campaigns against Apaches. Reconstructed buildings among fort ruins.

8. FORT VERDE STATE HISTORIC PARK

Camp Verde, (928) 567-3275

Served as staging base for military operations in surrounding countryside from 1865 to 1891. 3 historic house museums, officers quarters, interpretive exhibits, living history programs.

9. PICACHO PEAK STATE PARK

Picacho, (520) 466-3183

Site of Arizona's only Civil War battle—Picacho Pass—in April 1862. Historical markers, re-enactments.

10. PIMA AIR & SPACE MUSEUM

Tucson, (520) 574-0462

More than 250 aircraft on display over 80 acres of museum grounds. 5 hangars with aircraft, engines, models, interpretive exhibits and space gallery. Highlights include tram rides for outdoor aircraft, President Kennedy's Air Force One and SR-71 Blackbird spy plane. On the grounds, the **390TH MEMORIAL MUSEUM,** *(520) 574-0287,* honors WWII 390th Bombardment Group and includes restored B-17, Gen. James Doolittle exhibit, models, artifacts and library. Tours of **AEROSPACE MAINTENANCE & REGENERATION CENTER** ("Airplane Graveyard/ Boneyard") at Davis-Monthan AFB are available by reservation at *(520) 618-4800.*

11. TITAN MISSILE MUSEUM

Green Valley, (520) 625-7736

Only Titan II Intercontinental Ballistic Missile (ICBM) not dismantled and destroyed. Guided tours include 6-story view of missile in its silo, rocket engines, re-entry vehicle, launch control center and simulated missile launch.

12. TUBAC PRESIDIO STATE HISTORIC PARK

Tubac, (520) 398-2252

Spanish post that protected colonists from 1752 to 1776, and from 1787 to 1848, when it was attacked by Apaches and abandoned. Visitor center, museum, underground archaeological display of original structure.

13. U.S. ARMY INTELLIGENCE MUSEUM

Fort Huachuca (Huachuca City), (520) 533-3638

Traces art of U.S. Army intelligence, including Korea, Vietnam and human intelligence "tradecraft" artifacts.

ARKANSAS

Though the Revolutionary War did touch the Natural State—remembered at the Arkansas Post National Memorial—the state's primary war history is the Civil War. Five sites interpret battles of this war, including those from the Red River Campaign and the well-preserved Pea Ridge National Military Park.

Little Rock

NATIONAL PARK SERVICE

Arkansas Post National Memorial, Gillett

※ ※ ※
DID YOU KNOW?
In April 1783, the Colbert Raid, a skirmish between British partisans and American-sympathizing Spanish troops, occurred at Arkansas Post in Gillett. It was the westernmost battle of the Revolution.

1. ARKANSAS AIR MUSEUM
Fayetteville, (479) 521-4947
Exhibits, which include Vietnam-era Army helicopters and a Navy carrier fighter, are housed in 1940s-era aircraft hangar. Most planes maintained in flying condition.

2. ARKANSAS INLAND MARITIME MUSEUM
North Little Rock
(501) 371-8320
Tours of *USS Razorback's* seven watertight compartments tell the story of the submarine's wartime service, Cold War and Vietnam activities, and her service in the Turkish Navy.

3. ARKANSAS NATIONAL GUARD MUSEUM
North Little Rock
(501) 212-5215
Covers history of state units from territorial militia in 1804 to today's Army and Air Guard. Displays cover Americans at war from Mexican War through Persian Gulf War (except Vietnam), plus story of Camp Robinson.

4. ARKANSAS POST MUSEUM
Gillett, (870) 548-2634
5 buildings include local military memorabilia from Civil War through WWII.

5. ARKANSAS POST NATIONAL MEMORIAL
Gillett, (870) 548-2207
Site of 1783 "Colbert Incident," the state's only Revolutionary War action. Fort Hindman was built and destroyed at site during Civil War. Visitor center, exhibits, film, self-guided tours.

6. FORT SMITH NATIONAL HISTORIC SITE
Fort Smith, (479) 783-3961
One of the first military posts in Louisiana Territory, it enforced federal Indian policy, 1817-1896. Site includes remains of 2 forts and a federal court. Visitor center, exhibits, self-guided tours, walking trail with wayside exhibits.

USS Razorback. Arkansas Inland Maritime Museum, North Little Rock

Union General Samuel Curtis' coat on display at Pea Ridge National Military Park, Rogers

7. JACKSONVILLE MUSEUM OF MILITARY HISTORY

Jacksonville, (501) 241-1943
Features artifacts from Civil War, WWI, WWII and Vietnam, plus history of the Arkansas Ordnance Plant and Titan II missiles in Arkansas.

8. JENKIN'S FERRY STATE PARK

near Leola, (501) 844-4176
Site of April 1864 Union Red River Campaign battle. Interpretive markers. Exhibits and artifacts from battle in Grant County Museum in Sheridan, (870) 942-4496.

9. MACARTHUR MUSEUM OF ARKANSAS MILITARY HISTORY

Little Rock, (501) 376-4602
Formerly Little Rock Arsenal, was birthplace of Gen. Douglas MacArthur. Interprets state military history from territorial period to present. Exhibits include Arsenal's contribution to the Civil War, state's contribution to WWI and a WWII Gallery.

10. MARKS' MILLS STATE PARK

Fordyce, (501) 682-1191
Site of April 1864 Red River Campaign battle. Interpretive markers.

11. OLD STATE HOUSE MUSEUM

Little Rock, (501) 324-9685
The state museum houses a collection of Confederate battle flags.

12. PEA RIDGE NATIONAL MILITARY PARK

Rogers, (479) 451-8122
Site of March 1862 battle that gave the Union control of Missouri. One of the best-preserved Civil War battlefields. Visitor center, museum, reconstructed Elkhorn Tavern, 2 memorials, 7-mile self-guided driving tour and segment of "Trail of Tears."

13. POISON SPRING STATE PARK

Camden, (870) 685-2748
Site of April 1864 Red River Campaign battle. Interpretive markers, diorama.

14. PRAIRIE GROVE BATTLEFIELD STATE PARK

Prairie Grove, (479) 846-2990
Site of December 1862 battle. Visitor center, 19th century museum village, monument. Museum with diorama of battle, Civil War artifacts and displays on soldier life. One-mile walking trail, 6-mile driving tour.

CALIFORNIA

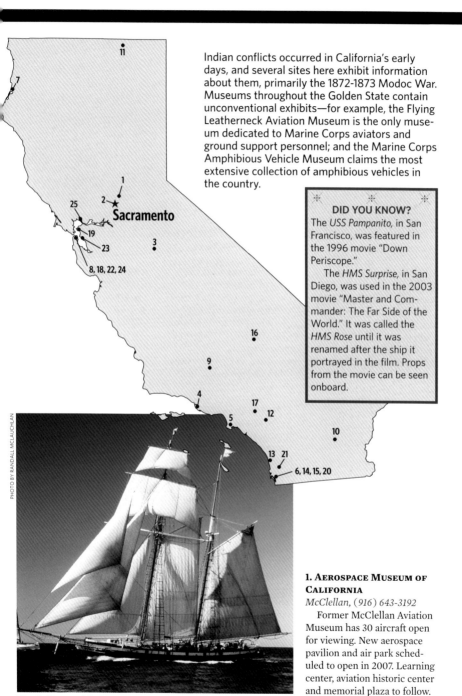

Indian conflicts occurred in California's early days, and several sites here exhibit information about them, primarily the 1872-1873 Modoc War. Museums throughout the Golden State contain unconventional exhibits—for example, the Flying Leatherneck Aviation Museum is the only museum dedicated to Marine Corps aviators and ground support personnel; and the Marine Corps Amphibious Vehicle Museum claims the most extensive collection of amphibious vehicles in the country.

> ### DID YOU KNOW?
> The *USS Pampanito,* in San Francisco, was featured in the 1996 movie "Down Periscope."
> The *HMS Surprise,* in San Diego, was used in the 2003 movie "Master and Commander: The Far Side of the World." It was called the *HMS Rose* until it was renamed after the ship it portrayed in the film. Props from the movie can be seen onboard.

PHOTO BY RANDALL MCLAUCHLAN

The *Californian,* Maritime Museum of San Diego

1. AEROSPACE MUSEUM OF CALIFORNIA
McClellan, (916) 643-3192

Former McClellan Aviation Museum has 30 aircraft open for viewing. New aerospace pavilion and air park scheduled to open in 2007. Learning center, aviation historic center and memorial plaza to follow.

Lava Beds National Monument, Tulelake

2. CALIFORNIA MILITARY MUSEUM

Sacramento, (916) 442-2883

3 floors covering state military history from Spanish California through U.S. peacekeeping mission in the Balkans. Extensive library and research center.

3. CASTLE AIR MUSEUM

Atwater, (209) 723-2178

Indoor Museum housed in converted WWII barracks building and features exhibits on Air Force history, including WWI, Tuskegee Airmen and WASPs. 47 WWII, Korean War and Vietnam aircraft on outdoor display.

4. CIVIL ENGINEERING CORPS/SEABEE MUSEUM

Naval Base Venture County (Port Hueneme) (805) 982-1249

Artifacts and memorabilia from history of CEC/Seabees, with extensive medal, uniform and arms exhibits. New U.S. Navy Seabee Museum will replace current museum in 2009.

5. DRUM BARRACKS CIVIL WAR MUSEUM

Wilmington, (310) 548-7509

Original junior officers quarters of Camp Drum is only Civil War-era U.S. Army building still standing in Southern California. Furnished rooms, camp model, weapons and artifacts.

6. FLYING LEATHERNECK AVIATION MUSEUM

San Diego, (877) 359-8762

Only museum dedicated to Marine Corps aviators and ground support personnel. Exhibits and artifacts cover history of Marine aviation, including nation's only exhibit on the history of women Marines. 25 vintage aircraft on outdoor display.

7. FORT HUMBOLDT STATE HISTORIC PARK

Eureka, (707) 445-6567

Served as a buffer between settlers and Indians from 1853 until 1870. Original post hospital houses museum with pre-Civil War military artifacts. Reconstructed surgeon's quarters.

8. FORT POINT NATIONAL HISTORIC SITE

San Francisco, (415) 556-1693

Coastal fortification at foot of Golden Gate Bridge built in 1850s to guard entrance to San Francisco Bay until 1886. Cannon-loading demonstrations, tours.

9. FORT TEJON STATE HISTORIC PARK

Lebec, (661) 248-6692

Manned 1854-64 to protect and control Indians on Sebastian Indian Reservation. Restored buildings, visitor center, museum.

10. GEORGE S. PATTON MEMORIAL MUSEUM

Chiriaco Summit (760) 227-3483

Exhibits display memorabilia from life and career of Gen. Patton and cover military life with focus on the Desert Training Center and WWII soldiers.

Battery Chamberlin in the Presidio, San Francisco

Captain Jack (Kintpuash)

❋   ❋   ❋

THE MODOC WAR

In 1864, the Modoc Indians signed a treaty agreeing to move to the Klamath Indian reservation. Unwilling to live with their traditional enemies, some Modocs, led by Captain Jack, left and returned to their native land. U.S. troops from Fort Klamath in Oregon were ordered to return the Modocs to the reservation. On the morning of Nov. 29, 1872, fighting broke out and a soldier was killed.

The victorious Modocs fled to the lava beds, where they took sanctuary in a protected area now known as Captain Jack's Stronghold.

The Army attacked Jan. 17, 1873, losing 35 men while the Modocs lost none. The group of some 50 Modocs held off the growing army—eventually up to 20 times larger—for more than 4 months.

During peace talks on April 11, 1873, Captain Jack shot and killed Gen. Edward Canby, while another Indian killed one of the other peace commissioners.

Captain Jack and his followers escaped, but were caught on June 4. They were convicted of murder and hanged at Fort Klamath on Oct. 3, 1873. Their graves are still on the grounds of the fort.

11. LAVA BEDS NATIONAL MONUMENT

Tulelake, (530) 667-2282, ext. 232

Includes Captain Jack's Stronghold (a natural fortress) from the 1872-73 Modoc War. The Historic Trail consists of 23 points of interest. Also, Thomas-Wright Battlefield and visitor center.

12. MARCH FIELD AIR MUSEUM

March ARB (Moreno Valley) (951) 697-6600

Housed in 26,800-sq.-ft. Hangar 1, displays cover history of March Field from 1918 to the present, with artifacts, more than 60 historic aircraft, films, library and a G-force flight simulator.

13. MARINE CORPS AMPHIBIOUS VEHICLE MUSEUM

Camp Pendleton (Oceanside) (760) 725-2418

Most extensive collection of amphibious vehicles in the country on outdoor display. More than 30 LVTs (Landing Vehicles, Tracked) dating from WWII through Vietnam.

14. MARINE CORPS RECRUIT DEPOT (MCRD) COMMAND MUSEUM

San Diego, (619) 524-6038

Exhibits in 22,200-sq.-ft. space include 6th Marine Division, Marine Raiders, weapons, the Recruit Depot, model of barracks, and medals and decorations. Marine Corps in War gallery covers WWI through Iraq.

15. MARITIME MUSEUM OF SAN DIEGO

San Diego, (619) 234-9153

HMS Surprise (formerly known as *HMS Rose* or Tall Ship Rose) is a 179-ft., full rigged replica of an 18th century Royal Navy frigate used in the Revolution. Onboard exhibits include artifacts, costumes, weapons and a re-created gun deck.

16. NAVAL MUSEUM OF ARMAMENT & TECHNOLOGY

China Lake (Ridgecrest) (760) 939-3511

Covers tactical air weaponry and technology from WWII rockets to today's guided missiles.

17. PLANES OF FAME AIR MUSEUM

Chino, (909) 597-3722

Specializes in military aviation, with WWII aircraft, vehicles and a working Sherman tank.

San Pasqual Battlefield State Historic Park, Escondido

USS Hornet, Alameda

20. SAN DIEGO AIR & SPACE MUSEUM
San Diego, (619) 234-8291
Includes galleries on WWI, WWII and the space age, plus classic military aircraft of WWII, Korea and Vietnam.

21. SAN PASQUAL BATTLEFIELD STATE HISTORIC PARK
Escondido, (760) 737-2201
Site of 1846 Mexican War clash with Spanish settlers. Visitor center, 3 memorials.

22. TROPHY ROOM MUSEUM
San Francisco (War Memorial Veterans Building)
(415) 861-4920
Small museum includes weapons, medals and insignia from various wars. Occasional special exhibits and DAR-provided docent tours. Call for days and hours.

23. USS HORNET
Alameda, (510) 521-8448
Guided and self-guided tours of WWII aircraft carrier.

24. USS PAMPANITO
San Francisco, (415) 775-1943
WWII submarine museum and memorial open for tours at Fisherman's Wharf. Nearby, WWII Liberty Ship **SS JEREMIAH O'BRIEN,** *(415) 544-0100,* is open for tours.

25. VALLEJO NAVAL & HISTORICAL MUSEUM
Vallejo, (707) 643-0077
5 galleries include history of naval shipyard at Mare Island—the first naval base in the western U.S.—with model of USS *Saginaw* bow, murals and a submarine periscope with views of the city.

18. PRESIDIO
San Francisco, (415) 561-4323
Military base from 1776-1994. 1,500-acre park features 470 historic structures dating back to 1861, coastal defense structures and ordnance, historic barracks, guided walks. Visitor center, San Francisco National Cemetery, memorial to missing of Pacific WWII.

19. ROSIE THE RIVETER/WWII HOME FRONT NATIONAL HISTORIC PARK
Richmond, (510) 236-7435
Tells story of local and national WWII home front experience. Visitor center, shipyard, *SS Red Oak Victory,* memorial, historic buildings.

✳   ✳   ✳
DID YOU KNOW?
The USS *Hornet* is reported to be haunted. More than 200 "sightings" have been reported since 1995.

COLORADO

Home to the U.S. Air Force Academy, the Centennial State features a number of aviation museums, including the Peterson Air & Space Museum on Peterson Air Force Base.

Travelers also can get a feel for the various Indian conflicts that took place in Colorado at sites such as Beecher Island Battlefield and the Fort Sedgwick Museum.

Air Force Academy Visitor Center, Colorado Springs

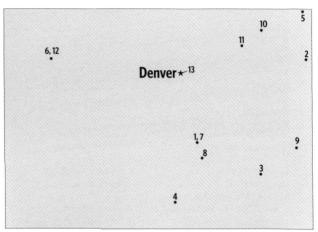

1. BARRY GOLDWATER AIR FORCE ACADEMY VISITOR CENTER
Colorado Springs
(719) 333-2990
Exhibit area features displays on academy history and cadet life with video and static displays.

2. BEECHER ISLAND BATTLEFIELD
Beecher Island, (970) 332-5063
Site of September 1868 battle between Col. George Forsyth's Scouts and Plains Indians. Monument, interpretive markers.

3. BENT'S OLD FORT NATIONAL HISTORIC SITE
La Junta, (719) 383-5010
Served as center for trade with Plains Indians and trappers, 1833-49. Staging base for Col. Stephen Kearny's Army of the West during Mexican War, 1846-48. Reconstructed adobe fort with furnished rooms, exhibits, information center and a film.

Bent's Old Fort National Historic Site, La Junta

4. FORT GARLAND MUSEUM
Fort Garland, (719) 379-3512
Adobe post established in 1858 to protect settlers in San Luis Valley. Last command of Col. Kit Carson. Museum exhibits include Carson's life and black troops during Indian wars. Restored fort, museum. Summers only.

5. FORT SEDGWICK MUSEUM
Julesburg, (970) 474-2061
Fort protected settlers and overland route to Denver, 1864-71. Attacked by southern Plains Indians in January 1865. Museum covers fort history.

Monument at Summit Springs Battlefield, near Atwood

6. MILK CREEK BATTLEFIELD

Meeker, (970) 878-9982

Site of 1879 battle between Maj. Thomas Thornburgh's troops and Ute Indians in which Thornburgh was killed. 2 monuments.

7. PETERSON AIR & SPACE MUSEUM

Peterson AFB (Colorado Springs), (719) 556-4915

Two buildings of exhibits cover air defense, history of the base and the North American Aerospace Defense Command (NORAD). Displays include WWII POWs, the WWII home front, model aircraft and Cheyenne Mountain. Airpark includes 16 aircraft and 4 missiles. Call at least 1 day in advance to arrange base access.

8. PUEBLO WEISBROD AIRCRAFT MUSEUM

Pueblo, (719) 948-9219

Features more than 20 aircraft on outdoor static display. Indoor displays in the International B-24 Memorial Museum include B-24 technical and design data, uniforms, airborne radio equipment, photographs and military aviation memorabilia.

9. SAND CREEK MASSACRE NATIONAL HISTORIC SITE

east of Eads, (719) 438-5916

Site of U.S. Army massacre of 150 Southern Cheyenne and Arapaho Indians, Nov. 29, 1864. New site is open weekends with ranger-led history talks.

10. SUMMIT SPRINGS BATTLEFIELD

near Atwood, (970) 522-3895

Site of July 1869 battle between 5th Cavalry and Cheyenne Indians. Last Plains Indian battle in Colorado. Relics from battle at Overland Trail Museum in Sterling. 2 monuments, 2 markers.

11. UNITED STATES MILITARY HISTORICAL MUSEUM

Fort Morgan, (970) 867-5520

Museum's 6,000 square feet cover Revolutionary through Persian Gulf wars. 5,000-sq.-ft. addition houses military vehicles, including Korean War jeep and Huey helicopter. Displays include 75 life-sized mannequins with uniforms, weapons, supplies and memorabilia. By appointment only.

12. WHITE RIVER MUSEUM

Meeker, (970) 878-9982

Exhibits include military uniforms from every branch dating back to WWI and Ute Indian uprising. Housed in original 1880 Army officer quarters.

13. WINGS OVER THE ROCKIES AIR & SPACE MUSEUM

Denver, (303) 360-5360

Seventeen military aircraft and special exhibits, including WWI uniform and memorabilia collection.

CONNECTICUT

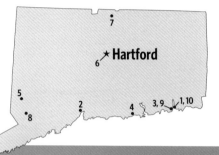

Revolutionary War enthusiasts will enjoy coverage of the Constitution State's colonial heritage. Other sites of note are the U.S. Coast Guard Museum and the U.S. Navy Submarine Force Museum.

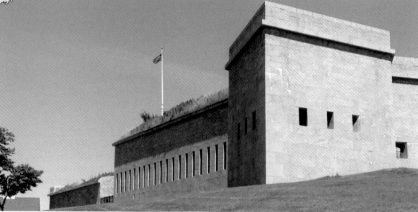

COURTESY JOHN HANRANHAN

Fort Trumbull State Park, New London

1. FORT GRISWOLD BATTLEFIELD STATE PARK
Groton, (860) 449-6877

Site of Sept. 6, 1781, Benedict Arnold-led massacre of 70 colonials. Earthwork fort with signage, guided tours in summer. Monument House with exhibits on massacre, 135-foot Groton Monument.

2. FORT NATHAN HALE
New Haven, (203) 946-6970

Site includes reconstructed wooden Revolutionary Black Rock Fort (attacked by British, July 5, 1779) and partially restored Civil War facility Fort Nathan Hale. Visitor booth, self-guided tours.

3. FORT TRUMBULL STATE PARK
New London, (860) 444-7591

1852 masonry fort operated through the Cold War. Features restored living quarters, mock laboratory, 1950s-era office, informational markers, cannon and artillery display, and gun emplacements. 4,500-sq.-ft. visitor center covers 225 years of military history from the Revolution to the Cold War through interactive exhibits, 3-D models, graphics and text panels. Themes include 1781 Ft. Griswold massacre, WWII U-Boats and Cold War anti-submarine efforts.

4. MILITARY HISTORIANS MUSEUM
Westbrook, (860) 399-9460

Contains one of the largest collections of military uniforms in the U.S. Exhibits on medals, awards and military bands, plus vehicles from WWII to the Persian Gulf War.

5. MILITARY MUSEUM OF SOUTHERN NEW ENGLAND
Danbury, (203) 790-9277

Galleries cover 10th Mountain Division, WWII life-size dioramas, heavy fighting vehicles and artillery pieces. Tanks, armored vehicles and artillery from WWII, Korea and Vietnam on outdoor display.

Putnam Memorial State Park, Redding

6. MUSEUM OF CONNECTICUT HISTORY
Hartford, (860) 757-6535

Military collection covers state's contributions to Revolutionary War through Persian Gulf War, including mementos preserved by Connecticut soldiers in the Civil War's Andersonville prison.

7. NEW ENGLAND AIR MUSEUM
Windsor Locks, (860) 623-3305

Military aircraft, vehicles, exhibits and artifacts focus on WWII.

8. PUTNAM MEMORIAL STATE PARK
Redding, (203) 938-2285

Site of Continental Army's 1779 winter encampment. Restored palisade and block-houses, museum, interpretive trail.

9. U.S. COAST GUARD MUSEUM
New London, (860) 444-8270

Located on grounds of U.S. Coast Guard Academy. Covers history of Coast Guard and Revenue-Cutter, Lighthouse and Life-Saving services.

10. U.S. NAVY SUBMARINE FORCE MUSEUM & USS NAUTILUS
Groton, (860) 694-3174

Only submarine museum operated by U.S. Navy. Traces sub development from Revolution to the present through models, films and equipment. More than 18,000 artifacts, 20,000 documents and 30,000 photos. Self-guided tours of world's first nuclear-powered submarine include replicas of torpedo room, attack center, control room, officer and crew living quarters, and dining areas.

U.S. Coast Guard Museum, New London

DELAWARE

Although the First State played a small role in the Revolutionary War compared to other northeastern states, it is home to the site of the Battle of Cooch's Bridge, which is said to be the first battle in which the Stars and Stripes was carried.

Fort Delaware State Park, Delaware City

1. AIR MOBILITY COMMAND MUSEUM
Dover AFB (Dover)
(302) 677-5938
Exhibits include WASPs, Korean War, Berlin Airlift, nose art, flight simulator, Tuskegee airmen, aircraft construction and Hall of Heroes. Aircraft on outdoor display.

2. BATTLE OF COOCH'S BRIDGE
Newark, (302) 655-7161
Site of September 1777 battle. The only Revolutionary War engagement in the state and said to be first battle in which the Stars & Stripes was carried. Marker, monument, cannon. Best view from tower in nearby Iron Hill Park.

3. DELAWARE HISTORY MUSEUM
Wilmington, (302) 656-0637
Distinctively Delaware exhibit features displays on state's role in Revolutionary War, including 1777 Battle of Cooch's Bridge, with interactive map and artifacts, plus section on Civil War with artifacts, artwork and videos.

4. FORT DELAWARE STATE PARK
Delaware City, (302) 834-7941
Site of 1813 earthwork and 1821 masonry forts. Standing 1859 granite fort once held Confederate POWs. Parade ground, officers quarters and mess hall remain. Orientation room with diorama, exhibits and artifacts. Accessible only by boat.

5. FORT DUPONT STATE PARK
Delaware City, (302) 834-7941
Fort active from Civil War through WWII. Earthworks, interpretive signs, WWI and WWII-era gun emplacements.

6. FORT MILES HISTORICAL AREA
Lewes (Cape Henlopen State Park), (302) 644-5007
WWII coastal defense fort features batteries, barracks and observation tower.

7. ZWAANENDAEL MUSEUM
Lewes, (302) 645-1148
Historic maritime and military artifacts dating from 1631 and including the British bombardment of Lewes during the War of 1812, and artifacts from a sunken British navy vessel.

21

FLORIDA

A heavy involvement in both the Second Seminole War and the Civil War makes the Sunshine State a rich source of military history. The 12 forts in this state include three Second Seminole War battle sites and the oldest masonry fort in the United States, the Castillo de San Marcos National Monument. Florida also is home to two nationally renowned museums—the Air Force Space & Missile Museum and the National Museum of Naval Aviation.

Air Force Space & Missile Museum, Cape Canaveral

1. AIR FORCE ARMAMENT MUSEUM

Eglin Air Force Base (Fort Walton Beach)
(850) 651-1808

Only U.S. museum dedicated to Air Force armaments. Exhibits include nearly 30 restored aircraft, plus missiles, bombs, rockets, weapons and a film on the history of Eglin AFB.

2. AIR FORCE SPACE & MISSILE MUSEUM

Cape Canaveral
(321) 853-9171

Covers U.S. space programs through missiles, rockets, models and exhibits. Features blockhouse and control rooms for Space Launch Complex 26, restored with much of original equipment, plus full-scale Explorer 1 model and "astro chimps" display. Exhibit hall includes displays on role of the Air Force in development of space exploration. 55 rockets on outdoor display.

3. CAMP BLANDING MUSEUM & MEMORIAL PARK

Starke, (904) 682-3196

Museum houses a refurbished WWII barracks and exhibits remembering the WWII training center. Florida Regimental Memorial includes roster of state National Guardsmen killed on duty. Memorial Park features monuments to various units, POWs and medal recipients.

Castillo de San Marcos National Monument, St. Augustine

4. CASTILLO DE SAN MARCOS NATIONAL MONUMENT

St. Augustine, (904) 829-6506

Oldest masonry fort in the U.S. (built 1672-95) and Spain's northernmost holding. Tours of original fort include rooms with exhibits tracing the fort's history, a video presentation on request, and living history demonstrations on weekends and holidays.

5. DADE BATTLEFIELD STATE HISTORIC SITE

Bushnell, (352) 793-4781

Site of December 1835 battle marking the beginning of the Second Seminole War (1835-42). Includes reproductions of log breastworks used in battle, monuments, visitor center with exhibits and artifacts, and interpretive trail marking the military road and battlefield.

Fort Caroline National Memorial, Jacksonville

6. FORT BARRANCAS (GULF ISLANDS NATIONAL SEASHORE)

Pensacola, (850) 455-5167

Built in 1839. Held by Confederates in 1861-62; exchanged fire with nearby Fort Pickens. Interpretive center with displays on the Civil War and coast artillery. Video and tours of fort.

7. FORT CAROLINE NATIONAL MEMORIAL

Jacksonville, (904) 641-7155

Site of French colony established in 1564. Captured by Spanish in 1565, attacked and burned by French in 1568. Reconstructed fort, visitor center with exhibits and interpretive trail.

> ✳ ✳ ✳
> **DID YOU KNOW?**
> During the Civil War, Fort Jefferson was used as a Union military prison for captured deserters. It also held 4 men convicted of complicity in Abraham Lincoln's assassination in 1865.

Fort Matanzas, St. Augustine

> ✳ ✳ ✳
> **DID YOU KNOW?**
> On Dec. 25, 1837, a force of 2,000 U.S. Army soldiers and Alabama Volunteers arrived 20 miles east of Orlando to construct a fort, which was aptly named Fort Christmas.

Fort Christmas, Christmas

8. FORT CHRISTMAS MUSEUM

Christmas, (407) 568-4149

Built in 1837-38 during the Second Seminole War. Reconstructed fort with 2 blockhouses containing exhibits on the Seminole Indian wars.

9. FORT CLINCH STATE PARK

Fernandina Beach (904) 277-7274

Brick and masonry fort was begun in 1847 but never completed. Preserved fort, visitor center, tours, monthly living history demonstrations.

10. FORT FOSTER STATE HISTORIC SITE (HILLSBOROUGH RIVER STATE PARK)

Thonotosassa, (813) 987-6771

Active 1836-38. Repeatedly attacked during the Second Seminole War. Reconstructed fort with seasonal guided tours, interpretive center with exhibits.

11. FORT GADSDEN HISTORIC SITE

Sumatra, (850) 643-2822

Built by British during War of 1812. Taken over by Indians and escaped slaves, and known as the "Negro fort." Attacked and destroyed in June 1816. Trenches and earthen outlines of old fort remain. Guided tours, interpretive signs.

12. FORT JEFFERSON NATIONAL MONUMENT (DRY TORTUGAS NATIONAL PARK)

Florida Keys (70 miles west of Key West), (305) 242-7700

Constructed between 1846-1876, but was never completed. Largest masonry fort in the Western Hemisphere. Visitor center with exhibits, brief audiovisual presentation, self-guided tours. Accessible by boat or air-taxi only.

13. FORT MATANZAS NATIONAL MONUMENT

St. Augustine, (904) 471-0116

Well-preserved masonry watchtower fort built by Spanish in 1740-42. Small visitor center with exhibits on fort's history and 8-minute video. Fort accessible by passenger ferry. Guided boat tours available.

Fort Jefferson, Florida Keys

14. FORT PICKENS (GULF ISLANDS NATIONAL SEASHORE)
Pensacola, (850) 934-2600
Active 1829-1947. Site of Battle of Santa Rosa, the state's first Civil War battle, in the fall of 1861. Visitor center, museum, tours.

15. FORT ZACHARY TAYLOR HISTORIC STATE PARK
Key West, (305) 292-6713
Built 1845-66 to prevent hostile invasion. Cannons and ammunition buried in the walls represent the largest collection of Civil War armaments in the U.S. Guided and self-guided tours.

16. HURLBURT FIELD MEMORIAL AIR PARK
Fort Walton Beach (850) 884-6507
Features 16 aircraft on display and 18 Air Force special operations memorials, including those to the Iran hostage rescue, Operation Just Cause, Southeast Asia and Medal of Honor recipients from WWI, WWII, Korea and Vietnam.

17. MUSEUM OF FLORIDA HISTORY
Tallahassee, (850) 245-6400
Contains military exhibits "Florida in the Civil War" and "Florida Remembers WWII," plus small amount of material on the Second Seminole War (1835-42).

18. MUSEUM OF FLORIDA'S MILITARY
St. Augustine, (904) 824-2872
Part of Oldest House Museum Complex. Covers Florida soldiers from 1560s through the present.

19. NATIONAL MUSEUM OF NAVAL AVIATION
Naval Air Station Pensacola (850) 452-3604
Traces development of U.S. naval aviation with more than 140 restored aircraft. Exhibits portray a WWII carrier hangar bay, a South Pacific Sea island forward Marine base and parts of the "Hanoi Hilton" Vietnam prison. Other displays include a flight deck replica of the *USS Cabot*, aircraft carrier models, Medal of Honor recipients and personal items of Navy POWs in Vietnam. IMAX theater presents films.

NATIONAL MUSEUM OF NAVAL AVIATION

National Museum of Naval Aviation, Pensacola

20. NATURAL BRIDGE BATTLEFIELD HISTORIC STATE PARK

Woodville (near Tallahassee)
(850) 922-6007

Site of March 1865 Civil War battle. Confederate monument outlining battle, interpretive plaques.

21. OLUSTEE BATTLEFIELD HISTORIC STATE PARK

Olustee, (386) 758-0400

Site of state's largest Civil War battle, February 1864. Interpretive center with artifacts, 1-mile interpretive trail and monuments to Union and Confederate armies.

22. SAN MARCOS DE APALACHE HISTORIC STATE PARK

St. Marks, (850) 925-6216

Fort construction began 1739. Traded hands between Spain, England, Creek Indians, Confederates and the U.S. from 1763-1861. Remains of fort and earthworks. Interpretive center, military cemetery.

23. SPECIAL OPERATIONS MEMORIAL

MacDill AFB (Tampa)
(813) 281-8791

Marble wall with engraved names of special ops personnel who risked or gave their lives in action, plus soldier statue.

24. T. T. WENTWORTH, JR. FLORIDA STATE MUSEUM

Pensacola, (850) 595-5985

"Civil War Soldiers" exhibit includes documents and artifacts covering Pensacola and northwest Florida experiences during the war.

25. UDT-SEAL MUSEUM

Fort Pierce, (772) 595-5845

Depicts history and development of Navy's UDT (Underwater Demolition Teams), SEALs (Sea, Air, Land teams), Naval Combat Demolition Units, Scouts and Raiders. Exhibits include Medals of Honor, WWII, Korea, Vietnam, Grenada, Panama and Persian Gulf War. Outdoor displays feature small landing craft, helicopter and Apollo training module.

26. VALIANT AIR COMMAND WARBIRD MUSEUM

Titusville, (321) 268-1941

Restores, maintains and displays military aircraft from WWI to present. 30,000-sq.-ft. hangar contains aircraft displays. 15,000-sq.-ft. area displays memorabilia of those who flew or maintained the aircraft.

GEORGIA

Much of the military history of the Peach State is defined by the Civil War. Confederate forts and historical sites abound, such as Andersonville National Historic Site, the war's deadliest prisoner of war camp and also the grounds of the National POW Museum. A new National Infantry Museum also is in the works.

1. ALLATOONA PASS BATTLEFIELD
Cartersville, (770) 387-1357
Site of October 1864 battle that began the Nashville Campaign. 2 earthen forts, miles of trench works and interpretive trail markers.

2. ANDERSONVILLE NATIONAL HISTORIC SITE
Andersonville, (229) 924-0343
One of the largest Confederate military prisons, built in 1864. Serves as a memorial to all American POWs. One corner and north gate of prison stockade have been rebuilt. Audio driving tour, interpretive programs, national cemetery.

THE NATIONAL PRISONER OF WAR MUSEUM honors all American POWs from Revolutionary War to the present. Exhibits cover aspects of the POW experience, including capture, living conditions, morale, escape and freedom. Features a 27-minute audiovisual program, letters and videotapes of prisoners' firsthand accounts, and personal items of prisoners at Andersonville.

Andersonville National Historic Site, Andersonville

3. ATLANTA CYCLORAMA
Atlanta, (404) 658-7625
360-degree painting of the Battle of Atlanta (358 feet circumference and 42 feet high) is viewed from a revolving platform as music, lighting, sound effects and narration tell the story. Located in Grant Park, which also contains a Civil War museum, Old Fort Walker and Civil War breastworks.

> ❋ ❋ ❋
> **DID YOU KNOW?**
> Andersonville Prison was the deadliest prisoner of war camp during the Civil War with a total of nearly 13,000 deaths. Some 40% of all Union prisoners of war who died during the Civil War perished at Andersonville.

PHOTO BY TOM BOARDMAN

DID YOU KNOW?
Union soldiers occupying Fort Pulaski played baseball to pass the time. One of the first photographs taken of the game of baseball was captured at Fort Pulaski in 1863.

Fort Pulaski National Monument, Savannah

COURTESY FORT KING GEORGE STATE HISTORIC SITE

Fort King George State Historic Site, Darien

4. ATLANTA HISTORY CENTER

Atlanta, (404) 814-4000

Features largest collection of Civil War artifacts in Georgia (one of 5 largest in U.S.), plus major WWII exhibit and model of *USS Atlanta*.

5. BRIER CREEK BATTLE SITE

Sylvania, (912) 564-7878

Site of March 1779 Revolutionary War battle. Breastworks, detailed historical marker on Brannen's Bridge Road at Brier Creek, 11 miles northeast of town.

6. CHICKAMAUGA & CHATTANOOGA NATIONAL MILITARY PARK

Fort Oglethorpe, Ga.;
Chattanooga, Tenn.
(706) 866-9241

Oldest and largest national military park. Contains sites of September 1863 Battle of Chickamauga—the war's bloodiest 2-day battle—and November 1863 Battle of Lookout Mountain near Chattanooga, Tenn. Park features more than 1,600 markers, monuments, cannons and tablets.

Chickamauga site features self-guided 7-mile loop tour and visitor center that houses museum with Civil War exhibits and Fuller gun collection (shoulder arms dating 1600-1918), plus multi-media presentation on the battle. Lookout Mountain site features Point Park Walking Tour, visitor center with 7-minute audio program, and tours, talks and demonstrations during the summer.

Chickamauga & Chattanooga National Military Park, Fort Oglethorpe, Ga., and Chattanooga, Tenn.

7. DRUMMER BOY CIVIL WAR MUSEUM

Andersonville, (229) 924-2558

Exhibits include uniforms, weapons, documents, photos and a large diorama depicting Andersonville prison and village.

8. FORT FREDERICA NATIONAL MONUMENT

St. Simons Island
(912) 638-3639

One of the most important British fortifications in America, established 1736. Fort ruins with wayside exhibits, visitor center with museum and 23-minute film. Nearby is site of 1742 Bloody Marsh battle, considered the first great decisive battle fought in the New World, with wayside exhibit.

9. FORT KING GEORGE STATE HISTORIC SITE

Darien, (912) 437-4770

First English settlement in the state (1721-36). Reconstructed earthen palisades, blockhouse, barracks and officers quarters. Museum interpreting Indian, Spanish and British occupation, living history demonstrations most weekends.

10. FORT MCALLISTER STATE HISTORIC PARK

Richmond Hill, (912) 727-2339

Best-preserved Confederate earthwork fortification in the U.S. Withstood multiple Union Navy attacks, but fell to land forces in December 1864. Self-guided tours and Civil War museum that features a video and exhibits on artillery and history of the fort.

11. FORT MORRIS STATE HISTORIC SITE

Midway, (912) 884-5999

Built in 1776. Attacked twice during Revolutionary War and active during War of 1812. Visitor center, museum, video presentation and walking tours.

12. FORT PULASKI NATIONAL MONUMENT

Savannah, (912) 786-5787

Built 1829-47. Attacked with experimental rifled cannon fire in April 1862, forcing a Confederate surrender. Visitor center with exhibits and 17-minute film, ranger-led talks and demonstrations, and self-guided tours.

13. FORT STEWART MUSEUM
Fort Stewart (Hinesville)
(912) 767-7885
Traces history of 3rd Infantry Division and the installation, and features exhibits on equipment and campaigns from WWI to the present.

14. FORT TYLER
West Point, (706) 645-8378
Site of Battle of West Point, the last Civil War battle east of the Mississippi, April 16, 1865, one week after the war's official end. Interpretive signs provide a detailed tour.

15. GEORGIA VETERANS MEMORIAL STATE PARK
Cordele, (229) 276-2371
Established as a memorial to all American veterans. Park includes a museum that houses artifacts from the Revolutionary War through the Persian Gulf War. Aircraft, armored vehicles and guns from WWI through Vietnam also on display.

16. KENNESAW MOUNTAIN NATIONAL BATTLEFIELD PARK
Kennesaw, (770) 427-4686
Site of June-July 1864 battle. Three battlefield areas include 17 miles of interpretive walking trails with earthworks, cannon emplacements, interpretive signs and maps, and 3 monuments. Visitor center features museum and a short film. Self-guided auto tour includes 4 stops with wayside exhibits.

17. KETTLE CREEK BATTLEFIELD
Washington, (706) 678-2013
Site of one of the most important Revolutionary War battles in Georgia, February 1779. Monument, historical marker and several marked graves.

National Infantry Museum, Fort Benning

18. MIGHTY EIGHTH AIR FORCE MUSEUM
Pooler (near Savannah)
(912) 748-8888
90,000 square feet of exhibits include a Nissen hut where visitors experience a simulated briefing, and a mission-experience theater that re-creates a bombing mission. Command Gallery exhibits cover specific jobs and duties of airmen, the unit's major WWII raids, and features dioramas of life in a POW camp and survivors who bailed out over enemy territory. Vintage aircraft also on display.

19. MUSEUM OF AVIATION
Warner Robins
(478) 926-6870
Second-largest Air Force museum. 200,000 square feet display 93 aircraft and hundreds of exhibits in four buildings and hangars. Exhibits include dioramas, 60-foot cutaway replica of a B-17 bomber, Tuskegee Airmen, 14th Air Force Flying Tigers, flight simulator, interactive theater and films.

Port Columbus National Civil War Naval Museum, Columbus

20. NATIONAL INFANTRY MUSEUM
Fort Benning (Columbus)
(706) 545-2958
30,000 square feet cover the evolution of the infantry from 1521 (Spanish colonial) through Afghanistan and Iraq. Exhibits include weapons, uniforms and personal equipment of both U.S. infantrymen and their enemies, including 1,500 firearms. Military art gallery and a variety of films shown daily. (A new National Infantry Museum and Soldier Center is being built.)

COURTESY GEORGIA COASTAL HISTORICAL SOCIETY

Old Fort Jackson, Savannah

21. OLD FORT JACKSON
Savannah, (912) 232-3945
Original fort built in 1740s. Standing brick fort (oldest in Georgia) built in early 1880s. Garrisoned during the Revolutionary War, War of 1812 and Civil War. Exhibits, living history demonstrations.

22. PICKETT'S MILL BATTLEFIELD HISTORIC SITE
Dallas, (770) 443-7850
Site of May 1864 battle. One of the best-preserved battlefields in the U.S. Visitor center includes video and interactive museum on the battle and the Atlanta Campaign. Site features earthworks, interpretive walking trails and living history programs.

23. PORT COLUMBUS NATIONAL CIVIL WAR NAVAL MUSEUM
Columbus, (706) 327-9798
40,000 square feet cover Civil War naval history, including remains and re-creations of 5 ships and a multi-media show depicting battle aboard an ironclad.

24. SAVANNAH HISTORY MUSEUM
Savannah, (912) 651-6825
Stands on site of 1779 Revolutionary War Battle of Savannah and includes exhibits on the battle and siege.

25. SOUTHERN MUSEUM OF CIVIL WAR & LOCOMOTIVE HISTORY
Kennesaw, (770) 427-2117
Covers the role of railroad in the Civil War, soldier and citizen life, and the April 1862 Great Locomotive Chase, in which Union spies stole a Confederate train.

26. ST. MARY'S SUBMARINE MUSEUM
St. Mary's, (912) 882-2782
Displays items from U.S. and foreign military submarines, models and an operating, hands-on periscope.

27. U.S. ARMY SIGNAL CORPS MUSEUM
Fort Gordon (Augusta)
(706) 791-3856
Covers development of Signal Corps from its beginning in 1860. Exhibits cover circa-1870 meteorological office, Spanish-American War, trench warfare, Cold War, Vietnam POWs, Persian Gulf War and Signal Corps equipment.

28. U.S. NAVY SUPPLY CORPS MUSEUM
Athens, (706) 354-4111
Displays include *USS Supply*, artifacts from the *USS Maine* and ship models.

HAWAII

It comes as no surprise that most sites of military interest in the Aloha State focus heavily on WWII, including the *USS Arizona* Memorial, which commemorates the infamous attack on Pearl Harbor, and the Pacific Aviation Museum. Also of interest is the Nu'uanu Pali State Wayside, the site of a grisly 1795 battle between Polynesian King Kamehameha's forces and Oahu armies.

USS Arizona Memorial, Honolulu

> ✳   ✳   ✳
> **DID YOU KNOW?**
> Kahoolawe island range was once used as a target by the U.S. Navy and Air Force. Due to unexploded shells, no one is allowed ashore without permission.

Nu'uanu Pali State Wayside, Honolulu

1. BATTLESHIP MISSOURI MEMORIAL
Honolulu, 1-877-644-4896 (Foundation)

Ship tours include orientation center with video, surrender deck, and exhibits on life at sea and WWII era. Several guided tours available.

2. NATIONAL MEMORIAL CEMETERY OF THE PACIFIC (PUNCHBOWL)
Honolulu, (808) 532-3720

More than 33,000 gravesites. Honolulu Memorial inscribed with names of MIAs from Vietnam, Korea and WWII Pacific Theater (other than Southwest).

3. NU'UANU PALI STATE WAYSIDE
Honolulu, (808) 587-0300

Site of gruesome 1795 battle when King Kamehameha forced Oahu armies over steep cliffs to their deaths, uniting the Hawaiian Islands. One of the best views on Oahu. 2 plaques commemorate the battle and remains.

National Memorial Cemetery of the Pacific (Punchbowl), Honolulu

4. PACIFIC AVIATION MUSEUM
Ford Island (Honolulu)
(808) 836-7747

Hangar 37 covers attack on Pearl Harbor with a film, dioramas, aircraft, artifacts, re-created debris field and nine WWII aircraft. Hangars 79 and 54 are scheduled to open by 2009 and will cover the story of the WWII air war, Korea, Vietnam and the Cold War. Exhibits will include the major theaters of the Pacific war, a full-scale replica of a WWII aircraft carrier deck, technological advances in aviation since WWII and a re-created portion of the Hanoi Hilton.

5. PACIFIC SUBMARINE MUSEUM & USS BOWFIN MEMORIAL
Honolulu, (808) 423-1341

Submarine artifacts and submarine-service memorabilia from WWI through post-WWII era. WWII sub *USS Bowfin* available for self-guided tours. Japanese Kaiten "Human Torpedo" on display.

6. TROPIC LIGHTNING MUSEUM
Schofield Barracks (Honolulu)
(808) 655-0438

History of Schofield Barracks and 25th Infantry Division. Relics from wars of 20th century, emphasizing WWII through Vietnam.

7. U.S. ARMY MUSEUM OF HAWAII
Fort DeRussy (Honolulu)
(808) 438-2821

Covers state military history from 1775 to present, with emphasis on Army in Pacific and coast-defense artillery from 1898 to present.

8. USS ARIZONA MEMORIAL
Honolulu, (808) 422-2771

Commemorates Americans killed during 1941 Japanese attack on Pearl Harbor, with names of men from the battleship who died.

Lies over hull of the sunken ship. Accessible by boat. On-shore visitor center. Nearby *USS Utah* also available to see with special requirements.

IDAHO

In the late 1800s, several key Indian battles took place in the Gem State, as seen at Nez Perce National Historical Park, home to 38 historic sites (in four states) pertaining to war and the Nez Perce Indians. A driving tour of the original 24 sites of the park covers some 400 miles of northeast Idaho.

White Bird Battlefield overlook, Nez Perce National Historical Park, Grangeville

1. FARRAGUT STATE PARK
Athol, (208) 683-2425
Site of world's second-largest naval training center in 1940s. Exhibits on training station's role in WWII.

2. FORT SHERMAN MUSEUM
Coeur d'Alene, (208) 664-3448
Consists of 3 original buildings from 1880s-era fort with exhibits in former magazine.

3. IDAHO HISTORICAL MUSEUM
Boise, (208) 334-2120
Includes exhibits on Fort Boise and Boise Barracks (1863-1903) and changing exhibits on military history and firearms.

4. IDAHO MILITARY HISTORY MUSEUM
Boise, (208) 272-4841
Covers state military history, including Idaho Army National Guard involvement from Philippines War through Persian Gulf War. Features uniforms, field gear, firearms and vehicles.

Warhawk Air Museum, Nampa

Idaho Historical Museum, Boise

Old Idaho Penitentiary State Historic Site, Boise

Fort Farragut State Park, Athol

5. NEZ PERCE NATIONAL HISTORICAL PARK
Spalding, (208) 843-2261

Consists of 38 historic sites in 4 states relating to Nez Perce Indians and war. Park headquarters has exhibits of Nez Perce culture and area history. Self-guided driving tour of sites includes:

CLEARWATER BATTLEFIELD
Stites. Fought July 1877. Interpreted at roadside pullout on Highway 13. Panoramic view from Battle Ridge Road.

WHITE BIRD BATTLEFIELD
Grangeville. Fought June 1877. Interpretive shelter with exhibit panels overlooks battlefield from Highway 95. Interpretive trail onto battlefield.

6. OLD IDAHO PENITENTIARY STATE HISTORIC SITE
Boise, (208) 334-2844

J. Curtis Earl Memorial Exhibit features more than 5,000 square feet of historic arms and military memorabilia, including dioramas of a WWI trench and WWII European and Pacific action, weapons from countries involved in both world wars, Revolutionary War firearms, Civil War artifacts and items from American POWs captured at Wake Island.

7. WARHAWK AIR MUSEUM
Nampa, (208) 465-6446

Private museum preserves WWII and aviation history.

✳   ✳   ✳
DID YOU KNOW?
Bayview, Idaho, is home to the Navy's Acoustic Research Detachment test facility, the only large-scale model submarine acoustic testing facility in the world.

A fleet of remote-controlled, 88-foot-long model submarines navigate the deep waters of Lake Pend Oreille in the Naval Surface Warfare Center's continuing quest for the quietest sub.

ILLINOIS

The Prairie State is the birthplace of the Grand Army of the Republic (GAR), an organization for veterans of the Union Army founded in Decatur. Museums commemorate its founder and the organization. Illinois also is home to three 18th century forts, as well as many specialized museums, such as the Rock Island Arsenal Museum, the second oldest in the U.S. Army museum system. The private First Division Museum at Cantigny (in Wheaton) is a prime attraction.

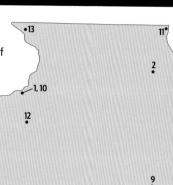

First Division Museum at Cantigny, Wheaton

© CANTIGNY FIRST DIVISION FOUNDATION

1. BLACK HAWK STATE HISTORIC SITE
Rock Island, (309) 788-9536
Site of westernmost battle of Revolutionary War at Saukenak in 1780. Descriptive plaque.

2. FIRST DIVISION MUSEUM AT CANTIGNY
Wheaton, (630) 668-5185
38,000-sq.-ft. facility honors the "Big Red One," including 10,000 square feet of interactive dioramas and re-created scenes—WWI, WWII, Cold War, Vietnam and Persian Gulf. Features maps, photographs, video, archives and outdoor tank park.

3. FORT DE CHARTRES STATE HISTORIC SITE
Prairie du Rocher
(618) 284-7230
French fort, 1720-1763. British garrison, 1765-72. Restored 1750 stone buildings, museum, interpretive center.

4. FORT KASKASKIA STATE HISTORIC SITE
Ellis Grove, (618) 859-3741
British fort until captured by Americans in 1778. Remains of earthworks and timber fort, self-guided tours, "Liberty Bell of the West."

Rock Island Arsenal Museum, Rock Island

5. FORT MASSAC STATE PARK
Metropolis, (618) 524-4712
1757 fort withstood Cherokee attack, was burned by Chickasaws, was rebuilt in 1794 and used until 1814. Reconstructed timber fort, museum with artifacts, costumes, photographs and video.

6. GENERAL JOHN A. LOGAN MUSEUM
Murphysboro, (618) 684-3455
Tells story of leader of Grand Army of the Republic and founder of Memorial Day through photographs, portraits, maps, political memorabilia, family antiques and Civil War weapons.

7. GRAND ARMY OF THE REPUBLIC (GAR) MEMORIAL MUSEUM
Springfield, (217) 522-4373
Tells the GAR story with encampment and Civil War memorabilia.

8. ILLINOIS STATE MILITARY MUSEUM
Springfield, (217) 761-3910
Covers history of state volunteers, militia and National Guard from 1809 to present. Collections include vehicles, aircraft, weapons, flags, uniforms, photographs and documents.

9. OCTAVE CHANUTE AEROSPACE MUSEUM
Rantoul, (217) 893-1613
Military exhibits include 8th Air Force memorial, Korean War, Military Aviation Hall of Fame of Illinois, Hall of WWII Allied Escape and Evasion Societies, and POWs/MIAs.

10. ROCK ISLAND ARSENAL MUSEUM
Rock Island, (309) 782-5021
Second-oldest U.S. Army museum (1905). Interprets history of Fort Armstrong, Black Hawk War and Confederate prison camp. 1,100 military firearms on display.

11. RUSSELL MILITARY MUSEUM
Zion, (262) 857-3418
Primarily outdoor museum features many vehicles and equipment on outdoor display, including a CH-54 Skycrane, C-130 Hercules, M-4 Sherman tanks, Vietnam-era river patrol boats, Huey helicopter and 2 HH-3 heavy lift helicopters.

DID YOU KNOW?
The "Liberty Bell of the West" at Fort Kaskaskia was cast in 1741 by King Louis XV of France as a gift to the people of the Illinois country. The village of Kaskaskia was ceded to Great Britain in 1763 and was under British rule until the Revolutionary War, when American Col. George Rogers Clark captured the town in a nighttime raid.
The next day, July 4, 1778, the villagers rang the bell to celebrate their liberation, and the bell became known as the "Liberty Bell of the West."

12. STOCKDALE SOLDIER CITIZEN MUSEUM
Galesburg, (309) 342-1181
Houses artifacts of Illinois National Guard from War of 1812 through Persian Gulf War.

13. ULYSSES S. GRANT HOME STATE HISTORIC SITE
Galena, (815) 777-0248
Contains many of Grant's possessions and original furnishings.

Santa Ana's leg at the Illinois State Military Museum, Springfield

37

INDIANA

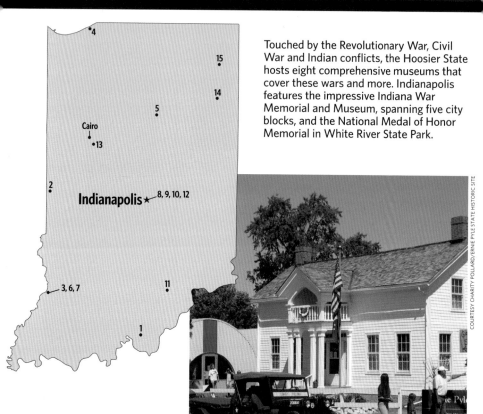

4

15

14

5

Cairo
• 13

2

Indianapolis ★ — 8, 9, 10, 12

3, 6, 7

11

1

Touched by the Revolutionary War, Civil War and Indian conflicts, the Hoosier State hosts eight comprehensive museums that cover these wars and more. Indianapolis features the impressive Indiana War Memorial and Museum, spanning five city blocks, and the National Medal of Honor Memorial in White River State Park.

COURTESY CHARITY POLLARD/ERNIE PYLE STATE HISTORIC SITE

Ernie Pyle State Historic Site, Dana

1. BATTLE OF CORYDON MEMORIAL PARK
Corydon, (812) 738-2137
Site of Indiana's only Civil War battle, July 9, 1863. Period cabin, cannon, memorials listing names of those killed.

2. ERNIE PYLE STATE HISTORIC SITE
Dana, (765) 665-3633
Restored farmhouse where he was born highlights life and career of Pulitzer Prize-winning newspaper correspondent during WWII. 2 Quonset huts serve as visitor center, with multi-media exhibits, life-size scenes interpreting Pyle's wartime experiences, and memorabilia.

3. GEORGE ROGERS CLARK NATIONAL HISTORICAL PARK
Vincennes, (812) 882-1776, ext. 110
Granite and marble memorial building commemorates George Rogers Clark campaign during the Revolutionary War. Visitor center, exhibits, 23-minute film.

4. GREAT LAKES MUSEUM OF MILITARY HISTORY
Michigan City, (219) 872-2702
15,000 square feet feature more than 5,000 items from Revolutionary War to present, including memorabilia, uniforms and medals.

5. GRISSOM AIR MUSEUM
Peru, (765) 689-8011
Covers WWII through Persian Gulf War with wide range of exhibits.

Indiana World War Memorial and Museum, Indianapolis

6. GROUSELAND

Vincennes, (812) 882-2096

Georgian home of war hero and President William Henry Harrison.

7. INDIANA MILITARY MUSEUM

Vincennes, (812) 882-8668

Covers Civil War through Persian Gulf War. Displays include George Field Army Air Forces Base, *USS Vincennes*, D-Day and POWs, plus battlefield relics and captured enemy souvenirs. Tanks, artillery and helicopters on outdoor display.

8. INDIANA STATE MUSEUM

Indianapolis, (317) 232-1637

Five cultural history galleries include military displays on George Rogers Clark at Fort Sackville in 1779, Battle of Tippecanoe in 1811, Civil War, WWI, WWII and Vietnam, plus scale models of *USS Indiana* and *USS Indianapolis*.

DID YOU KNOW?

North of West Lafayette, in the nearly abandoned town of Cairo, stands an old wooden watchtower that was used to watch for Soviet bombers during the Korean War.

It was the first of some 20,000 nationwide to be commissioned by the Air Force. The tower was manned 24 hours a day for over a year by some 90 volunteers, who rotated in 2-hour shifts. A monument and historical marker also are on site.

National Medal of Honor Memorial, Indianapolis

9. INDIANA WORLD WAR MEMORIAL & MUSEUM
Indianapolis, (317) 232-7615
Plaza of 5 city blocks with cenotaph honoring state's war dead, 100-ft. obelisk and memorial building. Museum covers history of Indiana veterans since 1811.

10. NATIONAL MEDAL OF HONOR MEMORIAL
Indianapolis (*White River State Park*), (317) 233-2434
3,410 recipient names are etched on 27 walls of curved glass, representing wars since the Civil War.

11. PIGEON ROOST STATE HISTORIC SITE
Scottsburg, (812) 265-3526
Site of massacre by Shawnee Indians prior to the War of 1812—the last Indian raid in the state. Obelisk monument, interpretive marker.

12. SOLDIERS' & SAILORS' MONUMENT
Indianapolis (*on War Memorial Plaza*) (317) 232-7615
284-ft. high monument dedicated in 1902 to commemorate Indiana war dead from 1776-1865. Col. Eli Lilly Civil War Museum chronicles experiences of Indiana residents.

13. TIPPECANOE BATTLEFIELD
Battle Ground, (765) 567-2147
Site of famous 1811 battle with Indians. 85-ft. marble obelisk, interpretive center museum with exhibits, audiovisual presentations and fiber-optic map of battle.

14. VETERANS NATIONAL MEMORIAL SHRINE
Fort Wayne, (260) 625-4944
Memorial dedicated to all U.S. war veterans. Museum includes more than 5,000 military artifacts from the Civil War to the present.

15. WORLD WAR II VICTORY MUSEUM
Auburn, (260) 927-9144
90,000 square feet display one of world's largest WWII artifact collections.

IOWA

Many Union soldiers during the Civil War hailed from the Hawkeye State, and a history of this participation along with the state's involvement in the Civil War can be seen at the State Historical Society of Iowa Museum. Three military forts, including Fort Madison, a site repeatedly attacked by Indians in 1812-13, also offer insight into frontier fort life.

Abbie Gardner Cabin State Historic Site, Arnolds Park

> ✴ ✴ ✴
> **DID YOU KNOW?**
> Fort Atkinson was the only fort ever built by the U.S. government to protect one Indian tribe from another. It guarded the relocated Winnebago tribe from the Sioux, Sauk and Fox tribes in the area.

1. ABBIE GARDNER CABIN STATE HISTORIC SITE
Arnolds Park, (712) 332-7248
Site of 1857 Spirit Lake Massacre, the bloodiest massacre in Iowa history. Cabin, interpretive center, graves, historic markers, monument.

2. FORT ATKINSON STATE PRESERVE
Fort Atkinson, (563) 425-4161
Active 1840-49. Reconstructed fort, museum.

3. FORT DODGE MUSEUM & FRONTIER VILLAGE
Fort Dodge, (515) 573-4231
Active 1850-1853. Reconstructed fort and museum with artifacts from Indian campaigns through WWII.

4. HISTORIC GENERAL DODGE HOUSE
Council Bluffs, (712) 322-2406
Restored 1869 residence of Civil War engineer general and railroad builder Grenville M. Dodge.

5. IOWA GOLD STAR MUSEUM
Johnston, (515) 252-4531
Covers state military history from 1846 to present, including service of residents. Uniforms, flags, medals, scale models and howitzers. Vehicles and aircraft from 1940 to present on outdoor display.

6. OLD FORT MADISON
Fort Madison, (319) 372-6318
First military post on upper Mississippi River, 1808-13. Attacked repeatedly by Indians. Reconstructed fort with 6 furnished structures, and costumed interpreters.

7. STATE HISTORICAL SOCIETY OF IOWA MUSEUM
Des Moines, (515) 281-6412
More than 350 artifacts—weapons, uniforms, artillery and battle flags—pertaining to Iowans' role in the Civil War.

KANSAS

Seven years before the Civil War broke out, Kansas and Missouri experienced their own vicious border war between anti-slavery and pro-slavery factions. Various sites in the Sunflower State commemorate these battles, including the Marais des Cygnes Massacre State Historic Site. In addition, two military museums on Fort Riley (including the U.S. Cavalry Museum) and the one-of-a-kind Frontier Army Museum on Fort Leavenworth stand out.

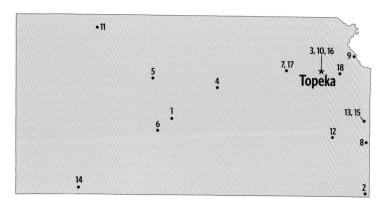

1. B-29 MEMORIAL PLAZA
Great Bend, (620) 792-9251
Tours of WWII-era Great Bend Airfield available by appointment.

2. BAXTER SPRINGS HERITAGE CENTER & MUSEUM
Baxter Springs, (620) 856-2385
Extensive Civil War display, including cannon, replication of Fort Blair on actual site, October 1863 Baxter Springs Massacre by William Quantrill, and driving tour showing events of massacre.

Fort Larned National Historic Site, Larned

3. COMBAT AIR MUSEUM
Forbes Field (Topeka)
(785) 862-3303
Covers WWI to space shuttle program. Missiles, military vehicles, aircraft engines, flight training simulators, field chapel and re-creation of German POW barracks.

4. FORT HARKER MUSEUM
Kanopolis, (785) 472-5733
Protected Kansas State Line and military wagon trains traveling Fort Riley Road and Smoky Hill Trail, 1864-72. Museum features horse-drawn ambulance, uniforms and equipment of local residents from WWI and WWII.

5. FORT HAYS STATE HISTORIC SITE
Hays, (785) 625-6812
Active 1867-89. Household furnishings, weapons and archaeological material. 4 original fort buildings, visitor center, 21 interpretive signs.

Kansas Museum of History, Topeka

6. FORT LARNED NATIONAL HISTORIC SITE

Larned, (620) 285-6911
Protected Santa Fe Trail, 1859-78. 9 restored original sandstone structures, visitor center, museum. Santa Fe Trail ruts nearby.

7. FORT RILEY REGIMENTAL MUSEUM

Fort Riley (Junction City) (785) 239-2737
Seven rooms of exhibits covering 1917 to present. Uniforms, equipment, unit Medal of Honor recipients, simulated WWI trench and Vietnam jungle. Vehicles and artillery on outdoor display.

8. FORT SCOTT NATIONAL HISTORIC SITE

Fort Scott, (620) 223-0310
Active 1842-73. Role in Mexican War, "Bleeding Kansas" border wars and post-Civil War West. 11 restored and reconstructed buildings, visitor center, self-guided tours.

9. FRONTIER ARMY MUSEUM

Fort Leavenworth (Leavenworth) (913) 684-3186
One of finest collections of 19th century military artifacts in the country. Exhibits cover exploration, expansion and protection of Trans-Mississippi West from 1804 Lewis and Clark Expedition to Pershing's 1917 Mexico Punitive Expedition. Weapons, uniforms, equipment and vehicles, including horse-drawn carriages.

10. KANSAS MUSEUM OF HISTORY

Topeka, (785) 272-8681
Extensive display on state's role in Indian campaigns and Civil War, plus smaller displays on Spanish-American War, WWI and WWII, including firearms, uniforms, flags, accoutrements and home-front artifacts.

DID YOU KNOW?
Fort Riley was the cradle of the U.S. Cavalry for 83 years. George Custer formed the famed 7th Cavalry there in 1866. Ten years later, at the Battle of the Little Big Horn, the 7th was virtually wiped out.

The only Cavalry survivor was a horse named Comanche, who is now stuffed and on display at the University of Kansas Natural History Museum in Lawrence.

U.S. Cavalry Museum, Fort Riley

Frontier Army Museum, Fort Leavenworth

11. LAST INDIAN RAID MUSEUM
Oberlin, (785) 475-2712
Exhibit on 1878 last Indian (Northern Cheyenne) raid in Kansas with artifacts and video. Additional exhibits cover other wars. Open May-November.

12. MAJOR GENERAL FREDERICK FUNSTON BOYHOOD HOME & MUSEUM
Iola, (620) 365-3051
Relocated and restored 1860 Victorian-style house on town square. Museum provides coverage of Philippines War (1899-1902) in which Funston was a hero.

13. MARAIS DES CYGNES MASSACRE STATE HISTORIC SITE
Pleasanton, (913) 352-8890
Site of May 1858 massacre—bloodiest single incident of Kansas-Missouri border wars. Museum in 1860s stone house. Interpretive signs.

14. MID-AMERICA AIR MUSEUM
Liberal, (620) 624-5263
Fifth-largest collection of military and civilian aircraft in U.S. Military displays cover WWII, Korean War and Vietnam, including interactive displays on Korea and Doolittle's 1942 raid on Tokyo.

15. MINE CREEK BATTLEFIELD STATE HISTORIC SITE
Pleasanton, (913) 352-8890
Site of only major Civil War battle in Kansas, October 1864. Visitor center with computerized animation of battle, walking trails on battlefield with interpretive signs.

16. MUSEUM OF THE KANSAS NATIONAL GUARD
Topeka, (785) 862-1020
Features memorabilia, artifacts, documentation and equipment of Kansas National Guard from Civil War through Iraq, including weapons, dioramas, photographs and vehicles on outdoor display. Extensive military research library.

17. U.S. CAVALRY MUSEUM
Fort Riley, (785) 239-2737
Displays cover entire history of the U.S. Cavalry from 1775 to 1950. Exhibits use full-size figures, dioramas and historical artifacts to explain evolution of horse-related equipment.

18. WATKINS COMMUNITY MUSEUM OF HISTORY
Lawrence, (785) 841-4109
Exhibits focus on Civil War with displays on Quantrill's Raid.

KENTUCKY

Civil War history buffs will enjoy the numerous Civil War-related sites the Bluegrass State has to offer, among them, Cumberland Gap National Historic Park. Other sites highlight the Revolution and Daniel Boone. Two museums tell the story of armor and airborne troops.

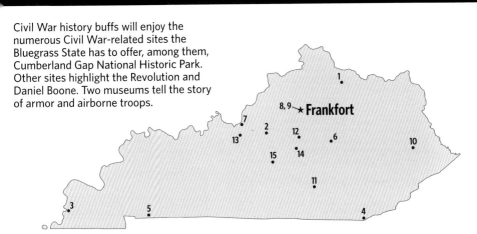

NATIONAL PARK SERVICE

Cumberland Gap National Historical Park, Middlesboro

1. BLUE LICKS BATTLEFIELD STATE RESORT PARK
Mount Olivet, (859) 289-5507

Site of deadly Revolutionary War battle in Kentucky, August 1782, in which Daniel Boone participated. Pioneer Museum features displays interpreting the 15-minute battle. Interpretive signs, burial site, monument.

2. CIVIL WAR MUSEUM
Bardstown, (502) 349-0291

With 8,500 square feet of space, this 4th-largest Civil War museum focuses on the war in the Western states, with artifacts, photos, cannons, battle wagons, weapons and personal items. Nearby are Women in the Civil War Museum and War Memorial of Mid-America.

3. COLUMBUS-BELMONT STATE PARK
Columbus, (270) 677-2327

Site of November 1861 battle. Massive chain and 6-ton anchor Confederates used to block passage of Union gunboats can still be seen, plus artillery relics and restored battle trenches. Museum in former Civil War infirmary.

45

Kentucky Military History Museum, Frankfort

4. CUMBERLAND GAP NATIONAL HISTORICAL PARK

Middlesboro, (606) 248-2817

Historic pass through Appalachian Mountains served as strategic point during the Civil War, changing hands 4 times without major battle. Earthwork fortifications remain. Visitor center contains museum with Civil War weapons.

5. DON F. PRATT MUSEUM

Fort Campbell (south of Hopkinsville), (270) 798-3215

Displays include military uniforms, weapons and photographs from Civil War to present, with emphasis on 101st Airborne Division. Outdoor exhibits.

6. FORT BOONESBOROUGH STATE PARK

Richmond, (859) 527-3131

Established in 1775 by Daniel Boone, served as trade center until 1820. Attacked by Indians in 1778. Reconstructed fort with cabins, blockhouses and furnishings. Nearby is 1863 Civil War Fort at Boonesboro.

7. FORT DUFFIELD

West Point, (502) 922-4574

1861 Union earthworks fortification. One of the best-preserved and largest forts in the state. Self-guided walking tour with interpretive signage.

8. KENTUCKY HISTORICAL SOCIETY HISTORY CENTER

Frankfort, (502) 564-1792

Civil War exhibit on Battle of Perryville. Revolutionary War, War of 1812, WWII and Vietnam are covered through their impact on the home front.

9. KENTUCKY MILITARY HISTORY MUSEUM

Frankfort, (502) 564-3265

Traces state's involvement in military conflict from Revolutionary War through Persian Gulf War. Displays feature uniforms, medals, flags and weapons, including a collection of automatic arms and Kentucky rifles. Housed in 1850s arsenal and Civil War ammunition factory.

10. MIDDLE CREEK NATIONAL BATTLEFIELD

Prestonsburg, 1-800-844-4704

Site of Jan. 10, 1862, battle featuring future President James A. Garfield. Features 2 loop trails with interpretive signage, information kiosk and 4-mile auto tour with 4 stops. (Not administered by the National Park Service.)

11. MILL SPRINGS BATTLEFIELD

Somerset, (606) 636-4045

Site of Jan. 19, 1862, battle, the first significant Union victory of the Civil War. Visitor center with video on battle, 13 interpretive signs, walking and driving tours with descriptive brochure, obelisk and grave markers.

Patton Museum of Cavalry & Armor, Fort Knox

Old Fort Harrod State Park, Harrodsburg

> ✳   ✳   ✳
> ### CIVIL WAR GUIDE
> For an in-depth look at Kentucky's Civil War history, get a copy of *Kentucky's Civil War Heritage Guide*, with a map and detailed descriptions of 34 Civil War-related sites, trails and driving tours. Call *1-800-225-8747* or visit *www.kentuckytourism.com* to order the free brochure.

12. OLD FORT HARROD STATE PARK
Harrodsburg, (859) 734-3314
First permanent settlement west of the Alleghenies, 1774. Served as haven for pioneers during Indian raids of Revolutionary War. Reconstructed fort with living history demonstrations. Mansion Museum houses Civil War artifacts and gun display.

13. PATTON MUSEUM OF CAVALRY & ARMOR
Fort Knox (Radcliff)
(502) 624-3812
One of largest facilities in Army Museum System. Features 40,000 square feet of armored equipment, vehicles, weapons, art and memorabilia chronologically presenting the development of the Armor branch (WWI-present), plus "Patton Gallery." Outdoor displays, Armor Memorial Park.

14. PERRYVILLE BATTLEFIELD STATE HISTORIC SITE
Perryville, (859) 332-8631
Site of the state's most significant Civil War battle, October 1862. Museum features battle artifacts, dioramas, Civil War display and map with layout of battle. Self-guided battlefield walking tour, self-guided driving tour, monuments.

15. TEBBS BEND BATTLEFIELD
Campbellsville, (502) 465-8726
Site of July 4, 1863, battle. Atkinson-Griffin House, the Confederate field hospital, at nearby Green River Reservoir houses a museum of the battle, with photographs, uniforms and a diorama. Historical marker and 10-stop Morgan-Moore Trail driving tour.

LOUISIANA

Despite the devastation of the 2005 hurricane season, Louisiana's most famous city still boasts the National WWII Museum. Originally focusing on D-Day in Europe, it now covers all the war's campaigns. Further back in history, the Pelican State features three battle sites from the Civil War and one from the War of 1812.

* Sites still affected by 2005 hurricane damage.

Baton Rouge ★—18

New Orleans
4, 5, 8, 11, 14, 16

LOUISIANA OFFICE OF TOURISM

National WWII Museum, New Orleans

1. 2ND ARMORED CAVALRY REGIMENT (REED) MUSEUM
Fort Polk (southeast of Leesville), (337) 531-4840

Tells history of the longest actively serving cavalry regiment in the U.S. Army, from Indian wars in the 1830s to the present. Outdoor vehicle park.

2. 8TH AIR FORCE MUSEUM
Barksdale AFB (Bossier City) (318) 456-3067

3,000 square feet of exhibits focus on strategic bombardment, 2nd Bombardment Wing and "Mighty 8th" Air Force.

3. CAMP MOORE CONFEDERATE MUSEUM & CEMETERY
Tangipahoa, (985) 229-2438

Training camp for Civil War soldiers. Museum features Civil War artifacts, medical equipment and musical instruments. Cemetery and research library.

JIM PIERCE/CAMP MOORE CONFEDERATE MUSEUM & CEMETERY

Camp Moore Confederate Museum & Cemetery, Tangipahoa

Fort St. Jean Baptiste State Historic Site, Natchitoches

4. CHALMETTE BATTLEFIELD & NATIONAL CEMETERY (JEAN LAFITTE NATIONAL HISTORICAL PARK AND PRESERVE)

New Orleans, (504) 589-3851

Site of 1815 Battle of New Orleans, the last major land battle of the War of 1812. Visitor center contains exhibits and audiovisual program. 1.5-mile tour road features 6 interpretive stops on battlefield. Monument, national cemetery.

5. CONFEDERATE MUSEUM

New Orleans, (504) 523-4522

Oldest museum in Louisiana and 2nd largest Confederate collection in the country. Features primarily Confederate memorabilia and artifacts, with personal effects of Southern generals and the common soldier.

6. FORT JACKSON

Buras, (985) 657-7083

1832 fort was site of April 1862 battle and later used as WWI training base. Walking tours of original fort. Museum in former powder magazine features fort artifacts and displays on the Battle of New Orleans.

7. FORT JESUP STATE HISTORIC SITE

Many, (318) 256-4117

Frontier fort, 1822-46. Original log kitchen building and reconstructed officers quarters house visitor information, interpretive exhibits, maps, images and diorama. Living history demonstrations.

8. FORT PIKE STATE HISTORIC SITE*

New Orleans, (504) 662-5703

Established in 1819 and played part in 1830s Seminole Wars, Mexican War and Civil War. Much of citadel, casement and exterior walls remain. Museum, self-guided tours.

9. FORT POLK MILITARY MUSEUM

Leesville, (337) 531-7905

Covers 12 U.S. divisions that have served at the fort, with emphasis on the 5th Infantry Division (Mechanized). Vehicles and equipment on outdoor display.

10. FORT ST. JEAN BAPTISTE STATE HISTORIC SITE

Natchitoches, (318) 357-3101

Reconstruction of 1732 French fort and trading post includes barracks, warehouse, chapel, mess hall and powder magazine. Interpretive programs.

11. JACKSON BARRACKS MILITARY MUSEUM*

New Orleans, (504) 278-8242

More than 10,000 square feet feature dioramas, artifacts, letters and personal mementos dating back to the Revolutionary War, with major focus on the Louisiana National Guard. Grounds display includes tanks, planes, helicopters, anti-aircraft batteries and cannons. Expected to reopen in 2010.

12. LOUISIANA MANEUVERS & MILITARY MUSEUM

Pineville, (318) 641-5733

Features WWII Maneuvers-era arms, uniforms and equipment, plus an extensive collection of military artifacts from colonial Louisiana through the Persian Gulf War.

13. LOUISIANA MILITARY MUSEUM

Ruston, (318) 251-5099

Covers Civil War through war on terrorism. Includes military artifacts and more than 300 weapons, with tanks and helicopter on outdoor display.

Louisiana State Museum Cabildo, New Orleans

14. LOUISIANA STATE MUSEUM

New Orleans, (504) 568-6968

Series of museums includes the Cabildo, which houses displays on the War of 1812 and the Civil War in Louisiana history. Louisiana State Museum-Baton Rouge in the capital includes "Louisiana at War" exhibit.

15. MANSFIELD STATE HISTORIC SITE

Mansfield, (318) 872-1474

Site of April 1864 Red River campaign battle. Museum features battle relics, maps, interpretive programs and monuments. Self-guided driving tours and interpretive trails.

16. NATIONAL WWII MUSEUM

New Orleans, (504) 527-6012

Designated by Congress as the nation's WWII museum. Stories of WWII soldiers told through 70,000 square feet of artifacts, film footage, photographs, personal effects, diaries and oral histories. Interactive galleries cover early days of war through D-Day to victory in Europe. Pacific theater gallery includes photos, video presentations, Japanese artifacts and 60-square-foot animated map.

Chalmette Battlefield & National Cemetery, New Orleans

USS *Kidd* Veterans Memorial & Museum, Baton Rouge

17. PORT HUDSON STATE HISTORIC SITE

Zachary, (225) 654-3775

Site of longest siege in U.S. history—48 days in 1863. Interpretive center with museum and audiovisual program, elevated boardwalks over breastworks, 3 observation towers and 6 miles of trails.

18. USS KIDD VETERANS MEMORIAL & MUSEUM

Baton Rouge, (225) 342-1942

Features WWII destroyer *USS Kidd*, observation tower and museum complex. Exhibits include model ship collection, maritime artifacts, Louisiana Veterans Hall of Honor and Vietnam Veterans Memorial Wall replica.

MAINE

Maine's strategic significance can be seen in the 19 forts, utilized from pre-Revolutionary times through WWI, that dot its coast from Kittery to Eastport. From the archaeological ruins of the 1635 Fort Pentagoet in Castine to the massive granite Fort Knox, the Pine Tree State is the fort-lover's paradise.

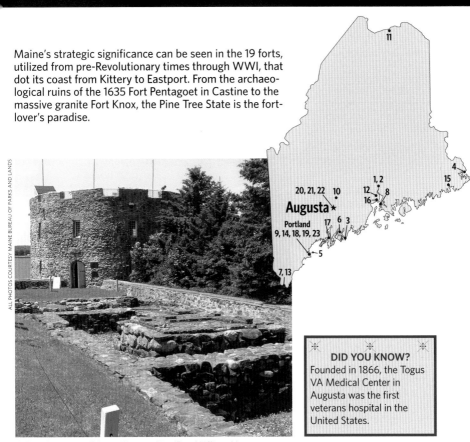

ALL PHOTOS COURTESY MAINE BUREAU OF PARKS AND LANDS

Colonial Pemaquid State Historic Site/Fort William Henry, Pemaquid Point

> ✳ ✳ ✳
> **DID YOU KNOW?**
> Founded in 1866, the Togus VA Medical Center in Augusta was the first veterans hospital in the United States.

1. BANGOR MUSEUM & CENTER FOR HISTORY
Bangor, (207) 942-1900
   Includes collection of Civil War artifacts from local Grand Army of the Republic and Sons of Union Veterans.

2. COLE LAND TRANSPORTATION MUSEUM
Bangor, (207) 990-3600
   Includes hundreds of military artifacts from Civil War through WWII, including fire, personnel and armored vehicles, plus several state memorials.

3. COLONIAL PEMAQUID STATE HISTORIC SITE/FORT WILLIAM HENRY
Pemaquid Point (New Harbor), (207) 677-2423
   Foundations of 17th and 18th century structures, officers quarters. Adjacent reconstruction of 1692 fort, museum with exhibits and artifacts. Guided tours in summer.

4. EASTPORT BARRACKS MUSEUM
Eastport, (207) 853-2328
   Building served as 1809 officers quarters of Fort Sullivan. Includes military exhibits and artifacts from the fort.

5. FIFTH MARINE REGIMENTAL MUSEUM
Peaks Island, (207) 766-3330
   Exhibits cover Marine Corps' Fighting Fifth and the 1942-46 Peaks Island Military Reservation. 2-hour self-guided tour of reservation available.

6. FORT EDGECOMB STATE HISTORIC SITE
Edgecomb, (207) 882-7777,
(207) 624-6080 off-season
1809 fort attacked during War of 1812. Original octagonal wooden blockhouse, reconstructed palisade, earthwork remains, interpretive panels.

7. FORT FOSTER PARK
Kittery, (207) 439-0333
1900s concrete fortifications. Historical information available at gate house.

8. FORT GEORGE
Castine, (207) 326-4502
1779 British earthworks with seasonal historic signage. Also in town are 1811 earthworks of **FORT MADISON** and archaeological ruins of 1635 **FORT PENTAGOET,** both with seasonal historic signage.

9. FORT GORGES
Portland, (207) 874-8793
1858 stone fort accessible by private boat.

10. FORT HALIFAX STATE HISTORIC SITE
Winslow, (207) 941-4014
1754 blockhouse was oldest in U.S. until torn apart by 1987 flood. Reconstruction using original timbers is all that remains of the fort.

11. FORT KENT STATE HISTORIC SITE
Fort Kent, (207) 941-4014
Hand-hewn timber 1839 blockhouse with interpretive panels. Boy Scout-run interpretive center.

12. FORT KNOX STATE HISTORIC SITE
Prospect, (207) 469-7719
Maine's largest historic fort, built 1844-64, was never completed. Pentagon-shaped granite fort includes 4 batteries, 64 cannon mounts, passageways and many rooms for touring. Guided tours in summer.

Fort Baldwin near Fort Popham State Historic Site, Phippsburg

Fort Edgecomb State Historic Site, Edgecomb

Fort Kent State Historic Site, Fort Kent

13. FORT MCCLARY STATE HISTORIC SITE
Kittery, (207) 384-5160
Small fort utilized in 5 wars, from Revolution through WWI. 1846 blockhouse, Rifleman's House, original granite walls, earthworks, powder magazine. Interpretive panels.

14. FORT MCKINLEY
Portland, (207) 766-5814
Restored 1900 brick fort buildings on private property. Museum. Tours by appointment only.

15. FORT O'BRIEN STATE HISTORIC SITE
Machiasport, (207) 941-4014
Original Fort Machias built 1775, destroyed 1814 by British. Well-preserved earthworks erected in 1863. First naval engagement of Revolution fought off-shore June 12, 1775. Interpretive panel.

16. FORT POINT STATE PARK
southeast of Stockton Springs
(207) 941-4014
Remains of 1759 Fort Pownall earthworks with interpretive panels.

Fort McClary State Historic Site, Kittery

Fort Popham State Historic Site, Phippsburg

Fort Knox State Historic Site, Prospect

> ✳   ✳   ✳
> ### DID YOU KNOW?
> A flood in 1987—the most destructive in Maine's history—tore apart the blockhouse at Fort Halifax, which sat at the confluence of the Kennebec and Sebasticook rivers.
>   Crews recovered logs from the blockhouse as far as 40 miles downstream and reassembled the structure on its original site, where it stands today.

17. FORT POPHAM STATE HISTORIC SITE
Phippsburg, (207) 389-1335
1862 granite fort used in Civil War, Spanish-American War and WWI. Nearby are remains of **FORT BALDWIN.**

18. FORT SCAMMEL
Portland, (207) 799-8188
Multi-level stone 1808 fort on House Island reconstructed after Civil War. 70 gun casements, subterranean vaults, tunnels and stairways. Accessible by appointment.

19. FORT WILLIAMS
Cape Elizabeth, (207) 799-7652
Remains of 6 batteries with pictorial plaques, officers quarters and remains of Goddard Mansion.

20. MAINE MILITARY HISTORICAL SOCIETY MUSEUM (MAINE NATIONAL GUARD)
Augusta, (207) 626-4338
Includes artifacts, displays and exhibits from Revolution through Persian Gulf War. Open by appointment only.

21. MAINE STATE MUSEUM
Augusta, (207) 287-2301
"Struggle for Identity" exhibit covers state's internal military history from 1675 to 1842 (border dispute with New Brunswick). Rotating exhibit of Civil War flags, weapons and equipment. Large collection covering Revolution through Persian Gulf War available to researchers by appointment.

22. OLD FORT WESTERN
Augusta, (207) 626-2385
Said to be country's oldest wooden fort, established 1754. Replicas of original blockhouses and palisades, plus surviving garrison house. Costumed interpreters.

23. PORTLAND HARBOR MUSEUM
South Portland
(207) 799-6337
Housed in former building of historic Fort Preble, built in 1808. Museum tours include information on fort, with guided tours of fort available.

MARYLAND

The bloodiest single-day battle in American history, on Sept. 12, 1862, is remembered at Antietam National Battlefield in the Old Line State. The War of 1812's Fort McHenry, the site that inspired the writing of "The Star-Spangled Banner," is another famous attraction that shouldn't be missed.

Antietam National Battlefield, Sharpsburg

1. AIRMEN MEMORIAL MUSEUM
Suitland, (301) 899-3500, ext. 229

Covers history of enlisted airmen from 1907 to the present. Exhibits include WWI era, Cold War orderly room, the atomic missions, WWII color photography, aviation art and airmen mannequins with artifacts from WWI through Persian Gulf War.

2. ANTIETAM NATIONAL BATTLEFIELD
Sharpsburg, (301) 432-5124

Site of Sept. 17, 1862 battle—the bloodiest day of the Civil War, with more than 23,000 casualties. Visitor center with exhibits, interpretive talks, 26-minute film and 1-hour documentary. More than 350 monuments, tablets and markers and 41 cannons throughout battlefield. Self-guided 8.5-mile driving tour with 11 stops, including national cemetery.

3. BAINBRIDGE NAVAL TRAINING CENTER MUSEUM
Port Deposit, (410) 378-4641

Includes artifact displays, ship and airplane models, replica of base's main gate, mannequins and Navy bunks with authentic bedding. Open weekends only.

USS Torsk at the Baltimore Maritime Museum

4. BALTIMORE CIVIL WAR MUSEUM

Baltimore, (410) 385-5188

Site of first bloodshed (4 soldiers and 12 rioters killed) of Civil War, April 19, 1861, at President Street Station. Museum includes exhibits, interpretive programs and living history on Baltimore's role in the Civil War.

5. BALTIMORE MARITIME MUSEUM

Baltimore, (410) 396-3453

Includes WWII submarine *USS Torsk*, which fired last torpedoes of WWII, and Coast Guard cutter *Taney*, the last ship afloat that survived the attack on Pearl Harbor. Self-guided tours, exhibits and interpretive materials throughout ships.

6. BOONSBOROUGH MUSEUM OF HISTORY

Boonsboro, (301) 432-6969

Housed in 2-story Victorian house, military displays consist primarily of one-of-a-kind Civil War artifacts, including items from Antietam and Gettysburg, plus various items from other wars. Open Sundays or by appointment.

7. CALVERT MARINE MUSEUM

Solomons, (410) 326-2042

Includes small exhibits on the War of 1812's Battle of the Patuxent and the area's WWII amphibious training base.

8. CLARA BARTON NATIONAL HISTORIC SITE

Glen Echo, (301) 320-1410

Last home of American Red Cross founder. Served as early headquarters for the organization, which today continues to coordinate relief efforts for victims of war and natural disasters. 11 restored rooms with personal artifacts.

9. FLAG HOUSE & STAR-SPANGLED BANNER MUSEUM

Baltimore, (410) 837-1793

1793 home of Mary Pickersgill where she sewed the Star-Spangled Banner in 1813. Museum includes exhibits on the War of 1812 with video on the Battle of Baltimore.

DID YOU KNOW?
Six brigadier and major generals were killed or mortally wounded during the Battle of Antietam on Sept. 17, 1862. Of the 6 fallen officers, 3 were from the Union Army (Mansfield, Richardson and Rodman) and 3 were Confederates (Starke, Anderson and Branch).

The spot where each was killed is marked by a "Mortuary Cannon," a cannon tube, muzzle down, in a block of stone.

Fort McHenry National Monument & Historic Shrine, Baltimore

10. FORT CUMBERLAND

Cumberland, (301) 777-5132

Wooden fort built 1754 and site of George Washington's first military headquarters. Attacked by Indians between 1755 and 1758. Washington's 1-room HQ is only remaining structure. Walking trail with 28 plaques. Fort model and tour tunnels in Emmanuel Episcopal Church on fort site.

11. FORT FOOTE PARK

Oxon Hill, (301) 763-4600

Active 1863-1878 to protect river entrance to ports. Intact earthworks considered best-preserved Civil War fort in region. 6 interpretive panels, 2 15-inch Rodman guns. Maintained by National Park Service.

12. FORT FREDERICK STATE PARK

Big Pool, (301) 842-2155

1756 frontier fort protected settlers during French and Indian War, was involved in Revolutionary War and was attacked by Confederates in December 1861. Stone wall and 2 barracks are restored to 1758 appearance and contain exhibits. Visitor center with 10-minute film and displays.

13. FORT GEORGE G. MEADE MUSEUM

Fort Meade (Annapolis Junction), (301) 677-6966

Includes items related to Ft. Meade, early American armor and the local region from the Revolutionary War through Vietnam. Indoor and outdoor exhibits include uniforms, tanks, missiles, personnel carrier, helicopter, monuments and memorials.

14. FORT MCHENRY NATIONAL MONUMENT & HISTORIC SHRINE

Baltimore, (410) 962-4290

Built 1798-1803. Resistance to 25-hour British bombardment (in 1814) during War of 1812 inspired Francis Scott Key to write "The Star-Spangled Banner." Used as a prison for Confederate soldiers and sympathizers.

Fort restored to pre-Civil War appearance with historical and military exhibits, and nation's largest display of 15-inch Rodman coastal guns. Includes second war memorial constructed on U.S. soil, to those killed in the 1814 battle. Self-guided tours.

Fort Washington Park, Fort Washington

DID YOU KNOW?
The flag flown at Fort McHenry that inspired Francis Scott Key to compose "The Star-Spangled Banner" was the largest battle flag ever flown, measuring 30 feet wide by 42 feet long. It was sewn by Mary Pickersgill of Baltimore, and today hangs in the Smithsonian National Museum of American History in Washington, D.C.

15. FORT WASHINGTON PARK
Fort Washington
(301) 763-4600
First fort built 1809 and destroyed during War of 1812. 1824 brick fort (only permanent fortification built to protect the capital) features visitor center with exhibits and audiovisual program. Guided tours. Maintained by National Park Service.

16. GATHLAND STATE PARK
Burkittsville, (301) 791-4767
Site of memorial arch dedicated to Civil War war correspondents in 1896, designed and built by Civil War journalist George Alfred Townsend. Park museum at Crampton's Gap includes exhibits on Townsend and the 1862 Battle of South Mountain.

17. GLENN L. MARTIN AVIATION MUSEUM
Middle River, (410) 682-6122
Located at Martin State Airport. Covers history of Maryland aviation and aircraft manufacturer Glenn L. Martin Company through models, restored aircraft and photographs. 11 military aircraft on outdoor display.

Gathland State Park, Burkittsville

18. JEFFERSON PATTERSON PARK & MUSEUM
St. Leonard, (410) 586-8500
Site of June 1814 Battle of St. Leonard Creek, the largest naval engagement in state history. Museum includes introductory video with section on War of 1812. Walking/driving tour with 11 interpretive panels on War of 1812 and battle.

USS Constellation, Baltimore

19. MARYLAND HISTORICAL SOCIETY MUSEUM
Baltimore, (410) 685-3750

"Looking for Liberty" exhibit on state history features section on defense and protection that includes War of 1812 artifacts, such as a uniform, a bomb shot at Ft. McHenry and the original manuscript of "The Star-Spangled Banner."

20. MARYLAND NATIONAL GUARD MUSEUM
Baltimore, (410) 576-1496

Covers Guard's history chronologically from 1634 to the present, with emphasis on its involvement in major wars, and includes the war on terrorism. Call prior to visit.

21. MONOCACY NATIONAL BATTLEFIELD
Frederick, (301) 662-3515

Site of the "Battle That Saved Washington," July 9, 1864. Gambrill Mill Visitor Center includes electric map orientation program, historical artifacts and interpretive displays of battle. 4-mile driving tour and 2 trails around battlefield with wayside exhibits.

National Cryptologic Museum, Fort Meade

22. NATIONAL CRYPTOLOGIC MUSEUM
Fort Meade (Annapolis Junction), (301) 688-5849

Covers history of the cryptologic profession with thousands of artifacts on the people, places, machines, devices and techniques. Includes exhibits on computer development, women in cryptology and on major wars from the Civil War through the Cold War. Adjacent is **NATIONAL VIGILANCE PARK AND AERIAL RECONNAISSANCE MEMORIAL,** showcasing two reconnaissance aircraft.

23. NATIONAL MUSEUM OF CIVIL WAR MEDICINE
Frederick, (301) 695-1864

Nearly 7,000 square feet on 2 floors cover aspects of Civil War medicine through re-created scenes, display cases and interpretive panels. Exhibits include recruiting and enlisting, camp life, evacuation of the wounded, a field dressing station, field and pavilion hospitals, nursing, embalming, and modern battlefield medicine's ties to Civil War advancements.

U.S. Naval Academy Museum, Annapolis

24. PATUXENT RIVER NAVAL AIR MUSEUM

Lexington Park, (301) 863-7418
Covers history of research, development, testing and evaluation of Navy aircraft since 1911. Includes hands-on displays, video presentation, flight trainers and aircraft on outdoor display.

25. POINT LOOKOUT STATE PARK

Scotland, (301) 872-5688
Area raided by British during Revolutionary War and War of 1812. Site of Civil War's largest POW camp (it held Confederates). Earthworks of Civil War's Fort Lincoln still visible. Re-created barracks, officer quarters and portion of prison pen. Park visitor center and Civil War museum with exhibits on the prison is open seasonally. Memorial, cemetery.

26. SOUTH MOUNTAIN STATE BATTLEFIELD

Boonsboro, (301) 432-8065
Site of state's first major Civil War battle, Sept. 14, 1862. 17-stop driving tour with some signage, monuments. Tour brochure available at Washington Monument State Park visitor center (near Boonsboro), which features exhibits on Civil War artillery.

27. U.S. ARMY ORDNANCE MUSEUM

Aberdeen, (410) 278-3602
Traces development of 20th century weaponry with extensive collection of small arms, library and small theater. 230 items on outdoor display, including tanks, artillery, WWI and WWII foreign weapons, and an atomic cannon.

28. U.S. NAVAL ACADEMY MUSEUM

Annapolis, (410) 293-2108
Four galleries totaling 12,000 square feet cover U.S. naval history from the Revolutionary War through Vietnam, plus the role of the Navy and Academy graduates in the Spanish American War, WWII, the Cold War and the space program. Exhibits include 108 ship models, 1,210 commemorative coin medals, 600 historic American and captured enemy flags, and prominent American naval heroes.

29. USS CONSTELLATION

Baltimore, (410) 539-1797
Last all-sail warship launched by U.S. Navy (1797) and last Civil War-era ship still afloat. Offers hands-on activities and demonstrations daily, plus self-guided audio tours. Artifacts on display include a Navy cutlass, leg irons and navigation instruments.

MASSACHUSETTS

Forts utilized from the 17th to 19th centuries dot the terrain of Massachusetts, where the first blood of the Revolutionary War was shed at Lexington Battle Green. With its oceanside location, the Bay State captures early naval history through the Charlestown Navy Yard, and is home to at least six historic ships, including the *USS Constitution,* or "Old Ironsides," the oldest commissioned ship still afloat in the world.

Battleship Cove, Fall River

1. ANCIENT & HONORABLE ARTILLERY COMPANY OF MASSACHUSETTS MUSEUM
Boston, (617) 523-1300

Located on 4th floor of Faneuil Hall with relics and memorabilia from all engagements involving members of the company (the nation's oldest continuously existing).

2. BATTLESHIP COVE
Fall River, (508) 678-1100

Collection of historic 20th-century naval ships, including: Battleship *USS Massachusetts* (Big Mamie) with ship tours, PT boat museum and scale model aircraft exhibit; destroyer *USS Joseph P. Kennedy Jr.,* with Admiral Arleigh Burke National Destroyermen's Museum; WWII attack sub *USS Lionfish;* restored WWII PT torpedo boats; and 10 memorials.

DID YOU KNOW?
The town of Woburn proudly displays a ventilator cowl (one of the "horns" that stick out of ship decks) from the *USS Maine,* salvaged after the *Maine* sank in Havana Harbor in 1898. It is sealed in a large glass case in the town square with a printed description.

Bunker Hill Monument, Charlestown

USS Constitution at Charlestown Navy Yard, Boston

3. BLOODY BROOK MASSACRE SITE

Deerfield, (*413*) *774-7476, ext. 10*

Site of Sept. 19, 1676, battle in which 76 colonial militiamen were killed by Indians during King Philip's War. Monument dedicated in 1838.

4. BUNKER HILL MONUMENT

Charlestown (*Boston*)
(*617*) *242-5641*

221-ft. granite obelisk marks site of Battle of Bunker Hill, June 17, 1775—the first major battle of the Revolution. Lodge at base contains dioramas and exhibits on the battle. Unit of Boston National Historical Park. Names of dead are listed at Winthrop Square.

5. CHARLESTOWN NAVY YARD

Boston, (*617*) *242-5601*

Active 1800-1974. Visitor center offers multi-media presentation on Battle of Bunker Hill, plus others. Restored destroyer **USS CASSIN YOUNG,** (*617*) *242-5629,* and the world's oldest commissioned ship (1797) afloat **USS CONSTITUTION,** (*617*) *242-5670,* both available for tours. **USS CONSTITUTION MUSEUM,** (*617*) *426-1812,* traces ship's 200+ year history through artifacts, computer-simulated re-enactments and historical interpreter presentation. Unit of Boston National Historical Park.

6. COMMONWEALTH MUSEUM

Boston, (*617*) *727-9268*

Under renovation, scheduled to open winter 2007. Focuses on how American rights developed, including original foundation documents and coverage of Revolutionary War, Civil War and area Indian conflicts.

7. FORT INDEPENDENCE (CASTLE ISLAND)

Boston, (*617*) *727-5290*

Pentagon-shaped, 5-bastioned granite fort built 1834-1851. Self-guided tours with interpretive signs. Guided tours in summer.

North Bridge at Minute Man National Historic Park, Concord

8. FORT PHOENIX
Fairhaven, (508) 979-4085
1778 fort active through 1876. Stone parapet, powder magazine and cannons remain. Interpreters give tours, tell history of fort and give musket-firing demonstrations 3 days a week.

9. FORT PICKERING
Salem, (978) 745-9430
Located on Winter Island. Begun in 1643 and frequently rebuilt. Manned during War of 1812, Spanish-American War and Civil War. Fort remnants adjacent to lighthouse.

10. FORT SEWALL
Marblehead, (781) 631-0000
Established in 1644, enlarged in 1742, 1794 and during Civil War. Fort embankments, paved walkway, historical plaque. Open seasonally.

11. FORT TABER PARK
New Bedford, (508) 994-3938
Located at Fort Rodman. Earthen Fort Taber constructed in 1861 and demolished when granite Fort Rodman was completed in 1863. Fort Taber Military Museum located in 1917 PX building, with fort model, photos, uniforms and mementos from Revolutionary War through Iraq. Park plans for interpretive signs.

12. FORT WARREN
Boston, (617) 223-8666
Massive granite fort on Georges Island in Boston Harbor was built 1834-67. Housed Confederate prisoners and was active during Spanish-American War, WWI and WWII. Ranger-led tours. Other Boston Harbor Island forts include **FORT STANDISH** on Lovells Island and **FORT ANDREWS** on Peddocks Island.

DID YOU KNOW?
In the mid-1850s, 200-million-year-old dinosaur bones were uncovered during a blasting operation at the watershops of the Springfield Armory. The bones of the anchisaurus polyzelus are considered one of the earliest dinosaur discoveries in North America.

13. LEXINGTON BATTLE GREEN
Lexington, (781) 862-1450
Site of first blood spilled in Revolution, April 19, 1775. Visitor center features diorama on Battle of Lexington. Revolutionary Monument is oldest war memorial in the country, built in 1799.

✳   ✳   ✳

**Massachusetts Native:
WALTER BRENNAN**

As an enlisted man in C Battery, 101st Field Artillery Regt., 26th Inf. Div., Brennan was in France November 1917-April 1919. His division fought in 4 major offensives with C Battery engaged at St. Mihiel and Verdun, among other battles.

First to win 3 Academy Awards as best supporting actor, this Swampscott, Mass., native appeared in 186 films, 5 TV movies and 3 TV series between 1929 and 1974. He has been called the most successful character actor of American sound films.

Fort Warren, Boston

14. MASSACHUSETTS NATIONAL GUARD MUSEUM
Worcester, (508) 797-0334
Housed in 1891 armory. Covers history of state National Guard, from 1636 to the present. Includes military records of all state sailors and soldiers from 1775-1940, plus rooms on the Civil War, Americal (23rd Inf.) and Yankee (26th Inf.) divisions.

15. MEMORIAL HALL MUSEUM
Deerfield, (413) 774-3768, ext. 10
Includes exhibit on 1704 Deerfield Raid and military room, with guns, uniforms and accessories from Revolution through Spanish-American War.

16. MINUTE MAN NATIONAL HISTORICAL PARK
Concord, (978) 369-6993
Commemorates opening battles of Revolution, April 19, 1775. Includes **MINUTE MAN VISITOR CENTER,** *(781) 674-1920,* with exhibits and 25-minute multi-media presentation; the North Bridge, the site of "the shot heard 'round the world"; **NORTH BRIDGE VISITOR CENTER,** *(978) 318-7810,* which features 12-minute video on North Bridge fight, exhibits and artifacts; and 5-mile interpretive Battle Road Trail.

17. OLD STATE HOUSE
Boston, (617) 720-1713
1713 building houses Bostonian Society Museum, with exhibitions on the Revolution.

18. SPRINGFIELD ARMORY NATIONAL HISTORIC SITE
Springfield, (413) 734-6478
Site established by George Washington as country's first arsenal in 1794. Current 1840s facility houses world's largest collection of American military firearms. Includes orientation exhibit, 18-minute film, computer-generated graphic videos and self-guided walking tour of historic buildings surrounding armory.

19. USS SALEM & UNITED STATES NAVAL SHIPBUILDING MUSEUM
Quincy, (617) 479-7900
USS Salem, said to be world's only preserved heavy cruiser gunship, open for tours. Exhibits onboard include Navy cruiser sailors, *USS Newport News, USS Saint Paul* and Navy SEALs.

MICHIGAN

Attractions in Michigan include sites related to Pontiac's Rebellion of 1763, as well as a deadly War of 1812 battle. The Wolverine State also hosts three air museums and a unique VFW Post military museum.

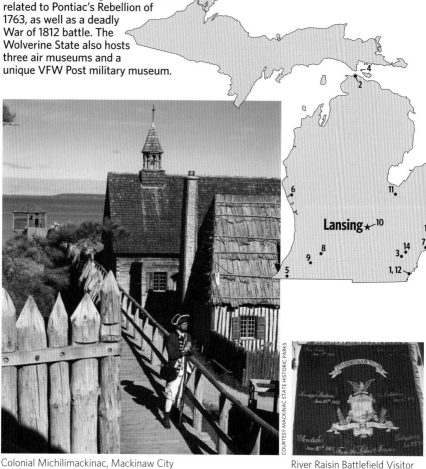

Lansing ★ 10

Colonial Michilimackinac, Mackinaw City

River Raisin Battlefield Visitor Center, Monroe

COURTESY MACKINAC STATE HISTORIC PARKS

1. CAPTAIN NORMAN W. HECK PARK & VIETNAM VETERANS MUSEUM
Monroe, (734) 457-0282

Museum covers Vietnam experience through uniforms, weapons, dioramas of field sites, aircraft and vehicle models, and artifacts. Open Wed. and Sat., May-October. Park includes Vietnam memorials, Cobra gunship and Huey helicopter.

2. COLONIAL MICHILIMACKINAC
Mackinaw City
(231) 436-4100

Built by French in 1715; occupied by British 1761-81. Site of 1763 Indian attack during Pontiac's Rebellion. Reconstructed buildings, audiovisual program, exhibits and costumed interpreters.

3. FORT CUSTER MILITARY MUSEUM
Augusta, (269) 731-3501

Fully restored WWII barracks features exhibits on Michigan in the Civil War, the history of Ft. Custer since 1917 and the history of the Michigan Army National Guard, 1865-present.

USS Silversides at Great Lakes Naval Memorial & Museum, Muskegon

4. FORT MACKINAC
Mackinac Island
(906) 847-3328
British fort, 1780-81. Active for U.S. until 1895. Original buildings, period exhibits, audiovisual presentations, costumed interpreters and demonstrations.

5. FORT ST. JOSEPH MUSEUM
Niles, (269) 683-4702
French fort in 1691. Seized by Indians during Pontiac's Rebellion of 1763. Museum with 10,000 historical items.

6. GREAT LAKES NAVAL MEMORIAL & MUSEUM
Muskegon, (231) 755-1230
Consists of *USS LST 393*, Coast Guard cutter *McLane* and submarine *USS Silversides*.

7. HISTORIC FORT WAYNE
Detroit, (313) 833-1805
Built in 1845. Original 1848 limestone barracks and other restored buildings remain. **MUSEUM OF THE TUSKEGEE AIRMEN,** *(313) 843-8849,* features model aircraft, uniforms, photos and video presentation.

8. KALAMAZOO AIR ZOO
Portage, (269) 382-6555
120,000 square feet include aircraft used in Korea and Vietnam. Also features National Guadalcanal Memorial Museum.

9. MARCELLUS VFW POST 4054 MILITARY MUSEUM
Marcellus, (269) 646-3498
3,000 square feet of exhibits in this VFW Post cover Civil War through Persian Gulf War, with thousands of artifacts, 30 uniformed mannequins and 15 murals depicting scenes from the wars. 2 tanks and a Huey helicopter on outdoor display.

10. MICHIGAN HISTORICAL MUSEUM
Lansing, (517) 373-3559
Military exhibits include residents' involvement in Civil War and WWI, plus a gallery on Michigan's WWII home-front role.

11. MICHIGAN'S OWN, INC., MILITARY & SPACE MUSEUM
Frankenmuth, (989) 652-8005
Honors Michigan's war veterans, from the Spanish-American War through the present. Unique display on 339th Infantry Regiment, which served in North Russia, 1918-19.

> ✳   ✳   ✳
> **DID YOU KNOW?**
> The oldest building in Michigan is the 1780 Officers Stone Quarters at Fort Mackinac.

12. RIVER RAISIN BATTLEFIELD VISITOR CENTER
Monroe, (734) 243-7136
Site of Jan. 22, 1813 battle of the War of 1812. Exhibits include dioramas, maps, mannequins and a 15-minute fiber-optic map presentation. Historical walking trail, markers, monument, driving tour.

13. SELFRIDGE MILITARY AIR MUSEUM
Selfridge Air National Guard Base (Harrison)
(586) 307-5035
Covers history of Michigan Air National Guard, WWI through Iraq. Air park displays more than 30 aircraft.

14. YANKEE AIR MUSEUM
Belleville, (734) 483-4030
Located at Willow Run Airport. Burned down in 2004, but heart of the aircraft collection—including restored B-17, C-47 and B-25—was saved. Closed to the public, but rebuilding is under way.

MINNESOTA

Southwest Minnesota was ravaged by the Sioux conflict of 1862 with some 400 settlers being killed. Two battle sites are interpreted, and the Brown County Historical Museum offers extensive coverage of the war. The North Star State also was the boyhood home of Charles Lindbergh, and his contributions to the Air Force are documented at his home and attached visitor center. Another state claim to fame is the Battle of Leech Lake in 1898—the very last of the U.S. Army's Indian fights. Don't miss Fort Snelling.

Historic Fort Snelling State Historic Site, St. Paul

1. BATTLE POINT (BATTLE OF SUGAR POINT)
Leech Lake
Site of last battle between Army and Indians, October 1898, in which 6 soldiers were killed. Historical marker near the town of Whipholt at a wayside on the lakes's south shore.

2. BIRCH COULEE BATTLEFIELD STATE HISTORIC SITE
Morton, (507) 697-6321
Site of September battle of 1862 Sioux War. Self-guided trail, interpretive signs. Nearby is **LOWER SIOUX AGENCY STATE HISTORIC SITE,** site of first organized Indian attack of 1862 Sioux War.

3. BROWN COUNTY HISTORICAL MUSEUM
New Ulm, (507) 233-2616
Extensive exhibits on Sioux conflict of 1862, including firearms, photographs, uniforms, artwork and artifacts. Interpretive signs throughout town, which was attacked twice during war. Defenders Monument to killed residents in front of county courthouse.

Charles A. Lindbergh Historic Site, Little Falls

DID YOU KNOW?

Though there is some controversy, Camp Ripley is said to be the birthplace of the Army Jeep. Minneapolis-Moline Power Implement Company converted a farm tractor into an artillery prime mover and collaborated with the Minnesota National Guard to test it at Camp Ripley. Sgt. James T. O'Brien is credited with calling the machine "Jeep"—not a contraction of the term General Purpose (GP), but after a character in the then-popular Popeye comic strip.

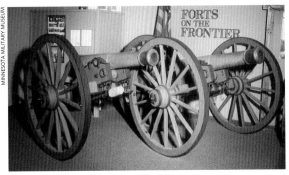

Minnesota Military Museum, Little Falls

Brown County Historical Museum, New Ulm

4. CHARLES A. LINDBERGH HISTORIC SITE

Little Falls, (320) 616-5421

Boyhood home and visitor center tell story of Lindbergh's life, including his contribution to the U.S. Army Air Forces in WWII. Hundreds of photographs and artifacts. Full-scale replica of Spirit of St. Louis. Summers only.

5. FORT RIDGELY STATE HISTORIC SITE

Fairfax, (507) 697-6321

Active 1853-1867. Attacked twice in 1862 Sioux War. Restored Commissary with exhibits, interpretive signs, diorama of 2 battles fought there. Summers only.

6. HISTORIC FORT SNELLING STATE HISTORIC SITE

St. Paul, (612) 726-1171

Established 1819; training installation, 1861-1946. Restored and re-created fort, guided tours, living history demonstrations.

7. MINNESOTA AIR GUARD MUSEUM

St. Paul, (612) 713-2523

Features artifacts, memorabilia and photos of Minnesota Air National Guard, 1921-present. 18 aircraft on outdoor display. Saturdays only.

8. MINNESOTA MILITARY MUSEUM (CAMP RIPLEY)

Little Falls, (320) 632-7374

Covers major wars since Minnesota became a state in 1858, Minnesota National Guard, state frontier forts, military small arms development, Minnesotans who received Medal of Honor and military decorations. Outdoor vehicle, aircraft and artillery exhibits.

MISSISSIPPI

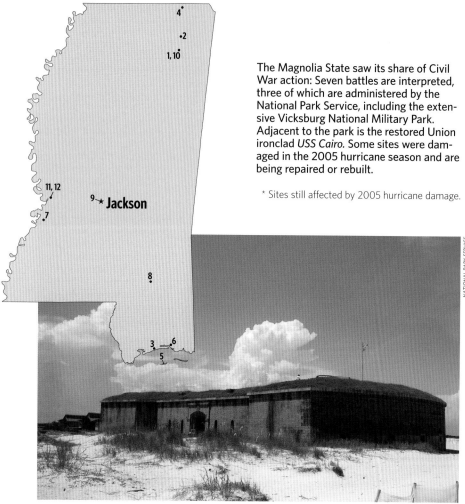

The Magnolia State saw its share of Civil War action: Seven battles are interpreted, three of which are administered by the National Park Service, including the extensive Vicksburg National Military Park. Adjacent to the park is the restored Union ironclad *USS Cairo*. Some sites were damaged in the 2005 hurricane season and are being repaired or rebuilt.

* Sites still affected by 2005 hurricane damage.

Fort Massachusetts, Ship Island

1. ACKIA BATTLEGROUND NATIONAL MONUMENT
Tupelo, (662) 680-4025

Site of significant battle between French and Chickasaws in 1736. Sign in town and wayside with map depicting battle along with monument between US 78 and SR 6. (Absorbed by Natchez Trace Parkway site Chickasaw Village.)

2. BRICES CROSS ROADS NATIONAL BATTLEFIELD
Baldwyn, (662) 365-3969

Site of June 1864 Civil War battle features 1.5-mile walking trail with interpretive signs, cemetery and memorial. Visitor center includes audiovisual program, artifacts, interactive exhibits and 1,500-piece miniature battlefield model.

3. CEC-SEABEE MUSEUM*
Gulfport, (228) 865-0480

Torn down due to 2005 hurricane damage. Command Historical Exhibit will open in new building in 2009 and will cover history of Navy's Civil Engineer Corps and Seabees.

Tupelo National Battlefield, Tupelo

Mississippi Native: ELVIS PRESLEY

Presley served in Germany for 18 months between Oct. 1, 1958 and March 2, 1960. Stationed at Friedberg, he was a jeep driver in Recon Plt., C Co., 1st Med. Tank Bn., 32nd Armor, 3rd Armored Div. He was a sergeant when discharged.

The Tupelo, Miss., native sold more than 1 billion records and made 32 financially successful movies.

4. CORINTH CIVIL WAR INTERPRETIVE CENTER
Corinth, (662) 287-9273

Exhibits focus on war in Corinth area, including photos, souvenirs and 2 films. Self-guided walking and driving tours of city. Nearby are Battery Robinett, a reconstruction of an earthen battery that was site of 1862 Battle of Corinth, and the well-preserved Battery F.

5. FORT MASSACHUSETTS
Ship Island (Gulf Islands National Seashore)
(228) 875-9057

Pre-Civil War fort was one of the last masonry forts built and was the site of a brief Civil War skirmish, July 1861. Remains mostly intact with magazines, cannon, shot furnace, guardrooms, half-bastions and casements. Self-guided tours, with guided tours March-October. Accessible only by boat.

6. GI MUSEUM
Ocean Springs, (228) 872-1943

1,600-sq.-ft. museum includes 16,000 items, mostly from WWI and WWII. Some items from Iraq on display.

7. GRAND GULF MILITARY PARK
Port Gibson, (601) 437-5911

Site of April 1863 shelling of forts Cobun and Wade. Park includes forts, trails, cemetery, observation tower and a museum, half of which is dedicated to the Civil War.

DID YOU KNOW?
Union siege lines and Confederate defensive lines at Vicksburg were marked in the early 1900s by veterans who had fought there. This made Vicksburg National Military Park one of the most accurately marked military parks in the world.

Vicksburg National Military Park, Vicksburg

USS *Cairo* Museum, Vicksburg

8. MISSISSIPPI ARMED FORCES MUSEUM
Camp Shelby (Hattiesburg)
(601) 558-2757

Traces role of state's veterans and training facilities from War of 1812 through the war on terrorism in Afghanistan with more than 15,000 pieces of military memorabilia. Galleries include life-size and immersive exhibits covering WWI trench warfare, WWII Battle of the Bulge, Korea's Chosin Reservoir and a Vietnam medical evacuation diorama.

9. OLD CAPITOL MUSEUM*
Jackson, (601) 576-6920

Covers state involvement in all major wars with emphasis on the Mexican and Civil wars. Includes laser disc display of procession of Civil War battles through the state. Will reopen in 2007. New building will be called Museum of Mississippi History 2012.

10. TUPELO NATIONAL BATTLEFIELD
Tupelo, 1-800-305-7417

Site of last major Civil War battle in Mississippi, July 1864. A cannon and monument commemorate the battle.

11. VICKSBURG BATTLEFIELD MUSEUM
Vicksburg, (601) 638-6500

Displays largest collection of Civil War gunboat models with paintings, reference files and artifacts pertaining to warships. Features 250-square-foot diorama containing miniature layout of Vicksburg battlefield with 2,500 miniature soldiers.

12. VICKSBURG NATIONAL MILITARY PARK
Vicksburg, (601) 636-0583

Site of decisive 3-month campaign, March 29-July 4, 1863, that included at least 5 battles and a 47-day siege. Park includes a 16-mile tour road with 15 interpretive stops and exhibits, 1,330 historic monuments and markers, 20 miles of reconstructed trenches and earthworks, 144 emplaced cannon and a national cemetery. Visitor center features film and exhibits. **USS CAIRO MUSEUM,** *(601) 636-2199,* displays artifacts recovered from the sunken Union ironclad, restored and on display next to the museum.

MISSOURI

Twelve battle sites and/or museums commemorating the Civil War are located in Missouri, including Wilson's Creek National Battlefield. Three key military figures—Gen. John Pershing, President Harry Truman and President Ulysses Grant—also called the Show Me State home. Homes and museums commemorating them can be found here. The new National World War I Museum at Liberty Memorial in Kansas City is the only museum in the U.S. devoted solely to WWI.

National WWI Museum at Liberty Memorial, Kansas City

1. BATTLE OF ATHENS STATE HISTORIC SITE
Kahoka, (660) 877-3871
Site of northernmost Civil War battle west of the Mississippi, August 1861. Thome-Benning House serves as visitor center and museum. Exhibits and tours interpret battle.

2. BATTLE OF CARTHAGE CIVIL WAR MUSEUM
Carthage, (417) 237-7060
Features historic relics, mural, prints and souvenirs.

3. BATTLE OF CARTHAGE STATE HISTORIC SITE
Carthage, (417) 682-2279
Site of July 1861 battle. Interpretive shelter with displays.

4. BATTLE OF LEXINGTON STATE HISTORIC SITE
Lexington, (660) 259-4654
Site of September 1861 "Battle of Hemp Bales." Restored 1853 Anderson House was used as a field hospital. Visitor center with exhibits and audiovisual programs, self-guided walking trail.

5. BATTLE OF WESTPORT
Kansas City, (816) 561-1821
Largest Civil War engagement west of Missouri River, October 1864. Thirty-two-mile self-guided driving tour with 25 interpretive markers. Self-guided walking tours marked through Byram's Ford and Big Blue Battlefield.

6. BUSHWACKER MUSEUM
Nevada, (417) 667-9602
Includes artifacts from Bushwacker Jail and Civil War memorabilia related to Bushwackers.

Jefferson National Expansion Memorial, St. Louis

7. CENTRALIA HISTORICAL SOCIETY MUSEUM

Centralia, (573) 682-5711

Civil War exhibit includes information on September 1864 Battle of Centralia and massacre.

8. CONFEDERATE MEMORIAL STATE HISTORIC SITE

Higginsville, (660) 584-2853

Site is on grounds of former Confederate Home of Missouri, which housed dependent Confederate veterans and their families. Restored historic chapel, cemetery, interpretive exhibits.

9. FORT DAVIDSON STATE HISTORIC SITE

Pilot Knob, (573) 546-3454

Site of September 1864 battle. Visitor center and museum featuring exhibits, research library, audiovisual presentation and fiber-optic diorama of battle. Self-guided driving tour with 13 historical markers.

10. FORT OSAGE

Sibley, (816) 650-5737

Served as government fur-trading post, 1808-27. One of first outposts in Louisiana Territory. Reconstructed fort, visitor center, museum, living history demonstrations.

DID YOU KNOW?
Gen. John Pershing's nickname was "Black Jack" because he had commanded a unit of the U.S. Army's all-black 10th Cavalry Regiment (Buffalo Soldiers). He was an outspoken advocate of the value of black soldiers in the military.

11. GEN. JOHN J. PERSHING BOYHOOD HOME STATE HISTORIC SITE

Laclede, (660) 963-2525

Preserved boyhood home, bronze statue with Wall of Honor, and exhibit gallery in 1-room Prairie Mound School, where he once taught.

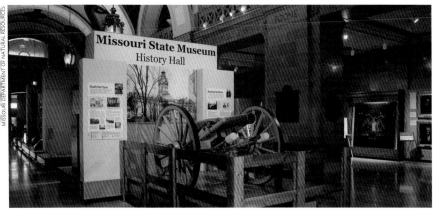

Missouri State Museum, Jefferson City

Gen. John J. Pershing Boyhood Home State
Historic Site, Laclede

Anderson House at Battle of Lexington State
Historic Site, Lexington

12. JEFFERSON BARRACKS HISTORIC PARK

St. Louis, (314) 544-5714

Served as major military installation from 1826 to 1946, and as a Union hospital during Civil War. Museum in 1857 powder magazine depicts barracks history. 1851 ordnance building houses special exhibits on military history. Restored 1851 Laborers House, stable. 1878 stable with visitor center. Memorials on grounds.

13. JEFFERSON NATIONAL EXPANSION MEMORIAL

St. Louis, (314) 655-1700

Museum of Westward Expansion, located under the Gateway Arch, chronicles exploration in West, including clashes with Indians.

14. LONE JACK BATTLEFIELD MUSEUM

Lone Jack, (816) 697-8833

Museum sits on site of August 1862 battle. Covers county Civil War history and Battle of Lone Jack, with weapons, uniforms, diorama, exhibits on soldier life and 6 cases of battlefield artifacts.

15. MISSOURI STATE MUSEUM

Jefferson City, (573) 751-4127

Military exhibits cover role of state residents in wars from the Revolutionary War through WWII, including weapons, pictures and dioramas, plus 6-ft. model of *USS Missouri*.

16. MUSEUM OF MISSOURI MILITARY HISTORY

Jefferson City, (573) 638-9603

Covers history of militia/National Guard and its role in Missouri from 1780 through Iraq. Exhibits include artifacts, uniforms, weapons and photographs.

17. NATIONAL WWI MUSEUM AT LIBERTY MEMORIAL

Kansas City, (816) 784-1918

Only public U.S. museum dedicated solely to WWI. 30,000 square feet of exhibits include interactive map, uniforms, weapons, medals and field hospital diorama. 217-ft. monument.

✳ ✳ ✳
Missouri Native:
HARRY TRUMAN

Truman served in France from April 13, 1918, through April 9, 1919. As captain of D Battery, 129th Field Artillery Regt., 35th Inf. Div., he fought in the Vosges Mountains and St. Mihiel and Meuse-Argonne offensives.

A biographer wrote, "The decision to go into the Army during WWI was the crucial event in Harry Truman's life." Truman agreed: "My whole political career is based upon my war service and war associates." He was a lifetime VFW member.

Ranked No. 7 (a "near great") among U.S. presidents, this Lamar, Mo., native brought the Pacific war to a swift end, launched the Truman Doctrine, authorized the Marshall Plan, helped establish NATO and presided over the Berlin Airlift.

Truman's Army uniform at Truman Presidential Library & Museum, Independence

Ulysses S. Grant National Historic Site, St. Louis

18. SOLDIERS' MEMORIAL MILITARY MUSEUM

St. Louis, (314) 622-4550

Exhibits include weapons, photographs, medals, uniforms, souvenirs, banners and memorabilia of St. Louis military history since 1800. Memorial bears names of 1,075 local soldiers killed in WWI. Memorials to those killed in WWII, Korea and Vietnam across the street.

19. STARS & STRIPES MUSEUM & LIBRARY

Bloomfield, (573) 568-2055

Covers history of Stars and Stripes newspaper from original issue printed by Union soldiers in 1861 to present. Exhibits include military uniforms, printing equipment, dark room, howitzers and Huey helicopter.

20. TRUMAN PRESIDENTIAL MUSEUM & LIBRARY

Independence, (816) 268-8200

Includes WWI artifacts from President Harry Truman's war service, and covers WWII, Korea and the Cold War. Highlights Truman's decision to use nuclear weapons, wartime propaganda and the Berlin Airlift.

21. ULYSSES S. GRANT NATIONAL HISTORIC SITE

St. Louis, (314) 842-3298

Park commemorates Grant's life, military career and presidency. 5 historic structures, visitor center with exhibits and library.

22. U.S. ARMY CHEMICAL CORPS MUSEUM

Ft. Leonard Wood
(573) 596-0131 (ext. 68844)

Traces history of Chemical Corps from 1919 to the present. More than 5,000 artifacts from history and development of chemical, biological and nuclear warfare, plus the corps' role in 20th century conflicts. Exhibits include protective masks, decontamination equipment, uniforms and supplies from WWI to present. Outdoor exhibits.

23. U.S. ARMY ENGINEER MUSEUM

Ft. Leonard Wood
(573) 596-8015

Covers history of Fort Leonard Wood and American military engineering. Exhibits include land mine warfare, tactical bridging, topographic engineering, special weapons and engineering equipment. 13 restored WWII mobilization barracks and large outdoor vehicle park.

Wilson's Creek National Battlefield, Republic

Soldier's Memorial Military Museum, St. Louis

> ✳   ✳   ✳
> **DID YOU KNOW?**
> More than 1,000 Civil War
> battles were fought in
> Missouri — only Tennessee
> and Virginia saw more.

24. U.S. ARMY MILITARY POLICE CORPS REGIMENTAL MUSEUM

Ft. Leonard Wood
(573) 596-0604

Covers history of military police from 1776 to present, with uniforms, field equipment, documents, weapons and combat art from WWI to Persian Gulf War and beyond.

25. VETERANS MEMORIAL MUSEUM

Branson, (417) 336-2300

More than 2,000 exhibits in 18,000 square feet of space cover the wars and conflicts of the 20th century through sculpture, murals, artifacts and memorabilia. Features the world's largest war memorial bronze sculpture (70 feet long), depicting 50 life-size soldiers storming a beach. Names of all service members killed in the 20th century are displayed on the walls of the 10 exhibit halls.

26. WILSON'S CREEK NATIONAL BATTLEFIELD

Republic, (417) 732-2662

Site of first major Civil War battle west of the Mississippi, August 1861. Visitor center features museum, film and battle map. Five-mile self-guided driving tour passes eight wayside exhibits, 12 displays and walking trails. Restored Ray House served as temporary field hospital during battle.

27. WILSON'S CREEK MUSEUM OF CIVIL WAR HISTORY

Republic, (417) 732-1224

Features Civil War collection from west of the Mississippi, with more than 50 displays on Bushwackers, a Mississippi gunboat, weapons, uniforms, photos and flags.

MONTANA

Four major battles between the U.S. Army and Indians occurred in the Treasure State. Two are preserved in national parks.

Best known, of course, is the famous place of Custer's last stand at Little Bighorn Battlefield National Monument.

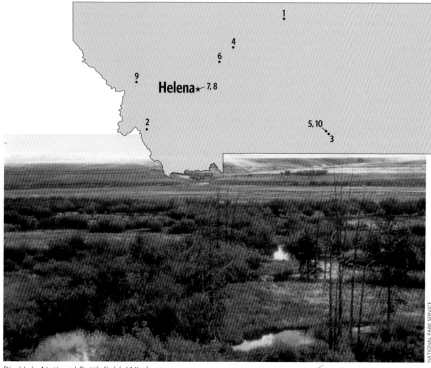

Big Hole National Battlefield, Wisdom

NATIONAL PARK SERVICE

1. BEAR PAW BATTLEFIELD
Chinook, (406) 357-3130
Site of final battle of Nez Perce War, September/October 1877, after which Chief Joseph surrendered and Indians moved to a reservation. Self-guided trail, interpretive signs and markers. Interim visitor center in **BLAINE COUNTY MUSEUM,** *Chinook,* *(406) 357-2590.*

2. BIG HOLE NATIONAL BATTLEFIELD
Wisdom, (406) 689-3155
Site of August 1877 battle of Nez Perce War in which 31 Army soldiers and 90 Nez Perce Indians were killed. Visitor center overlooks battlefield on which trails lead to areas of interest. Displays include video, photos, quotations and personal belongings of battle participants and non-combatants.

3. CUSTER BATTLEFIELD MUSEUM
Garryowen, (406) 638-1876
Houses extensive exhibit of artifacts, clothing and photographs associated with Battle of Little Bighorn and Plains Indian wars.

4. FORT BENTON
Fort Benton, (406) 622-5316
Originally a fur-trading post built in 1846. Occupied by Army, 1869-75. Partially reconstructed fort with exhibits, 2 museums. Lewis and Clark memorial nearby.

Malmstrom Air Force Base Museum, Great Falls

* * *
DID YOU KNOW?
During WWII, a secret operation was planned for the Army's First Special Service Force using teams of sled dogs in Norway. These men and dogs were trained at Camp Rimini in the mountains near Helena. Learn more about the training center in Montana's Military Museum.

Little Bighorn Battlefield National Monument, Crow Agency

5. LITTLE BIGHORN BATTLEFIELD NATIONAL MONUMENT
Crow Agency, (406) 638-2621
Site of legendary June 1876 battle between 7th Cavalry and Sioux and Cheyenne Indians under Sitting Bull in which 268 U.S. cavalrymen were killed. Visitor center, museum, walking tour with interpretive markers, Custer National Cemetery, 4½-mile Battlefield Road that connects Custer and Reno-Benteen battlefields. New Indian memorial.

6. MALMSTROM AIR FORCE BASE MUSEUM
Great Falls, (406) 731-2705
Indoor displays include model aircraft, WWII-era barracks room, Lend-Lease diorama, survival equipment, and Minute Man I and II missile launch consoles and launch facility cutaway.

7. MONTANA HISTORICAL SOCIETY MUSEUM
Helena, (406) 444-4710
Covers Lewis and Clark, Indian wars of 1870s-80s, impacts of Spanish-American War and WWI on Montana life, and role of Montana units in conflicts from WWI through the present. Tribute to joint First Special Service Force of WWII.

8. MONTANA'S MILITARY MUSEUM
Fort Harrison (Helena) (406) 324-3550
Features chronological progression of military in Montana from 1805 (Lewis and Clark) through Persian Gulf War and 20th century peacekeeping operations. More than 6,000 artifacts. Serves as anchor to chain of military memorial sites throughout Helena, including Philippines War plaque and Civil War memorials.

9. ROCKY MOUNTAIN MUSEUM OF MILITARY HISTORY
Missoula, (406) 549-5346
Covers Montana military history and Montanans in battle from frontier period through war on terrorism with exhibits, dioramas and weapons. Housed in 2 buildings built in 1936 by Civilian Conservation Corps, also featured in an exhibit.

10. ROSEBUD BATTLEFIELD STATE PARK
near Crow Agency (406) 234-0900
Site of second battle in Army's 1876 campaign against Sioux and Cheyenne Indians, in June 1876. Small interpretive display.

NEBRASKA

Five frontier forts can be seen in the Cornhusker State, including Fort Atkinson State Historical Park. A variety of museums, such as the Museum of the Fur Trade and the Strategic Air & Space Museum, can satisfy a wide range of tastes.

COURTESY STRATEGIC AIR & SPACE MUSEUM

Strategic Air & Space Museum, Ashland

1. DAWSON COUNTY HISTORICAL MUSEUM
Lexington, (308) 324-5340
Displays on Plum Creek Massacre. Markers, cemetery, small monument at site of Indian attack on wagon train.

2. FORT ATKINSON STATE HISTORICAL PARK
Fort Calhoun, (402) 468-5611
First U.S. military post west of the Missouri River, 1820-27. Reconstructed fort, visitor center with displays, artifacts and theater.

3. FORT HARTSUFF STATE HISTORICAL PARK
Burwell, (308) 346-4715
Active 1874 to 1881. Nine restored original concrete buildings, visitor center with interpretive displays.

4. FORT KEARNY STATE HISTORICAL PARK
Kearney, (308) 865-5305
Protected Overland Trail, 1848-71. Was a Pony Express home station, outfitting depot for Indian campaigns and home to Pawnee Scouts. Reconstructed fort, visitor center, self-guided walking tours.

5. FORT ROBINSON STATE PARK
Crawford, (308) 665-2900
Active 1874-1948. A cavalry remount station, K-9 dog training center and WWII POW camp. Museum, many restored buildings, historic tours. Monuments to 5th Cavalry and Yellow Hair at nearby (20 miles) War Bonnet Creek.

6. FORT SIDNEY COMPLEX
Sidney, (308) 254-5851
Protected Union Pacific Railroad workers, 1867-94. Restored commander and officers quarters, museum.

Fort Kearny State Historical Park, Kearney

Museum of the Fur Trade, Chadron

7. FREEDOM PARK
Omaha, (402) 345-1959
Includes *USS Hazard* (WWII minesweeper), *USS Marlin* (training submarine) and *USS LSM-45* (WWII amphibious landing ship). Temporarily closed.

8. GENERAL CROOK HOUSE MUSEUM
Omaha, (402) 455-9990
Restored 1879 home of the "greatest Indian fighter in U.S. history." Military artifacts and exhibits, plus buildings of Historic Fort Omaha, built in 1868.

> ✳   ✳   ✳
> **DID YOU KNOW?**
> At its peak in 1945, the Naval Ammunition Depot in Hastings was the largest U.S. ordnance plant during WWII. It provided more than 40% of the Navy's ammunition during the war.

9. HEARTLAND MUSEUM OF MILITARY VEHICLES
Lexington, (308) 324-6329
Some 60 restored vehicles span more than half a century: jeeps, trucks, planes, helicopters, 2 Bradley Fighting Vehicles and an M-60 Main Battle Tank.

10. MUSEUM OF NEBRASKA HISTORY
Lincoln, (402) 471-4754
Covers state's role in Civil War, and overseas and homefront involvement of state residents during WWII.

11. MUSEUM OF THE FUR TRADE
Chadron, (308) 432-3843
Reconstructed 1837 Bordeaux Trading Post: 3 galleries cover history of North American fur trading, 1500-1900, and frontier weapons.

12. STATE ARSENAL MUSEUM
Lincoln, (402) 309-7545
Addresses military service of Nebraskans from first volunteer units in 1854 through Persian Gulf War. By appointment only.

13. STRATEGIC AIR & SPACE MUSEUM
Ashland, (402) 944-3100
300,000 square feet house a glass atrium, two aircraft display hangars, 200-seat theater and aircraft restoration gallery. Displays include aircraft, missiles and aerospace artifacts.

NEVADA

The career of the *USS Nevada,* severely hit at Pearl Harbor, is chronicled at the Nevada State Museum, and the Silver State's contributions to WWII also are on display. The little-known 1860 Pyramid Lake campaign against Paiute Indians is interpreted at Fort Churchill.

*Carson City

Fort Churchill State Historic Park, Silver Springs

NEVADA DIVISION OF STATE PARKS

Nevada State Museum, Carson City

NEVADA STATE MUSEUM

1. FORT CHURCHILL STATE HISTORIC PARK
Silver Springs, (775) 577-2345

Provided protection for settlers, Pony Express, etc., 1861-1869. Historical marker in town, adobe ruins and visitor center tell story of 1861 Pyramid Lake campaign against Paiute Indians. Interpretive trail.

2. NEVADA STATE MUSEUM
Carson City, (775) 687-4810

Features displays on career of *USS Nevada,* including artifacts and parts of the ship, and the state's contributions to WWII.

DID YOU KNOW?
Nevada's official state slogan is "The Battle Born State" because the state was admitted into the Union during the Civil War.

NEW HAMPSHIRE

Those with varied military interests will enjoy the hodge-podge of sites located in the Granite State, from a Navy submarine to an outdoor shrine to veterans.

Cathedral of the Pines, Rindge

American Independence Museum, Exeter

1. ALBACORE PARK
Portsmouth, (603) 436-3680
Year-round guided tours of U.S. Navy experimental submarine *USS Albacore.*

2. AMERICAN INDEPENDENCE MUSEUM
Exeter, (603) 772-2622
Ladd-Gilman House features exhibits on the state's role in the Revolution and its military, 18th century weapons, and the Society of the Cincinnati, the nation's first veterans organization.

3. CATHEDRAL OF THE PINES
Rindge, (603) 899-3300
Outdoor shrine honors all Americans killed in war and features a museum with war memorabilia.

4. FORT CONSTITUTION HISTORIC SITE
New Castle, (603) 436-1552
Site of first overt act of rebellion against British, Dec. 14, 1774, when rebels seized British powder and arms. Restored 1808 portcullis (iron grating) and gateway, powder magazine and heavy gun platform. Interpretive signs, self-guided tour.

Museum of New Hampshire History, Concord

5. FORT STARK HISTORIC SITE
New Castle, (603) 436-1552
Self-guided tour of remaining early 1900s batteries.

6. MUSEUM OF NEW HAMPSHIRE HISTORY
Concord, (603) 228-6688
Sections of "New Hampshire Through Many Eyes" exhibit cover Revolution, Civil War and WWI.

7. WOODMAN INSTITUTE
Dover, (603) 742-1038
Top floor houses War Memorial Museum.

8. WRIGHT MUSEUM
Wolfeboro, (603) 569-1212
Covers WWII on the home front, plus displays on Army Air Forces, Women Airforce Service Pilots (WASPs), and a large collection of fully operational military vehicles.

NEW JERSEY

An important theater during the Revolutionary War, New Jersey offers many exhibits and battlegrounds from this war, including the site of George Washington's historic crossing of the Delaware River, and Morristown National Historical Park, the site of two of the Continental Army's winter encampments. The Garden State also features a handful of naval sites like the New Jersey Naval Museum. The unique New Jersey Vietnam Veterans Memorial & Vietnam Era Education Center is in Holmdel.

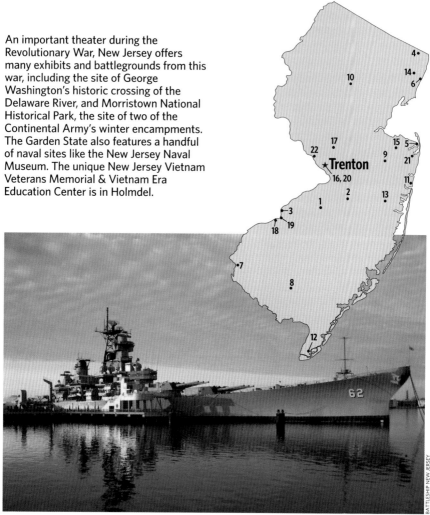

Battleship *New Jersey*, Camden

1. AIR VICTORY MUSEUM
Lumberton, (609) 267-4488
Features aviation artifacts, uniforms, engines and restored aircraft, including an F-14 Tomcat and an F-86 Sabre.

2. ARMY RESERVE MUSEUM OF MOBILIZATION (FORMERLY FORT DIX MUSEUM)
Fort Dix (*Wrightstown*) (609) 562-6983
Will open mid-2008. 8,000 square feet will cover Army Reserve mobilization from 1776 to the present.

3. BATTLESHIP NEW JERSEY
Camden, (856) 966-1652
U.S. Navy's most-decorated battleship served in WWII, Korea, Vietnam and Persian Gulf. 2-hour guided tours include displays and multimedia room. Firepower Tour focuses on ship's weapons systems. Self-guided tours also available.

Fort Lee Historic Park, Fort Lee

Air Victory Museum, Lumberton

✳   ✳   ✳

New Jersey Native: ZEBULON PIKE

Discoverer of Colorado's Pike's Peak in 1806, this Trenton, N.J., native explored the upper Mississippi River and the Southwest, particularly New Mexico. His 3-volume chronicle (1810) of his expeditions encouraged westward expansion.

Joining the U.S. Army at age 15, Pike soon served in at least 4 frontier forts in the hostile Ohio country during the late 1790s.

Pike was a brigadier general by the War of 1812, during which he was mortally wounded in April 1813.

4. BAYLOR MASSACRE BURIAL SITE

River Vale, (201) 336-7267

Commemorative plaques and gravesites detail Sept. 28, 1778, massacre of up to 22 Continental soldiers by British and Tories.

5. FORT HANCOCK

Highlands, (732) 872-5970

Fort built 1890. Fort Hancock Museum in former guardhouse has exhibits on New York Harbor coastal defenses, 1895-1974 (open weekends). Restored 1898 officer's row History House illustrates 1940s fort life. Interpretive signs, tours of Battery Potter, Sandy Hook Visitor Center.

6. FORT LEE HISTORIC PARK

Fort Lee, (201) 461-1776

Site of Continental Army batteries, with reproduction gun batteries accessible by short interpretive trails and a reconstructed 18th century hut. 11,000-sq.-ft. visitor center features 12-minute film and two floors of displays covering Revolutionary War in New Jersey.

7. FORT MOTT STATE PARK

Salem, (856) 935-3218

1896 fort built for Spanish-American War. Self-guided tours of remains with interpretive signs. N.J. Coastal Heritage Trail Welcome Center contains displays on fort's history.

8. MILLVILLE ARMY AIR FIELD MUSEUM

Millville, (856) 327-2347

Covers military aviation history and P-47 Thunderbolt. WWII artifacts and static displays.

9. MONMOUTH BATTLEFIELD STATE PARK

Freehold, (732) 462-9616

Site of one of the largest Revolutionary War battles, June 28, 1778. Restored 1710 farmhouse, visitor center with interpretive displays, fiber-optic map and artifacts from the battle.

New Jersey Vietnam Veterans Memorial & Vietnam Era Education Center, Holmdel

Morristown National Historical Park, Morristown

National Guard Militia Museum of New Jersey, Sea Girt

10. MORRISTOWN NATIONAL HISTORICAL PARK

Morristown, (973) 539-2016

Site of Continental Army's winter encampments, 1777 and 1779-80. Consists of **FORD MANSION** (Washington's Headquarters) with guided tours; **1777 FORT NONSENSE** with cannon, exhibits and fort outline; and **JOCKEY HOLLOW,** *(973) 543-4030,* with 5 re-created soldier huts and visitor center with displays and film. Washington's Headquarters Museum closed for renovation.

11. NATIONAL GUARD MILITIA MUSEUM OF NEW JERSEY

Sea Girt, (732) 974-5966

Exhibits cover early state militias, state's role in French & Indian and Revolutionary wars, Korean War, military medicine and weapons. Military vehicles and aircraft on outdoor display.

FIELD ARTILLERY ANNEX in *Lawrenceville, (609) 530-6802,* covers Revolutionary War to the present, with 2 rooms on Civil War, Sons of Union Veterans of the Civil War Camp No. 4 and Grand Army of the Republic.

12. NAVAL AIR STATION WILDWOOD AVIATION MUSEUM

Rio Grande, (609) 886-8787

92,000-sq.-ft. wooden hangar houses aircraft, aviation artifacts, military memorabilia and aircraft engines.

13. NAVY LAKEHURST HISTORICAL SOCIETY INFORMATION CENTER

Lakehurst, (732) 818-7520

Covers history of naval aviation of WWI, WWII, Korea, the Cold War and present day. Features Vietnam POW remembrance room, joint services room, and Army equipment. Tours by appointment only.

USS *Ling* at the New Jersey Naval Museum, Hackensack

Monmouth Battlefield State Park, Freehold

14. NEW JERSEY NAVAL MUSEUM

Hackensack, (201) 342-3268

Attractions include submarine *USS Ling* with guided tours, Vietnam-era PBR Mark II gunboat, Japanese Kaiten suicide torpedo and German 2-man coastal defense submarine. Museum features Navy SEAL delivery vehicle, artifacts and personal effects.

15. NEW JERSEY VIETNAM VETERANS MEMORIAL & VIETNAM ERA EDUCATION CENTER

Holmdel, (732) 335-0033

5,000-sq.-ft. exhibit area of education center features historical timeline with touchscreen computers and photographs, written eyewitness accounts and an oral history theater. Collection of memorabilia left at the memorial, temporary exhibits of artifacts and resource center.

16. OLD BARRACKS MUSEUM

Trenton, (609) 396-1776

1758 structure is only surviving British colonial barracks in the U.S. Used as military hospital in Revolutionary War. Museum features restored officer's quarters, soldier barracks room and hospital room. Costumed interpreters describe the Battle of Trenton and medical techniques of the time.

17. PRINCETON BATTLEFIELD STATE PARK

Princeton, (609) 921-0074

Site of Jan. 3, 1777, battle, the Continental Army's first victory against British regulars. Four-column battle memorial. 1772 Clarke House includes Revolutionary War exhibits. Princeton Battle Monument in town.

18. RED BANK BATTLEFIELD PARK

National Park, (856) 853-5120

Site of Fort Mercer and October 1777 battle. Restored 1748 Whitall House nearby served as military hospital after the battle. Museum with fort and battle relics, interpretive signs, monument.

19. TOWNSEND C. YOUNG VFW POST 3620 DONALD "DOC" DOHERTY VETERANS MUSEUM

Gloucester City, (856) 456-7135

Located on second floor of VFW Post. Includes artifacts from every conflict in which the U.S. was involved from 1674 to the present.

20. TRENTON BATTLE MONUMENT

Trenton, (609) 737-0623

150-ft. granite monument marks site of Continental Army artillery emplacement in Dec. 26, 1776, Battle of Trenton.

21. U.S. ARMY COMMUNICATIONS AND ELECTRONICS MUSEUM

Fort Monmouth (Longbranch) (732) 532-1682

Exhibits cover history of Fort Monmouth and development of military communications radars and sensors. Open by appointment.

22. WASHINGTON CROSSING STATE PARK

Titusville, (609) 737-9303

Site of George Washington's historic Delaware River crossing, Dec. 25, 1776. Interpretive signs. Visitor center museum's exhibits cover Revolution and "Ten Crucial Days" campaign.

NEW MEXICO

The development of an atomic bomb during WWII, a process known as the Manhattan Project, largely took place in New Mexico. Replicas of the atomic bombs used in WWII—Little Boy and Fat Man—are displayed at the National Atomic Museum, which also covers nuclear science history in the military. The Land of Enchantment also features a missile range museum and sites from the Civil War, the Mexican War and the Mexican border conflict of 1916.

Fort Union National Monument, Watrous

1. BATAAN MEMORIAL MILITARY MUSEUM & LIBRARY
Santa Fe, (505) 474-1670
Central focus on men of 200th Coast Artillery Regiment who spent years in Japanese captivity on Bataan, Philippines, during WWII. Housed in 1941 armory. Exhibits encompass 16th century through Persian Gulf War.

2. ERNIE PYLE HOME & LIBRARY
Albuquerque, (505) 256-2065
Memorabilia-filled home of Pulitzer Prize-winning WWII correspondent. Branch of Albuquerque Public Library.

3. FORT SELDEN STATE MONUMENT
Radium Springs (505) 526-8911
Protected settlers from outlaws and Apaches from 1865 to 1891. Visitor center, remains of adobe buildings.

New Mexico Native:
BILL MAULDIN

Pulitzer Prize-winning editorial cartoonist Bill Mauldin was born in Mountain Park, N.M., on Oct. 29, 1921.

His grandfather was a civilian cavalry scout in the Apache wars, and his father was an artilleryman in WWI. Mauldin entered the Army in 1940. He served with the 45th Infantry Division in WWII and received a Purple Heart. During the war, he created two cartoon infantrymen, Willie and Joe, who became synonymous with the average GI. Soon he began working for *Stars and Stripes,* and his cartoons were seen all over the world.

Mauldin won the Pulitzer Prize for his cartoons in 1945 at the age of 23.

After the war, Mauldin turned to drawing political cartoons, which he did for such publications as the *St. Louis Post-Dispatch* and the *Chicago Sun-Times,* where he worked for 29 years until his retirement in 1991. He died in 2003 from complications of Alzheimer's disease.

Kit Carson Home & Museum, Taos

Fort Selden State Monument, Radium Springs

6. GEN. DOUGLAS L. MCBRIDE MUSEUM
Roswell, (505) 624-8220
Museum at New Mexico Military Institute covers Corps of Cadets life and military conflicts in which alumni have served.

7. GOVERNOR BENT HOUSE & MUSEUM
Taos, (505) 758-2376
Site of January 1847 Mexican War skirmish in which Charles Bent, governor of New Mexico, was killed. Museum features 19th century artifacts of the area.

Ernie Pyle Home & Library, Albuquerque

4. FORT SUMNER STATE MONUMENT
Fort Sumner, (505) 355-2573
Built in 1862. Navajos held there during 1860s. Visitor center, historical exhibits and interpretive trail focus on Indians.

5. FORT UNION NATIONAL MONUMENT
Ft. Union (Watrous)
(505) 425-8025
Guarded Santa Fe Trail and served as military garrison, territorial arsenal and supply depot for Southwest from 1851 to 1891. Fort ruins, museum, tours.

8. KIT CARSON HOME & MUSEUM
Taos, (505) 758-4945
Contains portion of original home, plus artifacts and exhibits illustrating life story of the legendary scout, who served in Civil and Indian wars. He is buried in nearby **KIT CARSON MEMORIAL STATE PARK.**

White Sands Missile Range Museum, near Las Cruces

9. LAS VEGAS CITY MUSEUM & ROUGH RIDERS MEMORIAL COLLECTION
Las Vegas, (505) 454-1401, ext. 283

Features mementos, artifacts and photos of Theodore Roosevelt's cavalry regiment of Spanish-American War fame.

10. NATIONAL ATOMIC MUSEUM (NATIONAL MUSEUM OF NUCLEAR SCIENCE & HISTORY)
Kirkland AFB (Albuquerque) (505) 245-2137

Museum of nuclear science and history includes exhibits on Manhattan Project, WWII, the Cold War and history of arms control. Features replicas of WWII atomic weapons Little Boy and Fat Man.

11. PANCHO VILLA STATE PARK
Columbus, (505) 531-2711

Site of last armed invasion of continental U.S. when Mexican revolutionary Pancho Villa attacked city in March 1916. Impetus for Pershing's Punitive Expedition. Camp Furlong ruins, visitor center featuring artifacts, historic photos, exhibits, film.

12. PECOS NATIONAL HISTORICAL PARK
Pecos, (505) 757-6414

Site of March 1862 Civil War battle of Glorieta Pass. Park includes 2 units preserving battle sites. Marble plaque. Access to units by ranger-guided tour only. Call for reservations.

13. WAR EAGLES AIR MUSEUM
Santa Teresa, (505) 589-2000

Covers WWII and Korean War through 64,000 square feet of displays, including 28 historic aircraft, 5 military vehicles and special exhibits.

14. WHITE SANDS MISSILE RANGE MUSEUM
east of Las Cruces (505) 678-8824

Includes weapons systems, rocket technology and 1880 battle between 9th Cavalry and Apaches in Hembrillo Basin.

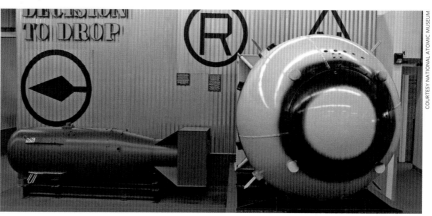

National Atomic Museum, Albuquerque

NEW YORK

During the French & Indian War, more battles were fought in New York than in any other state, represented by five battle sites. New York's location also made it a crossroads during the Revolutionary War and the War of 1812, and nearly 20 battle sites and museums covering these wars are open to visitors. Enthusiasts of historic forts will enjoy the Empire State, which hosts at least 14 from colonial times through the late 20th century.

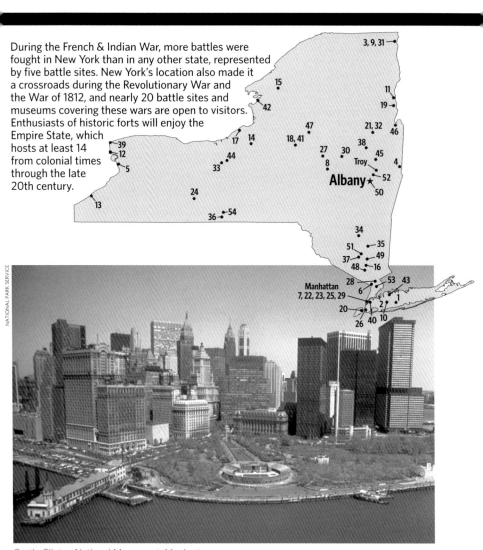

Castle Clinton National Monument, Manhattan

1. AMERICAN AIRPOWER MUSEUM
Farmingdale, (212) 843-8010
WWII hangar with operational era warplanes, including a B-17 Flying Fortress and a P-40 Warhawk. Control tower retrofitted to 1940s operations, fleet of vintage automobiles and trucks, interpreters and volunteers in period gear.

2. AMERICAN MERCHANT MARINE MUSEUM
Kings Point, (516) 773-5515
Includes displays on marine art, ship models and nautical artifacts.

3. BATTLE OF PLATTSBURGH INTERPRETIVE CENTER
Plattsburgh, (518) 566-1814
Allan S. Everest Gallery, with dioramas of both land and naval battles of 1814 and 10,000-sq.-ft. War of 1812 Museum. Provides map to tour city's key battle sites. Base's 1838 barracks also on site. 134-ft. battle monument in town.

4. BENNINGTON BATTLEFIELD STATE HISTORIC SITE

Hoosick, (518) 686-8266

Site of August 1777 battle. Interpretive signs, relief maps. 1830s Barnett Homestead features costumed interpreters and gallery on the battle.

5. BUFFALO & ERIE COUNTY NAVAL & MILITARY PARK

Buffalo, (716) 847-1773

Guided-missile cruiser *USS Little Rock,* destroyer *USS The Sullivans* and WWII submarine *USS Croaker* all open for self-guided tours. Exhibits cover Marine Corps memorabilia, women in the military, destroyer escort sailors, Vietnam vets and aircraft models. Other equipment on display includes armored personnel carrier, tank, Huey helicopter and fast patrol boat.

6. CAMP SHANKS WWII MUSEUM

Orangeburg, (845) 638-5419

Exhibits focus on WWII military life at camp, the largest Army embarkation port for the European theater.

7. CASTLE CLINTON NATIONAL MONUMENT

Manhattan, (212) 344-7220

1811 fort built to defend New York Harbor. Interpreters describe fort's construction and its role in the War of 1812. Park ranger-led programs and tours, self-guided tours.

8. CHERRY VALLEY MUSEUM

Cherry Valley, (607) 264-3303

Includes exhibit on Cherry Valley Massacre of Nov. 11, 1778, in which 700 Tories and Seneca Indians killed 48 settlers and Continental soldiers. Monument marks mass grave in city cemetery.

American Merchant Marine Museum, Kings Point

Buffalo & Erie County Naval & Military Park, Buffalo

9. CLINTON COUNTY HISTORICAL MUSEUM

Plattsburgh, (518) 561-0340

Contains diorama of battles of Valcour Island (1776) and Plattsburgh (1814) that explains strategic importance of Lake Champlain.

10. CRADLE OF AVIATION MUSEUM

Garden City, (516) 572-4066

Military collections include exhibits and aircraft from WWI, WWII and space exploration.

11. CROWN POINT STATE HISTORIC SITE

Crown Point, (518) 597-3666

Site of 1734 French Fort St. Frederic and 1759 British Fort Crown Point. Captured by colonists in 1775. Ruins of both forts include stonework, bastions and barracks. Museum with orientation film, exhibits, artifacts, electric map and models of both forts.

12. DEVIL'S HOLE MASSACRE SITE

Niagara Falls, (716) 284-4691

Site of Sept. 14, 1763, massacre in which 300 Seneca Indians ambushed a British supply train, killing 112 men and throwing their bodies into the gorge below. Parking lot off NB Robert Moses Parkway.

Fort Ontario State Historic Site, Oswego

13. DUNKIRK HISTORICAL LIGHTHOUSE & VETERANS PARK MUSEUM

Dunkirk, (716) 366-5050
Museum includes display rooms for Coast Guard, Marine Corps, Army, Navy, Air Force and Vietnam War.

14. FORT BREWERTON

Brewerton, (315) 668-8801
Reconstructed blockhouse museum with local artifacts from prehistoric times to WWI. Adjacent original earthworks of 1759 British fort.

15. FORT DRUM HISTORICAL HOLDING

Fort Drum (northeast of Watertown), (315) 772-9007
1,700-sq.-ft. indoor exhibit area illustrates history of fort, weapons, equipment and 10th Mountain Division in WWII. Tanks, helicopter, artillery and other equipment on outdoor display.

16. FORT MONTGOMERY STATE HISTORIC SITE

Bear Mountain (845) 446-2134
Site of Oct. 6, 1777, battle. Park includes fort ruins, Grand Battery, earthwork remains and interpretive trail.

17. FORT ONTARIO STATE HISTORIC SITE

Oswego, (315) 343-4711
Star-shaped fort was first fortified during French & Indian War and in use through WWII. Barracks, guard houses, powder magazine, officer's quarters, underground stone casements and grounds restored to 1868-72 appearance. Orientation exhibit in enlisted barracks and costumed interpreters tell history of fort.

National Park Service

General Grant National Memorial, Manhattan

18. FORT STANWIX NATIONAL MONUMENT
Rome, (315) 336-2090

Built during French & Indian War. Attacked by British, Tories and Indians in 1777, withstanding a 3-week siege. Reconstructed fort, visitor center with ranger-led orientation, museum with fort artifacts, 3 interpretive trails and living history programs. Marinus Willett Center features additional exhibits and audiovisual programs. Nearby is **TOMB OF THE UNKNOWN SOLDIER OF THE AMERICAN REVOLUTION.**

19. FORT TICONDEROGA
Ticonderoga, (518) 585-2821

Built in 1755, the French fort was captured by British in 1777. Site of 1758 battle and several Revolutionary War battles. Restored fort with guided and self-guided tours. Museum inside restored 1756 barracks building with more than 30,000 items on colonial and Revolutionary periods. Interpretive signs, costumed interpreters and weapons demonstrations. Research library.

20. FORT WADSWORTH
Staten Island, (718) 354-4500

Includes 1860 Fort Tompkins and Battery Weed, both available for guided tours. Visitor center features 12-minute orientation film, plus exhibits on harbor forts and coastal defense.

21. FORT WILLIAM HENRY MUSEUM
Lake George, (518) 668-5471

Replica 1755 fort contains barracks, stockades, dungeons, interpretive displays, audiovisual presentations and fort artifacts. Costumed interpreters lead guided tours and conduct weapons demonstrations. Museum with life-size mannequins re-creating daily British/militia soldier life.

Fort Jay at Governor's Island National Monument, Manhattan

Fort Ticonderoga, Ticonderoga

22. FORT WOOD

Manhattan, (212) 363-3200
1808 11-pointed star fort now serves as base of the Statue of Liberty. Interpretive sign.

23. GENERAL GRANT NATIONAL MEMORIAL

Manhattan, (212) 666-1640
Memorial to Ulysses S. Grant includes his tomb (the largest mausoleum in the U.S.), exhibits, artwork, ranger-guided tours and living history and weapons demonstrations.

Fort Wood, Manhattan

24. GLENN H. CURTISS MUSEUM

*Hammondsport
(607) 569-2160*
Dedicated to the "father of Naval aviation," museum includes a WWI area, a P-40 Warhawk and military artifacts.

25. GOVERNOR'S ISLAND NATIONAL MONUMENT

Manhattan, (212) 825-3045
Active military base from 1783-1996. Includes historic Fort Jay, Castle Williams, officers quarters and other structures. Open summers only for ranger-guided and self-guided tours.

26. HARBOR DEFENSE MUSEUM

*Fort Hamilton (Brooklyn)
(718) 630-4349*
Contains artifacts and exhibits on 1825 Fort Hamilton, defense of New York City, coast artillery, military-themed art, and models, dioramas and miniatures of New York soldiers through history. Research library.

27. HERKIMER HOME STATE HISTORIC SITE

Little Falls, (315) 823-0398
Home of Revolutionary War Gen. Nicholas Herkimer. House, visitor center with relics from his service in French & Indian War and Battle of Oriskany, cemetery with 60-ft. monument.

Mount Gulian, Fishkill

New York State Military Museum, Saratoga Springs

28. HISTORICAL SOCIETY OF TARRYTOWN MUSEUM
Tarrytown, (914) 631-8374
Features exhibits and
weapons from Revolutionary
War with emphasis on capture
of British spy Maj. John Andre
and military items from every
war since the Revolutionary
War.

29. INTREPID SEA-AIR-SPACE MUSEUM
Manhattan, (212) 245-0072
Aircraft carrier *USS Intrepid*
served in WWII, Cold War and
Vietnam. Hangar deck houses
exhibit halls, aircraft, artifacts,
models and dioramas. Flight
deck displays aircraft, including the F-14B Tomcat, A-12
Blackbird and the Concorde.
Guided-missile submarine *USS
Growler* open for tours. Closed
for renovation until fall 2008.

30. JOHNSTOWN BATTLEFIELD
Johnstown, (518) 762-8712
Site of last major land battle
of Revolutionary War, Oct. 25,
1781. Plaque in town.

31. KENT-DELORD HOUSE MUSEUM
Plattsburgh, (518) 561-1035
Served as British headquarters in War of 1812. Includes
exhibits on daily life during
the War of 1812 and Civil War.
Earthwork remains of Fort
Brown and plaque at south end
of city.

32. LAKE GEORGE BATTLEFIELD PARK
Lake George, (518) 668-3352
Site of September 1755
Battle for Lake George.
Interpretive signs throughout
park, support building founda-
tions and ruins of uncomplet-
ed bastion.

33. NATIONAL MEMORIAL DAY MUSEUM
Waterloo, (315) 539-0533
22-room brick 1835 mansion
covers history of Memorial
Day, including the Civil War
and the holiday's founding;
GAR and its successors,
including VFW; and service
and sacrifice of veterans,
including every major war
from Revolution through the
present.

34. MINISINK BATTLEGROUND PARK
*Highland, (845) 794-3000,
ext. 3066*
Site of July 22, 1779, battle.
Visitor interpretive center
with displays of historical
materials on the battle.
Battleground Trail highlights
Sentinel Rock, Hospital Rock
and Minisink Monument.

35. MOUNT GULIAN
Fishkill, (845) 831-8172
1783 birthplace of the
Society of the Cincinnati, the
country's first veterans organization. Society artifacts on display, 1-room exhibit.

36. NEWTOWN BATTLEFIELD STATE PARK
Elmira, (607) 732-6067
Site of August 1779 battle.
Battlefield overlook deck with
interpretive signs. Sullivan's
Monument.

Old Fort Niagara State Historic Site, Youngstown

37. NEW WINDSOR CANTONMENT STATE HISTORIC SITE

Vails Gate, (845) 561-1765

Site of last winter encampment of Continental Army and its disbandment. Costumed interpreters demonstrate 18th century military life. Visitor center with exhibits on Revolutionary War and cantonment. 7,500-sq.-ft. NATIONAL PURPLE HEART HALL OF HONOR shares stories of medal recipients.

38. NEW YORK STATE MILITARY MUSEUM

Saratoga Springs (518) 581-5100

Current exhibits include New York in the Revolutionary War, G.I. Joe, Civil War, and Vietnam war paintings and photos. WWI and WWII galleries focus on state participation, especially 27th and 77th divisions.

39. OLD FORT NIAGARA STATE HISTORIC SITE

Youngstown, (716) 745-7611

French post established 1679 and used by U.S. until 1963. 1726 "French Castle" has been restored and furnished to its 18th century appearance. Also features 2 original British redoubts, bakehouse and large powder magazine with archaeological displays. Living history programs.

40. OLD STONE HOUSE

Brooklyn, (718) 768-3195

Original 1699 Dutch farmhouse was site of valiant Maryland regiment attack on British troops during August 1776 Battle of Long Island, the "deadliest of the Revolution." Reconstructed house with interpretive center, exhibit on battle.

41. ORISKANY BATTLEFIELD STATE HISTORIC SITE

Rome, (315) 768-7224

Site of one of the bloodiest battles of the Revolutionary War, Aug. 6, 1777. Visitor center, interpretive signs, monument, guided tours.

42. SACKETS HARBOR BATTLEFIELD STATE HISTORIC SITE

Sackets Harbor (315) 646-3634

Site of northern Army and Navy headquarters, and May 29, 1813, battle. 15 interpretive displays highlight the battle. Guided and self-guided tours, demonstrations of 1812 Army camp life, restored 1850s Navy yard and commandant's house, and lieutenant's house with exhibits. Earthwork remains of Fort Volunteer (Pike) in town.

West Point Museum at U.S. Military Academy, West Point

43. SAGAMORE HILL NATIONAL HISTORIC SITE
Oyster Bay, (516) 922-4788

Home of veteran and president Theodore Roosevelt. 1885 house displays memorabilia. Visitor center, Old Orchard Museum with some military artifacts.

44. SAMPSON WWII NAVAL MUSEUM
Seneca Falls, (315) 585-6203

Features memorabilia, pictures and stories of life and training at Sampson Naval Training Base during WWII. Open summer weekends.

45. SARATOGA NATIONAL HISTORICAL PARK
Stillwater, (518) 664-9821, ext. 224

Site of Sept. 19 and Oct. 7, 1777, battles. Visitor center includes 20-minute orientation film, small museum with artifacts and thematic seasonal exhibits. 9.5-mile, self-guided driving tour with 10 stops. Park also includes **GEN. PHILIP SCHUYLER HOUSE** in Schuylerville and **SARATOGA MONUMENT** in nearby Victory.

46. SKENESBOROUGH MUSEUM
Whitehall, (518) 499-0716

Considered by some to be the birthplace of the U.S. Navy. Main exhibit is 16-ft. diorama of the 1776 Whitehall shipyard. Also includes models of 1812 shipyard, exhibit on Battle of Valcour Island and hull of *USS Ticonderoga*.

47. STEUBEN MEMORIAL STATE HISTORIC SITE
Remsen, (315) 831-3737

Large monument marks burial site of Maj. Gen. Baron von Steuben, "drillmaster of the American Revolution" and author of military "Blue Book." Replica cabin has displays on his life.

48. STONY POINT BATTLEFIELD STATE HISTORIC SITE
Stony Point, (845) 786-2521

Site of British fort and July 1779 battle. Earthen fort remains with historical markers and interpretive trail. Museum with exhibits, costumed interpreters, weapons and camp life demonstrations. Guided and self-guided tours.

49. U.S. MILITARY ACADEMY & WEST POINT MUSEUM
West Point, (845) 938-2638

Visitor center offers films, exhibits and replica cadet barracks room. Narrated bus tours of campus. Museum exhibits cover histories of West Point, the academy, warfare, American wars and the U.S. Army, plus the evolution of weapons. Trophy Point displays captured weapons from every American war beginning with Revolution. Restored 1778 **FORT PUTNAM** available for tours. **CONSTITUTION ISLAND** across the river features fortification remains.

50. USS SLATER
Albany, (518) 431-1943

Restored WWII destroyer escort open for tours.

51. WASHINGTON HEADQUARTERS STATE HISTORIC SITE
Newburgh, (845) 562-1195

1750 Hasbrouck House served as Washington's headquarters, April 1782-August 1783. House furnished as military headquarters. Separate museum contains exhibits on Continental Army. 1887 Tower of Victory monument.

Saratoga National Historical Park, Stillwater

Sagamore Hill National Historic Site, Oyster Bay

✳   ✳   ✳
New York Native:
THEODORE ROOSEVELT

During the Spanish-American War, Roosevelt led the 1st Volunteer Cavalry Regiment ("Rough Riders") on Cuba, participating in the battles of Las Guasimas and Kettle Hill. In January 2001, he was posthumously awarded the Medal of Honor. He was a life-long proponent of veterans, joining VFW in 1917.

Ranked No. 5 among U.S. presidents as a "near great," this New York City native oversaw building the Panama Canal, won the Nobel Peace Prize in 1906, served as assistant secretary of the Navy and created the modern police department.

52. WATERVLIET ARSENAL MUSEUM
Watervliet, (518) 266-5805
Nation's oldest continuously active arsenal, built in 1813. Exhibits on cannon development and equipment from 16th century to the present. Restored 1890s machine shop.

✳   ✳   ✳
DID YOU KNOW?
Fort Stanwix in Rome and Fort Necessity in Pennsylvania are the only French & Indian War sites in the entire National Park Service.

53. WHITE PLAINS NATIONAL BATTLEFIELD SITE
White Plains, (914) 995-8500
Site of Oct. 28, 1776, battle. Three monuments mark George Washington's position in the battle. Interpretive signs in **BATTLE-WHITNEY PARK** on Chatterton Hill.

54. WINGS OF EAGLES DISCOVERY CENTER
Horseheads, (607) 739-8200
Exhibits include military aircraft and artifacts from 1919 through Persian Gulf War. Restoration hangar and vintage aircraft rides.

NORTH CAROLINA

As the birthplace of flight, it is fitting that North Carolina features four aviation museums. The Tar Heel State also is teeming with battlefields from both the Civil and Revolutionary wars.

COURTESY AIRBORNE & SPECIAL OPERATIONS MUSEUM

Airborne & Special Operations Museum, Fayetteville

CIVIL WAR GUIDE
The North Carolina Civil War Tourism Council produces a brochure—*North Carolina Civil War Heritage Trails*—detailing eight Civil War trails covering 41 sites, including battlefields, forts, prison sites, plantations and museums. Call the Council at (919) 876-6067 to request a copy.

---

1. 82ND AIRBORNE DIVISION WAR MEMORIAL MUSEUM
Ft. Bragg (Fayetteville)
(910) 432-3443
15,000 square feet with some 3,000 artifacts tell unit's history from 1917 to the present. Memorials to unit members who died in WWI, WWII, Dominican Republic, Vietnam, Grenada, Panama, Persian Gulf War, Afghanistan and Iraq.

2. AIRBORNE & SPECIAL OPERATIONS MUSEUM
Fayetteville, (910) 483-3003
59,000 square feet commemorate Army airborne and special ops units from 1940 to the present through life-size dioramas, artifacts and interactive displays. Large-screen movie theater and motion simulator that takes visitors through parachute jumps and helicopter gunship attacks.

3. ALAMANCE BATTLEGROUND STATE HISTORIC SITE
Burlington, (336) 227-4785
Site of May 1771 battle between British militia and colonial reformers. Visitor center with audiovisual presentation on the battle, walking trail, monument, restored **JOHN ALLEN HOUSE.**

4. AVERASBORO BATTLEFIELD
Dunn, (910) 891-5019
Site of March 1865 battle, the first deliberate, tactical resistance to Union Gen. William T. Sherman's march through the Carolinas. Museum, interpretive driving tour, cemetery.

Battleship *North Carolina,* Wilmington

5. BATTLESHIP NORTH CAROLINA

Wilmington, (910) 251-5797

Commissioned in 1941, it participated in every major Pacific campaign of WWII. Visitor center with exhibits. Self-guided tours of battleship include portions of 9 decks with gun turrets, crew quarters, sick bay, an engine room, the bridge and the Roll of Honor Room with names of 10,000 North Carolinians killed in WWII.

6. BENNETT PLACE STATE HISTORIC SITE

Durham, (919) 383-4345

Restored Bennett House was site of final and largest Confederate troop surrender of Civil War on April 26, 1865—some 89,000 men. Visitor center with Civil War exhibits, guided tours.

7. BENTONVILLE BATTLEGROUND STATE HISTORIC SITE

north of Newton Grove (910) 594-0789

Site of largest Civil War battle in North Carolina and one of the war's last engagements, March 1865. Restored **HARPER HOUSE** furnished as Civil War field hospital. Visitor center with exhibits, fiber-optic map and 10-minute audiovisual program. Tour trail, monuments, earthworks and cemetery. Area roads marked with highway historical markers highlighting events of battle.

8. BRUNSWICK TOWN/FORT ANDERSON STATE HISTORIC SITE

Winnabow, (910) 371-6613

Major pre-Revolutionary War port razed by British in 1776. Confederates built Fort Anderson on the site in 1861 and were attacked in February 1865. Visitor center with Civil War artifacts, town ruins, well-preserved earthworks.

9. CSS NEUSE STATE HISTORIC SITE & GOVERNOR CASWELL MEMORIAL

Kinston, (252) 522-2091

Memorial building honors Richard Caswell, first governor of North Carolina, and contains remains of the hull of the Confederate ironclad with guided tour, limited displays and a 12-minute video.

THE MARINE CORPS MUSEUM OF THE CAROLINAS

✳ ✳ ✳
DID YOU KNOW?
The Marine Corps Museum of the Carolinas is scheduled to open in Jacksonville in 2009. Plans include a multi-media orientation, hall of honor and exhibits on Camp Lejeune, other Carolina bases, the Carolina Marine presence around the globe, non-warfare missions, the modern Marine Corps, and Marine stories and innovations. Those interested can check the museum's Web site, *www.mcmuseum.com*, or call (910) 937-0033 for details and updates.

COURTESY CSS NEUSE STATE HISTORIC SITE

CSS Neuse State Historic Site, Kinston

NATIONAL PARK SERVICE

Guilford Courthouse National Military Park, Greensboro

10. DARE COUNTY CIVIL WAR HERITAGE TRAIL
Buxton, (252) 473-5772 or 986-2131

80-mile self-guided driving tour travels from Hatteras to Roanoke Island and features 15 markers and wayside exhibits, including the first amphibious landing of the Civil War, the captures of Fort Hatteras and Fort Clark, and the naval engagement between *USS Albatross* and *CSS Beaufort*.

11. FORT DOBBS STATE HISTORIC SITE
Statesville, (704) 873-5866

Active 1756-64 during French & Indian War. No original structures remain. Archaeological sites, visitor center with artifacts, trails.

12. FORT FISHER STATE HISTORIC SITE
Kure Beach, (910) 458-5538

One of the largest Confederate earthwork forts. Attacked December 1864 and January 1865 in the war's largest naval assault. Portion of earthworks and restored wooden palisade on display. Visitor center with 15-minute audiovisual presentation, fiber-optic battle map and exhibits. Guided tours, trail with 12 wayside exhibits, restored gun emplacement and Confederate monument.

13. FORT MACON STATE PARK
Atlantic Beach, (252) 726-3775

Built in 1826-34. Well-preserved brick and stone fort attacked by Union forces March-April 1862, and regarrisoned during Spanish-American War and WWII. 26 restored casemates with exhibits and displays, including re-created Civil War and WWII barracks. Guided and self-guided tours available.

Fort Macon State Park, Atlantic Beach

14. FORT RALEIGH NATIONAL HISTORIC SITE

Manteo, (252) 473-5772

Site of first English attempts at colonization in North America, originally established in 1585. Reconstructed earthworks, visitor center, exhibits, 17-minute film and interpretive programs in the summer.

15. GENERAL WILLIAM C. LEE AIRBORNE MUSEUM

Dunn, (910) 892-1947

Housed in former home of Lee, known as "Father of the Airborne." Exhibits cover growth of airborne divisions and include WWII memorabilia, paratrooper equipment and uniforms.

16. GRAVEYARD OF THE ATLANTIC MUSEUM

Hatteras, (252) 986-2995

"Piracy and Warfare" gallery covers warfare off the eastern coast from colonial and Revolutionary times through WWII, including displays on Civil War blockade runners, the sinking of the *USS Monitor* and submarine attacks of both world wars.

17. GUILFORD COURTHOUSE NATIONAL MILITARY PARK

Greensboro, (336) 288-1776

Site of March 1781 Revolutionary War battle considered to have changed the course of the war. Visitor center with displays and films, self-guided 2.5-mile auto tour with 8 stops, wayside exhibits throughout battlefield, 28 monuments. Nearby city-owned **TANNENBAUM HISTORIC PARK** features buildings and exhibits on civilian life at time of battle.

✳ ✳ ✳
DID YOU KNOW?
At the Battle of Moores Creek (see page 102), a force of nearly 1,000 Patriots surprised charging Loyalists—mostly Scottish Highlanders, shouting "King George and broadswords!" —who were expecting a smaller Patriot contingent.

The short battle resulted in 30 Loyalists killed and 40 wounded, with only one Patriot killed and one wounded. Some 850 Loyalists surrendered or were captured, and British authority in the colony was effectively ended.

The Patriot victory greatly influenced North Carolina in becoming the first colony to vote for independence. Moores Creek is believed to be the last major broadsword charge in Scottish history.

Moores Creek National Battlefield, Currie

North Carolina Museum of History, Raleigh

20. NORTH CAROLINA AVIATION MUSEUM

Asheboro, (336) 625-0170

Focuses primarily on military aviation history with more than 12 planes from WWII and Korea, all of which still fly.

21. NORTH CAROLINA MILITARY HISTORY MUSEUM

Kure Beach, (910) 251-7325

Covers state military history from WWI through Vietnam with 1,000 square feet of displays. Helicopter, tanks and artillery on outdoor display.

18. JOHN F. KENNEDY SPECIAL WARFARE MUSEUM

*Ft. Bragg (Fayetteville)
(910) 432-4272*

Official museum of the Army Special Forces, but covers all Army special operations. Covers WWII through Afghanistan and Iraq, with exhibits on the Office of Strategic Services (OSS), Alamo Scouts and First Special Service Force. Weapons on outdoor display. Medal of Honor recipients exhibit in Bank Hall.

19. MOORES CREEK NATIONAL BATTLEFIELD

Currie, (910) 283-5591

Site of February 1776 battle that ended British authority in the colony and helped prevent a full-scale invasion of the South. Visitor center with exhibits and an audiovisual program, reconstructed earthworks, 6 monuments, 2 self-guided interpretive trails with wayside exhibits.

22. NORTH CAROLINA MUSEUM OF HISTORY

Raleigh, (919) 807-7900

"North Carolina and the Civil War" exhibit contains more than 300 rare artifacts in 3,500 square feet of exhibit space. Workshop of David Marshall "Carbine" Williams, developer of M-1 Carbine, also on display.

NORTH DAKOTA

Five forts built during frontier times dot the landscape of North Dakota. Most were used as protection for settlers against the Indians, including Fort Abercrombie State Historic Site, which was besieged by the Sioux for a month in 1862. The Peace Garden State also is home to two battlefields and two air museums.

* **DID YOU KNOW?**
One of North Dakota's nicknames is the Roughrider State, referring to the U.S. First Volunteer Cavalry that Theodore Roosevelt organized to fight in the Spanish-American War. The unit included several North Dakotans.

Fort Abraham Lincoln State Park, Mandan

1. DAKOTA TERRITORY AIR MUSEUM

Minot, (701) 852-8500
Military displays include a WWII-era C-47 Skytrain, C-47 cockpit display, A-7 Corsair II, P-40 Warhawk and WWII flight gear.

2. FARGO AIR MUSEUM

Fargo, (701) 293-8043
Military aircraft on display include a P-51 Mustang, F4U Corsair, Grumman TBM Avenger and C-47 Skytrain.

3. FORT ABERCROMBIE STATE HISTORIC SITE

Abercrombie, (701) 553-8513, (701) 553-8377 off-season
Active 1858-78. Besieged by Sioux for a month during Sioux War of 1862. Original guardhouse, reconstructed blockhouses and stockade. Visitor center, self-guided tours.

4. FORT ABRAHAM LINCOLN STATE PARK

Mandan, (701) 667-6340
Active 1872-91. Reconstructed complex includes commissary, granary, barracks and house where Custer stayed. Visitor center, museum, 75-minute guided tour, historic trails with interpretive signs.

North Dakota Heritage Center, Bismarck

Fort Union Trading Post National Historic Site, Williston

5. FORT BUFORD STATE HISTORIC SITE

Williston, (701) 572-9034

Active 1866-95. Under continual siege by Sioux for its first 4 years, though never directly assaulted. Restored buildings, museum, post cemetery, self-guided tours.

6. FORT TOTTEN STATE HISTORIC SITE

Devils Lake, (701) 766-4441

Active 1867-90. One of nation's best preserved forts of Indian Wars era, with 17 original buildings, exhibits, museum, video presentation.

7. FORT UNION TRADING POST NATIONAL HISTORIC SITE

Williston, (701) 572-9083

Active 1828-67. Reconstructed buildings, visitor center with exhibits on fur trade.

8. KILLDEER MOUNTAIN BATTLEFIELD STATE HISTORIC SITE

Killdeer, (701) 623-4355

Site of one of the largest pitched battles in Plains warfare, July 1864. Marker, gravestones of 2 soldiers killed in battle.

9. NORTH DAKOTA HERITAGE CENTER

Bismarck, (701) 328-2666

Military exhibits include artifacts, photos and documents from Indian Wars, Philippines War and *USS North Dakota*. State veterans memorial on site.

10. WHITESTONE HILL BATTLEFIELD STATE HISTORIC SITE

10 miles southeast of Kulm (701) 396-7731

Site of major September 1863 battle of Dakota War. Small museum, 2 monuments. Summers only.

OHIO

Not typically thought of as an arena of Indian warfare, Ohio is rich with such history. Five of the state's forts involved Indians, including two used to repulse British-led Indians in the late 18th and early 19th centuries. The Buckeye State also features three War of 1812 sites, three veteran-president homes and the U.S. Air Force Museum, the largest military aviation museum in the world.

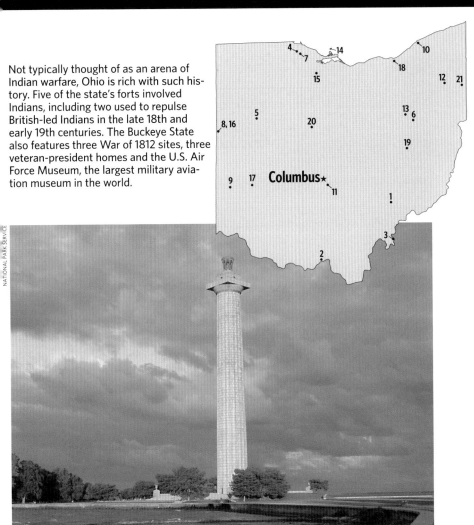

Perry's Victory & International Peace Memorial, Put-in-Bay

1. BIG BOTTOM STATE MONUMENT

Stockport, (614) 297-2630

Site of a January 1791 skirmish between settlers and Indians that marked the start of 4 years of frontier warfare in Ohio. Descriptive signs, 12-foot marble obelisk.

2. BONEYFIDDLE MILITARY MUSEUM

Portsmouth, (740) 353-8066

1,000-sq.-ft. historic building displays uniforms, equipment and artifacts from WWI to present. Open spring-fall weekends or by appointment.

3. BUFFINGTON ISLAND STATE MEMORIAL

Portland, (614) 297-2630

Site of only significant Civil War battle in Ohio, July 19, 1863. Descriptive signs, stone monument.

105

**Ohio Native:
JOHN GLENN**

In Korea between February and July 1953, Glenn flew 63 missions with Marine Fighter Squadron 311 based in Pohang, and 27 missions with the Air Force's 25th Fighter-Interceptor Squadron at Suwon. During WWII, he flew 59 missions over the Marshalls in 1944-45 and later patrolled North China. Altogether, he earned six Distinguished Flying Crosses.

As a test pilot, the Cambridge, Ohio, native set a transcontinental speed record in 1957 flying a supersonic jet. Serving in the Marine Corps through 1964, he then became a business executive for a decade, and was Ohio's first four-term senator. In 1998, at age 77, he became the oldest human to travel in space.

Motts Military Museum, Groveport

James A. Garfield National Historic Site, Mentor

4. FALLEN TIMBERS STATE MEMORIAL

Maumee, (419) 535-3050

Site of August 1794 battle and U.S. victory over Indians. Monuments to soldiers and Indians who died there, and Gen. Anthony Wayne.

5. FORT AMANDA STATE MEMORIAL

Lima, 1-800-283-8713

A major supply depot during the War of 1812 marked by a monument and burial ground.

6. FORT LAURENS STATE MEMORIAL

Bolivar, (330) 874-2059

Withstood a month-long siege by British-led Indians in 1778. Small museum commemorates the frontier soldier. Site of **TOMB OF AN UNKNOWN SOLDIER FROM THE REVOLUTIONARY WAR.**

7. FORT MEIGS STATE MEMORIAL

Perrysburg, (419) 874-4121

Built in 1813, fort was besieged twice by British and Canadian troops, assisted by Indians. 7 reconstructed blockhouses form one of the largest log forts in the country. Museum and Education Center's 3,000 square feet include soldier letters and diaries, weapons, maps and uniforms to describe fort's role during the War of 1812.

Fort Meigs State Memorial, Perrysburg

8. FORT RECOVERY STATE MEMORIAL

Fort Recovery, (419) 375-4649

Repulsed Indian attack in 1794, explained on outdoor plaques. Museum covers various campaigns and has soldier displays. Two reconstructed blockhouses with connecting stockade.

9. FORT ST. CLAIR PARK

Eaton, (937) 456-4125

Site of 1792 battle with Miami Indians. Plaques explain battle.

10. JAMES A. GARFIELD NATIONAL HISTORIC SITE

Mentor, (440) 255-8722

Restored home of the 20th U.S. President. Covers his time as a Civil War general.

11. MOTTS MILITARY MUSEUM

Groveport, (614) 836-1500

Covers military history from pre-Revolutionary War times through the present, including uniforms, weapons, vehicles and memorabilia.

12. NATIONAL MCKINLEY BIRTHPLACE MEMORIAL

Niles, (330) 652-1704

Marble statue of the 25th President and museum, with Civil War and Spanish-American War artifacts.

13. OHIO SOCIETY OF MILITARY HISTORY MUSEUM

Massillon, (330) 832-5553

Covers Ohio military history from Civil War through Persian Gulf War, with collections of medals, photographs, uniforms, letters, documents and memorabilia. Exhibits emphasize the individuals who served.

Fallen Timbers State Memorial, Maumee

14. PERRY'S VICTORY & INTERNATIONAL PEACE MEMORIAL

Put-in-Bay (South Bass Island), (419) 285-2184

Site of War of 1812 Battle of Lake Erie, Sept. 10, 1813. 352-foot pink granite monument with engraved names of American casualties. Interpretive talks and living history demonstrations available summers only.

U.S. Air Force Museum, Dayton

15. RUTHERFORD B. HAYES PRESIDENTIAL CENTER
Fremont, (419) 332-2081

Home of 19th President with displays on his Civil War service.

16. ST. CLAIR'S DEFEAT MEMORIAL
Fort Recovery (Monument Park), (419) 375-2530

Dedicated to the 643 soldiers killed in the worst defeat in U.S. Army-Indian warfare history, Nov. 4, 1791. Also commemorates Gen. Wayne's later victory.

Rutherford B. Hayes Presidential Center, Fremont

17. U.S. AIR FORCE MUSEUM
Dayton, (937) 255-3286

The oldest and largest military aviation museum in the world. Covers development of aviation from its origin with the Wright brothers through the Space Age. Features more than 300 aircraft and missiles in more than 17 acres of indoor exhibit space. Adjacent Memorial Park of statuary memorials, plaques and trees dedicated to Air Force units, organizations and individuals.

18. USS COD
Cleveland, (216) 566-8770

Self-guided tours of this fully intact WWII fleet submarine include torpedo room, engines and crew spaces.

19. USS RADFORD NATIONAL NAVAL MUSEUM
Newcomerstown (740) 498-4446

Covers involvement of Destroyer Squadron 21 in WWII, Korea, Vietnam and the Cold War, and history of *USS Radford.*

20. VETERANS MEMORIAL PARK
Marion, (740) 383-9062

Dedicated to veterans of all U.S. conflicts ever fought. Includes monuments for veterans from Revolutionary War through Persian Gulf War.

21. WWII VEHICLE MUSEUM
Hubbard, (330) 534-8125

Military vehicles and tanks, plus displays of weapons, uniforms and other military artifacts from various countries.

❄   ❄   ❄
DID YOU KNOW?
The Presidential and Research & Development galleries of the U.S. Air Force Museum, showcasing approximately 50 aircraft, are located in two hangers on the historic Wright Field flight line. Free shuttle bus service is provided to the hangers on a first-come, first-served basis.

OKLAHOMA

Indian Territory hosted both Civil War and Indian campaign battles. The Sooner State includes four frontier forts, three battlefields and the impressive 45th Infantry Division Museum, one of the largest military history museums in the country.

OKLAHOMA TOURISM & RECREATION DEPARTMENT

USS Batfish & War Memorial Park, Muskogee

1. 45TH INFANTRY DIVISION MUSEUM

Oklahoma City, (405) 424-5313

One of the nation's largest military history museums. Covers state military history from Spanish in 1541 to current activities of Oklahoma National Guard. 27,000 square feet include emphasis on 45th Division in WWII and Korea; largest public display in the world of artifacts once owned by Adolf Hitler; largest, most comprehensive American military firearms collection in Southwest; Bill Mauldin cartoon collection.

2. CABIN CREEK BATTLEFIELD

Pensacola

Site of July 1-2, 1863, battle. Wooded park, 11 granite markers detailing the battle, monument.

3. FORT GIBSON HISTORIC SITE

Fort Gibson, (918) 478-4088

Oldest military post in Oklahoma, active from 1824 to 1890. Exhibits cover Indian removals of 1830s and '40s to post-Civil War. Partially reconstructed fort (including 7 buildings), interpretive markers.

4. FORT SUPPLY HISTORIC SITE

Fort Supply, (580) 766-3767

Frontier Army fort from 1868 to 1894. Five restored buildings, replica stockade, visitor center with interpretive exhibits.

DID YOU KNOW?
Boise City, Okla., was bombed during WWII. On July 5, 1943, at 12:30 a.m., a B-17 bomber from Dalhart Army Air Base (50 miles south) mistakenly dropped 6 practice bombs on the sleeping town. No injuries were reported.

Fort Washita Historic Site, Durant

Fort Gibson Historic Site, Fort Gibson

7. HONEY SPRINGS BATTLEFIELD HISTORIC SITE

Rentiesville, (918) 473-5572

Site of territory's largest Civil War battle, in July 1863. Visitor center, monuments, 54 interpretive markers, trails. Battlefield tours available for groups.

8. OKLAHOMA HISTORY CENTER

Oklahoma City
(405) 522-5248

Includes displays on state military history from 1821 to the present, Indian veterans, WWI and WWII Indian code talkers, artifacts from *USS Oklahoma* (sunk at Pearl harbor), and digital veterans memorial.

9. U.S. ARMY FIELD ARTILLERY & FORT SILL MUSEUM

Fort Sill, (580) 442-5123

Occupies 26 original buildings (dating back to 1869), 7 of which are open to the public with displays, weapons and artifacts. Covers history of fort, Indian campaigns of the Southwest and evolution of field artillery pieces. Geronimo buried nearby.

10. USS BATFISH & WAR MEMORIAL PARK

Muskogee, (918) 682-6294

Submarine sank 14 Japanese vessels (including three submarines) during WWII, earning 9 battle stars. Tours of inside. Park features museum housing artifacts from WWI to present, static equipment, artillery displays, military memorabilia and veterans Walk of Honor.

11. WASHITA BATTLEFIELD NATIONAL HISTORIC SITE

Cheyenne, (580) 497-2742

Site of Custer's November 1868 attack on a Cheyenne village. Battlefield overlook, interpretive markers, trail.

5. FORT TOWSON HISTORIC SITE

Fort Towson, (580) 873-2634

Ruins of 1824-54 Army post, whose garrison patrolled the Red River and U.S.-Mexico border. Site of Confederate Civil War General Stand Watie's surrender in 1865. Fort ruins, museum.

6. FORT WASHITA HISTORIC SITE

Durant, (580) 924-6502

Protected peaceful Indian settlements from renegade tribes, 1842-1861. Used as supply depot by Confederate troops during Civil War. Well-preserved partially restored fort.

OREGON

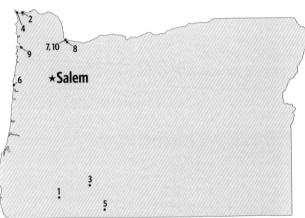

Oregon was involved in the Modoc War of 1872-73, which is covered in the Fort Klamath Museum and the Klamath County Museum. The Beaver State also is home to Fort Stevens State Park, the only fortification in the continental United States to be attacked since the War of 1812, when it was shelled by the Japanese in 1942.

Fort Clatsop National Memorial, Astoria

1. CAMP WHITE MILITARY MUSEUM
White City, (541) 826-2111, ext. 3674

Located on grounds of WWII training camp. Covers history of the 91st Infantry Division, from basic training through end of WWII, through wartime maps, charts, weapons and uniforms.

2. FORT CLATSOP NATIONAL MEMORIAL (LEWIS AND CLARK NATIONAL HISTORIC PARK)
Astoria, (503) 861-2471

Wintering spot of Lewis and Clark at the end of their 1804-06 expedition to the Pacific Ocean. Reconstructed fort, visitor center, museum, exhibits.

3. FORT KLAMATH MUSEUM
Fort Klamath, (541) 381-2230, (541) 883-4208 off-season

Housed in replica guardhouse of 1863 fort. Exhibits cover history of fort and Modoc Indian War of 1872-73.

Klamath County Museum, Klamath Falls

OREGON HISTORICAL SOCIETY

Oregon Historical Society Museum, Portland

COURTESY TILLAMOOK AIR MUSEUM

✳   ✳   ✳

DID YOU KNOW?
The Tillamook Air Museum is housed in a WWII blimp hanger, believed by some to be the largest wooden structure in the world.

4. FORT STEVENS STATE PARK

Hammond, (503) 861-3170

Protected Columbia River from invasion from Civil War through WWII. Shelled by Japanese in 1942; only continental-U.S. fortification to be attacked since War of 1812. Original fort buildings, museum, walking tours.

5. KLAMATH COUNTY MUSEUM

Klamath Falls, (541) 883-4208

Includes exhibits on Modoc Indian War.

6. OREGON COAST HISTORY CENTER

Newport, (541) 265-7509

Soldiers' uniforms, insignia, photographs and weapons, plus role of civilians (through civil defense and industry) during WWI and WWII.

7. OREGON HISTORICAL SOCIETY MUSEUM

Portland, (503) 222-1741

"Battleship *Oregon*" exhibit covers the ship's role in the Spanish-American War, her captain, life onboard, activities after the war and preservation efforts. "Oregon My Oregon" exhibit includes Indian Wars, WWII and shipyards.

8. OREGON MILITARY MUSEUM

Camp Withycombe (Clackamas), (503) 557-5359

State military history of 20th century, with 10,000 artifacts, 10,000 library items and photographic files dating back to 1898. Quonset hut (aviation items), 1911 barn (artillery exhibits), restoration shop, exterior exhibits.

9. TILLAMOOK AIR MUSEUM

Tillamook, (503) 842-1130

Includes more than 30 historic military aircraft plus a jet simulator.

10. USS BLUEBACK

Portland, (503) 797-4624

Guided tours of the Navy's last non-nuclear, fast attack submarine. Located at the Oregon Museum of Science and Industry.

PENNSYLVANIA

Significant battle sites from the French & Indian War, Revolutionary War and the Civil War abound in the Keystone State. Gettysburg National Military Park is the most famous, commemorating the largest and bloodiest battle of the Civil War in which more than 7,000 soldiers died. Fort Necessity National Battlefield tells the story of the French & Indian War. The Revolutionary War is remembered at Brandywine Battlefield Park and Valley Forge National Historic Park, the site of George Washington and the Continental Army's brutal six-month winter encampment.

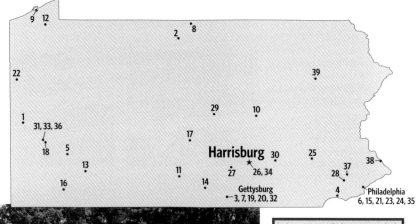

9 12
2 8
22
39
1
31, 33, 36
29 10
18 5
17
13
Harrisburg 30 25
11 27 26, 34 37 38
16 14 28
Gettysburg 4 Philadelphia
3, 7, 19, 20, 32 6, 15, 21, 23, 24, 35

Valley Forge National Historical Park, Valley Forge

✳   ✳   ✳
DID YOU KNOW?
A veteran of the War of 1812 and resident of Gettysburg, 72-year-old John Burns fought side-by-side with Union soldiers in the first day of the battle of Gettysburg in 1863 and was wounded several times. His service is commemorated by a battlefield statue at Gettysburg National Military Park.

1. AIR HERITAGE MUSEUM
Beaver Falls, (724) 843-2820
   Includes memorabilia and aircraft from WWII, Korea, Vietnam and Persian Gulf War.

2. ALLEGHENY ARMS & ARMOR MUSEUM
Smethport, (814) 362-2642
   Preserves and displays military vehicles, armor, aircraft, watercraft and weapons from Revolutionary War through Iraq. Displays include battle tank, Huey helicopters and captured equipment from Persian Gulf War.

3. AMERICAN CIVIL WAR MUSEUM
Gettysburg, (717) 334-6245
   Recounts Civil War period through more than 200 life-size figures and 30 re-created scenes. Multi-media program presents Battle of Gettysburg.

4. Brandywine Battlefield Park

Chadds Ford, (610) 459-3342

Site of Sept. 11, 1777, battle, the largest of the Revolutionary War. Visitor center includes museum with audiovisual presentation. Driving tour of battlefield with stops and interpretive signs, plus a walking trail. Reconstructed Washington's Headquarters open for guided tours.

5. Bushy Run Battlefield

Jeannette, (724) 527-5584

Site of August 1763 battle between British and Indians. Only historic site or museum in U.S. dealing exclusively with Pontiac's Rebellion. Visitor center with interpretive exhibits and fiber-optic map, self-guided battlefield tour with 9 stops, soldier graves, battle monument, guided tours and interpretive programs.

6. Civil War & Underground Railroad Museum of Philadelphia

Philadelphia, (215) 735-8196

Nine galleries of Civil War displays and exhibits include the cavalry, medicine, the Grand Army of the Republic, Union and Confederate regimental histories, *USS Monitor* and Gen. George Meade. Changing gallery and 7,000-volume library.

7. Eisenhower National Historic Site

Gettysburg, (717) 338-9114

Home and farm of famed general and President Dwight Eisenhower includes displays and programs on his military career. Accessible through **Gettysburg National Military Park** (see page 116).

U.S. Brig *Niagara* at Erie Maritime Museum, Erie

ERIE MARITIME MUSEUM

NATIONAL PARK SERVICE

Eisenhower National Historic Site, Gettysburg

BRANDYWINE BATTLEFIELD PARK

Brandywine Battlefield Park, Chadds Ford

8. Eldred WWII Museum

Eldred, (814) 225-2220

Covers war's history and its effect on the region through electronic exhibits, sound-and-light effects, dioramas, photos and documents. Displays include Sheridan tank, submarines, airplanes, Battle of Midway and Merchant Marines.

9. Erie Maritime Museum

Erie, (814) 452-2744

Homeport of reconstructed U.S. Brig *Niagara*, which won the War of 1812's Battle of Lake Erie on Sept. 10, 1813. Museum's multi-media presentations and interactive exhibits cover battle and War of 1812. Displays include reconstruction of cannon-damaged wooden warship and *USS Wolverine*.

10. Fort Augusta

Sunbury, (570) 743-4100

Built 1756 to protect against French invasion and was used in Revolutionary War. Powder magazine is only remaining structure. Hunter House serves as museum with fort artifacts, scale model of fort and research library.

11. Fort Bedford Museum

Bedford, (814) 623-8891

British stockade built 1758. Museum, housed in reproduction of fort blockhouse, includes large-scale model of original fort and exhibits depicting the time period the fort was operational. Open May-October.

Visitor Center at Fort Necessity National Battlefield, Uniontown

12. FORT LEBOEUF MUSEUM

Waterford, (814) 732-2573

Original fort built in 1753. Museum includes fort model and exhibits on fort history and Pontiac's Rebellion.

13. FORT LIGONIER

Ligonier, (724) 238-9701

1758 British fort attacked by Indians in 1763. Full-scale, on-site reconstruction with 9 interpreted buildings and life-size figures portraying fort life. Museum features video presentation, model of fort, artifacts and dioramas. Open May-October, by appointment rest of the year.

14. FORT LOUDON

Fort Loudon, (717) 369-3318

Built 1756. Reconstructed stockade. Restored 1798 Patton House with exhibits. Open summer weekends for self-guided tours.

15. FORT MIFFLIN

Philadelphia, (215) 685-4167

1771 British fort was involved in Revolutionary War and War of 1812, and used as a Civil War prison camp. Restored to 1834 appearance with 11 buildings. Tours, weapons demonstrations, and soldier life programs. Museum includes exhibits on 1777 siege, diorama of fort, displays and slide show. Open April-November.

16. FORT NECESSITY NATIONAL BATTLEFIELD

Uniontown, (724) 329-5512

Site of first battle of French & Indian War, July 3, 1754. Main park unit includes battle-field, reconstructed stockade, Mount Washington Tavern and visitor center. Braddock Grave unit has outdoor exhibits and monument to Gen. Edward Braddock. Jumonville Glen unit has interpretive signs on earlier skirmish.

17. FORT ROBERDEAU HISTORIC SITE

Altoona, (814) 946-0048

"Lead Mine Fort" con-structed in 1778. Recon-structed fort includes 6 build-ings. 1858 barn serves as visitor center with video and exhibits, and 1860 farmhouse is an edu-cation center. Open May-October.

18. FRENCH & INDIAN WAR MUSEUM & GALLERY

Braddock, (412) 351-5356

Small museum on second floor of Braddock Carnegie Library features artifacts and artwork of French & Indian War and 1755 Battle of the Monongahela.

Gettysburg National Military Park, Gettysburg

19. GENERAL LEE'S HEADQUARTERS MUSEUM

Gettysburg, (717) 334-3141

Early 19th century stone house served as Gen. Robert E. Lee's headquarters during Battle of Gettysburg. Displays include Union and Confederate equipment and Civil War artifacts. Open March-November.

20. GETTYSBURG NATIONAL MILITARY PARK

Gettysburg, (717) 334-1124, ext. 431

Site of largest and bloodiest battle of the Civil War, July 1-3, 1863, in which more than 7,000 men were killed. Visitor center with vast Civil War museum and electric map. Adjacent Cyclorama Center. 18-mile self-guided driving tour with 16 stops; more than 1,400 monuments, markers and memorials; national cemetery. Ranger-led walks, talks and programs during the summer. New museum and visitor center slated for 2008.

Hillcrest Memorial Park, Hermitage

21. GRAND ARMY OF THE REPUBLIC MUSEUM & LIBRARY

Philadelphia, (215) 289-6484

Housed in 1796 Georgian mansion, Union vet museum offers displays of Civil War artifacts, battle relics and personal memorabilia; educational programs; and research library. Open to the public first Sunday of every month. Group visits by appointment.

22. HILLCREST MEMORIAL PARK

Hermitage, (724) 346-3818

Features Avenue of 444 Flags—a U.S. flag for each day that 53 American hostages were held in Iran, 1979-80. Monument and eternal flame dedicated to 8 servicemen killed in rescue attempt, April 1980. **WAR ON TERROR VETERANS MEMORIAL,** with inscribed names of more than 4,300 GIs killed by terrorism since 1975, is updated regularly. Monuments throughout park recognize veterans.

Independence Seaport Museum, Philadelphia

National Civil War Museum, Harrisburg

23. INDEPENDENCE NATIONAL HISTORICAL PARK

Philadelphia, (215) 965-2305

Some 20 buildings associated with the colonial period include **NEW HALL MILITARY MUSEUM,** which commemorates the history of the U.S. Army, Navy and Marine Corps from 1775-1805. Features dioramas, weapons cases and scale model of the U.S. Brig *Raleigh.*

24. INDEPENDENCE SEAPORT MUSEUM

Philadelphia, (215) 925-5439

Military exhibits include 1892 cruiser *Olympia*—the oldest steel warship afloat in the world—with displays on Spanish-American War era, turn-of-the-century naval life and history of the ship. WWII/Cold War submarine *Becuna* also open for tours.

25. MID-ATLANTIC AIR MUSEUM

Reading, (610) 372-7333

Features more than 25 airplanes, rare and unusual military aircraft, and historical exhibits. Annual WWII weekend air show includes 80 aircraft, 200 period vehicles, 1,100 living history interpreters and entertainers, and features air show, military vehicle show, encampment displays and battle recreations.

26. NATIONAL CIVIL WAR MUSEUM

Harrisburg, (717) 260-1861

Only museum that interprets entire Civil War. 17 galleries—using artifacts, life-size dioramas and audiovisual presentations—cover formation of the armies, weapons and equipment, Civil War music, Gettysburg, women in the war, various campaigns and battles, and battle maps.

Tomb of the Unknown Soldier, Philadelphia

(vertical credit, right margin) EDWARD SAVARIA, JR. /PHILADELPHIA CONVENTION & VISITORS BUREAU

27. OMAR N. BRADLEY MUSEUM

Carlisle, (717) 245-3971

Located at **CARLISLE BARRACKS** in Upton Hall (home of one of the nation's largest collections of historical military documents, photos and books). Commemorates service of the 5-star general with military memorabilia and personal items. Nearby **HESSIAN POWDER MAGAZINE MUSEUM,** a structure built by Hessian prisoners in 1777, contains military artifacts and displays.

28. PAOLI MASSACRE SITE

Malvern (Malvern Memorial Park), (610) 644-2602

Site of Sept. 21, 1777, massacre in which more than 300 American soldiers were killed or wounded by British. Wooden-capped stone wall encloses burial mound with remains of 53 of the men killed. 6-ft. stone obelisk and 30-ft. monument.

29. PENNSYLVANIA MILITARY MUSEUM

Boalsburg, (814) 466-6263

Covers state military history, with emphasis on 20th century service of state residents and Pennsylvania-based units. Features full-scale WWI trench battlefield replica and vehicle and arms collections. Armored vehicles on outdoor display, plus shrine to 28th Infantry Division and memorials.

30. PENNSYLVANIA NATIONAL GUARD MILITARY MUSEUM

Annville, (717) 861-2402

Housed in 1941 barracks. Displays cover Civil War through the present, soldier life in the barracks, and history of state National Guard and Fort Indiantown Gap.

31. POINT STATE PARK

Pittsburgh, (412) 471-0235

Includes 1764 **FORT PITT BLOCKHOUSE** (*471-1764*) and **FORT PITT MUSEUM** (*281-9284*), located in one of 3 reconstructed bastions of 1759 Fort Pitt (attacked by Indians during Pontiac's Rebellion, 1763). Museum features 12,000 square feet of exhibits, artifacts, dioramas, audiovisual presentations and computer simulations depicting French & Indian War, Pontiac's Rebellion and Ohio Indian wars. Monuments, plaques and markers throughout park, plus a stone outline of 1754 Fort Duquesne. Park under construction until spring 2008.

32. SOLDIERS NATIONAL MUSEUM

Gettysburg, (717) 334-4890

Features artifacts and memorabilia from Revolutionary War through Persian Gulf War, with 10 miniature Civil War dioramas and narrated Confederate encampment.

Fort Pitt Museum at Point State Park, Pittsburgh

Soldiers & Sailors National Military Museum & Memorial, Pittsburgh

33. SOLDIERS & SAILORS NATIONAL MILITARY MUSEUM & MEMORIAL
Pittsburgh, (412) 621-4253
Exhibits cover Civil War through present day. Hall of Valor, captured war trophies, weapons, memorabilia and model of *USS Pittsburgh*. Bronze plaques list names of 25,920 Pennsylvania soldiers who served in the Civil War. Film presentations cover Revolutionary War through Vietnam. Films and guided tours by appointment.

34. STATE MUSEUM OF PENNSYLVANIA
Harrisburg, (717) 787-4980
Civil War gallery covers state's military and home-front contributions to the war effort. Includes 16x32-ft. painting of Pickett's Charge.

35. TOMB OF THE UNKNOWN SOLDIER
Philadelphia, Washington Square
Tomb honoring an unknown soldier from the Revolutionary War. Statue of George Washington and eternal flame.

36. USS REQUIN
Pittsburgh, (412) 237-1550
300-ft. WWII submarine in front of **CARNEGIE SCIENCE CENTER** is open for tours that re-create submariner life and show how subs are built.

37. VALLEY FORGE NATIONAL HISTORICAL PARK
Valley Forge, (610) 783-1077
Site of George Washington and the Continental Army's 6-month encampment, December 1777-June 1778. Visitor center includes exhibits, artifacts and 18-minute film. 10-mile self-guided tour visits reconstructed soldier huts, Washington's Headquarters, National Memorial Arch and original entrenchment lines and fortifications. Washington Memorial Chapel with Veterans Wall of Honor.
New **AMERICAN REVOLUTION CENTER** in planning stages.

✳   ✳   ✳
Pennsylvania Native: JAMES STEWART

Stewart served in the Army Air Forces, March 1941-September 1945. He flew 20 missions over Europe as captain of the 703rd Sqdn., 445th Bomb Grp. Later, he was operations officer for the 453rd Bomb Grp. In April 1945, he became chief of staff of the 2nd Combat Wing. The Indiana, Pa., native earned the Distinguished Flying Cross and four Air Medals. In addition, he flew combat missions over Vietnam as an Air Force Reserve general. The renowned movie star appeared in 93 films.

38. WASHINGTON CROSSING HISTORIC PARK
Washington Crossing (215) 493-4076
Park is dedicated to George Washington and 2,400 soldiers who crossed the Delaware River on Dec. 25, 1776. Two sections include 13 historic buildings, soldiers' graves and Memorial Building visitor center (under renovation) with limited exhibits and film.

39. WYOMING BATTLE MONUMENT
Forty Fort, 1-888-905-2872
62-ft. obelisk honors the 376 soldiers and settlers killed by Indians in 1778 battle and subsequent massacre.

RHODE ISLAND

As a New England state, Rhode Island played a part in the Revolutionary War with one land battle in August 1778 at Fort Butts. The Ocean State also features remains of several colonial forts, and the historic stone Fort Adams, in use through WWII, is said to be the largest coastal fort in the U.S. Other sites of note include the Naval War College Museum and the extensive military collection at Brown University's John Hay Library.

Providence ★——— 1, 9
10•
•5
6•
3, 7
2, 4, 8

COURTESY ANNE S.K. BROWN MILITARY COLLECTION

Napoleon's Toy Soldiers at the Anne S.K. Brown Military Collection, Brown University, Providence

1. ANNE S.K. BROWN MILITARY COLLECTION
Providence (John Hay Library Brown University)
(401) 863-2414

One of world's largest collections devoted to study of military uniforms, from 17th century to present. Also covers military tactics, history, ceremonies and biographies. Includes 12,000 books; 18,000 albums, sketchbooks, scrapbooks and portfolios; 13,000 individual prints, drawings and watercolors; and 5,000 miniature lead soldiers.

2. ARTILLERY COMPANY OF NEWPORT MILITARY MUSEUM
Newport, (401) 846-8488

Covers company's history from 1741 to the present. Includes uniforms, memorabilia, Civil War artillery pieces and artifacts of significance to state history and the company.

3. CONANICUT BATTERY HISTORIC PARK
Jamestown, (401) 423-0784

Park contains remains of 1776 fortifications and features well-marked trails with information on the site's history and earthworks.

Juliett 484 at the Russian Sub Museum, Providence

Naval War College Museum, Newport

6. FORT BUTTS
Portsmouth, (401) 683-3255
Site of state's only Revolutionary War land battle, Aug. 29, 1778. Redoubt on Butts Hill, marker describing battle.

7. FORT WETHERILL STATE PARK
Jamestown, (401) 423-1771
Original fort built 1776 and later abandoned. Current stone fort built in late 19th century. Remains open to the public.

8. NAVAL WAR COLLEGE MUSEUM
Newport, (401) 841-4052
Covers history of naval warfare, naval heritage of Narragansett Bay, the college itself, the Navy's origins in the region and the evolution of naval installations from the late 19th century to the present. Military ID required for admittance, or call one day in advance for pass to get on base.

9. RUSSIAN SUB MUSEUM
Providence, (401) 521-3600
Tours of Soviet Cold War cruise missile submarine *Juliett 484*. Located in Collier Point Park. As of April 18, 2007, museum closed for maintenance. Call for updates.

10. VARNUM MEMORIAL ARMORY
East Greenwich
(401) 884-4110
Includes military weapons and artifacts from 16th century to the present, with official museum collection of the 76th Infantry Division, WWI and WWII posters, artillery pieces, documents, medals and ribbons, and a library.

4. FORT ADAMS STATE PARK
Newport, (401) 841-0707
Historic stone fort built 1824-57 and active through WWII. Said to be largest coastal fort in the U.S. Tour highlights include barracks, casemates, bastions, tunnel system and museum exhibits.

5. FORT BARTON
Tiverton, (401) 423-1771
Site of 1777 redoubt featuring 30-foot observation tower and 3 miles of trails.

SOUTH CAROLINA

On April 12, 1861, the first shots of the Civil War rang out in South Carolina, now commemorated at Fort Sumter National Monument. However, South Carolina's military history is equally tied to the Revolutionary War. Many battle sites are dispersed throughout the Palmetto State, including Historic Camden Revolutionary War Site, the location of 14 battles during the war. Visitors also have 10 military museums to choose from—including the Charleston Museum, the first and oldest museum in the U.S., founded in 1773.

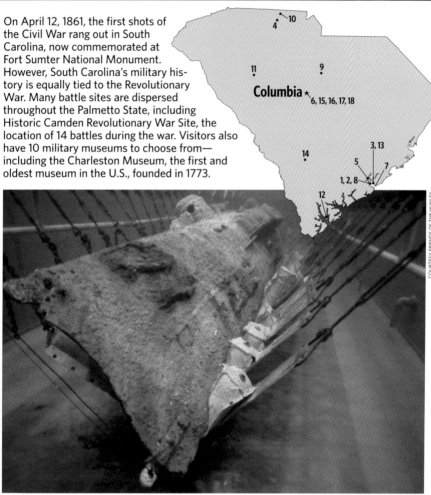

COURTESY FRIENDS OF THE HUNLEY

CSS H.L. Hunley, North Charleston

1. AMERICAN MILITARY MUSEUM
Charleston, (843) 723-9620

Features 70 display cases with 260 uniforms, 33 flags and hundreds of artifacts from Revolutionary War through Iraq, including 400 pieces of military headgear and 600 military miniatures and toy soldiers.

2. CHARLESTON MUSEUM
Charleston, (843) 722-2996

First and oldest museum in U.S., founded in 1773. Numerous displays are military-related, with a Revolutionary War exhibit and "City Under Siege," the largest Civil War collection in Charleston.

3. CONGRESSIONAL MEDAL OF HONOR MUSEUM
Mt. Pleasant, (843) 884-8862

Located on hangar deck of **USS YORKTOWN** at Patriot's Point. Features 4 exhibits on the Medal of Honor's origin, the toll of war and the bravery it evokes. Covers recipients from the medal's introduction during the Civil War through the war on terrorism. Renovated in 2007.

Fort Sumter National Monument, Charleston

71st Highlanders Badge from the Charleston Museum

DID YOU KNOW?

The palmetto tree has been a symbol of South Carolina since 1776 when the first Fort Moultrie was built of palmetto logs. The spongy logs proved useful during the Revolutionary War's 9-1/2 hour Battle of Sullivan's Island, and the British bombardment did little damage to the fort.

6. FORT JACKSON MUSEUM
Fort Jackson (Columbia)
(803) 751-7419

Details history of the Army training center and major units that have trained there, with more than 4,000 artifacts from WWI to the present. Vehicles and artillery pieces on outdoor display.

7. FORT MOULTRIE NATIONAL MONUMENT
Sullivan's Island (Charleston)
(843) 883-3123

Site of one of the first American victories in the Revolutionary War. Third fort, built in 1809, was involved in Confederate attack on Fort Sumter and still stands. Visitor center with exhibits and 20-minute film, self-guided tours with interpretive signs.

8. FORT SUMTER NATIONAL MONUMENT
Charleston, (843) 883-3123

Site of the first shots of the Civil War, April 12, 1861, when Confederates attacked and captured the fort. Fort ruins, cannons and monuments at site accessible only by boat.

FORT SUMTER VISITOR EDUCATION CENTER in Liberty Square, downtown Charleston, features interpretive exhibits and is the primary departure point for fort tours, which consist of a 75-minute narrated tour of Charleston Harbor and a 1-hour tour of the fort.

4. COWPENS NATIONAL BATTLEFIELD
Gaffney, (864) 461-2828

Site of January 1781 battle, considered one of the most important of the Revolutionary War. Visitor center with 13-minute fiber-optic map program and 22-minute laser disc presentation. Wayside exhibits along a 3.8-mile auto tour road and 1.5-mile walking trail.

5. CSS H.L. HUNLEY
North Charleston
(843) 722-2333

First submarine ever to sink an enemy ship. Was recovered intact from the ocean floor in 2000 and is undergoing preservation. Tours include viewing the *Hunley* in the conservation lab, a life-size model and an animated simulation of the recovery.

South Carolina Military Museum, Columbia

> ✦ ✦ ✦
> **DID YOU KNOW?**
> During the Siege of Ninety Six, Patriots built a 30-ft. Maham Tower, from which sharpshooters were able to fire into the Loyalist-held Star Fort. The Loyalists tried to burn down the tower, but it was made of green wood and would not burn. Ninety Six National Historic Site features a 10-ft. replica of the tower.

Kings Mountain National Military Park, Blacksburg

9. HISTORIC CAMDEN REVOLUTIONARY WAR SITE

Camden, (803) 432-9841

Site of 14 Revolutionary War battles. Features restored houses, reconstructed fortifications, powder magazine and reconstructed 1777 Kershaw-Cornwallis house. Self-guided tours.

10. KINGS MOUNTAIN NATIONAL MILITARY PARK

Blacksburg, (864) 936-7921

Site of October 1780 Revolutionary War battle that halted the British advance into North Carolina. Visitor center features a 27-minute film, museum and diorama of the battle. 1.5-mile self-guided loop trail around battlefield with wayside exhibits and monuments.

11. NINETY SIX NATIONAL HISTORIC SITE

Ninety Six, (864) 543-4068

Fort attacked twice by Cherokees in 1760. Site of first Revolutionary land battle south of New England in 1775, and the longest siege of the war, May-June 1781. Visitor center with museum and 10-minute video. Reconstructed stockade fort, Star Fort earthworks and self-guided 1-mile interpretive walking trail.

12. PARRIS ISLAND MUSEUM

Parris Island, (843) 228-2951

Covers region's military history and history of Marine Corps. Exhibits include Marines at Parris Island from Civil War to the present; 20th century involvement, including major wars, Nicaragua, Haiti, Dominican Republic and Lebanon; celebrity Marines; women in the Marines; and a weapons room.

USS Yorktown at Patriot's Point Naval & Maritime Museum, Mt. Pleasant

Confederate Relic Room & Museum, Columbia

13. PATRIOT'S POINT NAVAL & MARITIME MUSEUM

Mt. Pleasant, (843) 884-2727

Centerpiece is aircraft carrier **USS YORKTOWN.** Hangar bay includes exhibits of fighter planes, mementos and **CONGRESSIONAL MEDAL OF HONOR MUSEUM** (see page 122). Tours feature the ship's bridge, wheelhouse and flight deck. Exhibits include names of aircraft carrier personnel killed since WWII, Carrier Hall of Fame and relics from other carriers. Site also includes destroyer *USS Laffey,* Cold War submarine *USS Clamagore,* Coast Guard cutter *Ingham,* Vietnam base camp replica and **COLD WAR SUBMARINE MEMORIAL.**

14. RIVERS BRIDGE STATE HISTORIC SITE

Ehrhardt, (803) 267-3675

Site of one of Confederacy's last stands against Gen. William T. Sherman, February 1865. Only state historic site in South Carolina to commemorate Civil War. Earthworks, 11 wayside exhibits explaining the battle, memorial grounds.

15. SOUTH CAROLINA CONFEDERATE RELIC ROOM & MUSEUM

Columbia, (803) 737-8095

Covers state military history from Revolutionary War to the present, emphasizing the Confederate era, in 17,000 square feet of the old Columbia Mills building. Exhibits include a nationally known Civil War flag collection; South Carolina's involvement in the Spanish-American War, WWI and WWII; and a model of the *USS Columbia.*

16. SOUTH CAROLINA MILITARY MUSEUM

Columbia, (803) 806-4440

Tells history of South Carolina military from 1670 through Iraq and Afghanistan. Includes both Army and Air National Guard, plus state Medal of Honor recipients and South Carolina Gen. William C. Westmoreland.

17. SOUTH CAROLINA STATE MUSEUM

Columbia, (803) 898-4921

The former Columbia Mills building, built in 1894, houses four floors of exhibits. Military exhibits include arms and equipment from the Revolutionary War, state militia troops in the antebellum era, and from the Civil War.

18. U.S. ARMY CHAPLAIN MUSEUM

Fort Jackson (Columbia) (803) 751-8079

Covers the chaplaincy chronologically from its roots in 1775 through every major war from the Revolutionary War to the present.

SOUTH DAKOTA

Similar to its neighboring states, the Mount Rushmore State hosts sites of the Sioux campaigns, including Wounded Knee Battlefield. Also featured is the Cold War-era Minuteman Missile National Historic Site, which opened in 2004.

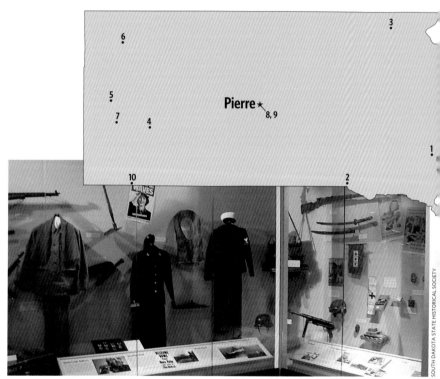

South Dakota State Historical Society Museum, Pierre

1. BATTLESHIP SOUTH DAKOTA MEMORIAL
Sioux Falls, (605) 367-7141, (605) 367-7060 off-season

Most-decorated battleship of WWII. Memorial is a 680-ft.-long concrete outline of the ship with gun turrets and barrels, anchor cast and propeller. Museum housing historical memorabilia. Open summers only.

2. FORT RANDALL
Pickstown, (605) 773-3458

Active 1856-92. Remains of old parade ground, building foundations and standing ruins of post chapel. Walking tour with interpretive panels.

3. FORT SISSETON STATE PARK
Lake City, (605) 448-5474, (605) 448-5701 off-season

Active 1864-88. Well-preserved stone fort, visitor center, museum, guided walking tours.

4. MINUTEMAN MISSILE NATIONAL HISTORIC SITE
near Wall, (605) 433-5552

Site features missile silo, unarmed Minuteman II missile and underground control center from Cold War era. Exhibits and 12-minute orientation film. Limited tours available by reservation.

Fort Sisseton State Park, Lake City

Minuteman Missile National Historic Site, near Wall

☀   ☀   ☀

DID YOU KNOW?

The Flaming Fountain on Capitol Lake at the South Dakota State Capitol is fed by an artesian well with natural gas content so high that it can be lit. The fountain glows perpetually as a memorial to all veterans.

7. SOUTH DAKOTA AIR & SPACE MUSEUM

Ellsworth Air Force Base (northeast of Rapid City)
(605) 385-5188

Exhibits include more than 25 historic bombers, fighters, utility aircraft, missiles and other aviation memorabilia. Bus tours to Minuteman missile silo and base available.

8. SOUTH DAKOTA NATIONAL GUARD MUSEUM

Pierre, (605) 224-9991

8,000 square feet of indoor displays include memorabilia and artifacts from Dakota Militia of 1860s through the present. 10,000 square feet of outdoor exhibits include A-7-D jet, Sherman tank, cannon, howitzer, anti-aircraft guns and an armored personnel carrier.

9. SOUTH DAKOTA STATE HISTORICAL SOCIETY MUSEUM

Pierre, (605) 773-3458

Covers state's military roles in WWI, WWII, Korea, Vietnam, Cold War and Persian Gulf. Includes coverage of state bases, missile sites, women in the military, Indian code talkers and home-front support.

10. WOUNDED KNEE BATTLEFIELD

Pine Ridge, (605) 773-3458

Site of last armed conflict between Sioux and U.S. Army, December 1890. Interpretive marker, monument that marks mass grave of Indian victims.

5. OLD FORT MEADE MUSEUM

Fort Meade (east of Sturgis)
(605) 347-9822,
(605) 347-2818 off-season

Active 1878-1944. Cavalry saddles, Indian artifacts, historical letters from Battle of the Little Bighorn.

6. SLIM BUTTES BATTLEFIELD

Reva, (605) 773-3458

Site of September 1876 battle of the Dakota War. Historic marker and obelisk.

TENNESSEE

Civil War history permeates the Volunteer State, with three national battlefields, smaller state battlegrounds and forts, and museums with extensive collections. Three military heroes—Andrew Jackson, Davy Crockett and Alvin York—from Tennessee are remembered.

The Hermitage, Hermitage (northeast of Nashville)

1. BATTLES FOR CHATTANOOGA MUSEUM

Chattanooga, (423) 821-2812
Covers battles for city through 480-sq.-ft., 3-dimensional electronic battle map of 480 square feet. Also features a weapons and relic collection.

2. BRITTON LANE BATTLEFIELD

Medon, (731) 935-2209
Site of September 1862 battle. Monuments, mass Confederate grave, restored cabin, church with graffiti of Federal prisoners held there.

3. CHATTANOOGA REGIONAL HISTORY MUSEUM

Chattanooga, (423) 265-3247
Extensive Civil War collection, including weapons, uniforms, photographs, diaries and letters.

4. DAVID CROCKETT STATE PARK

Lawrenceburg, (931) 762-9408
Museum exhibits cover Crockett's life as a soldier.

5. DAVY CROCKETT BIRTHPLACE STATE PARK

Limestone, (423) 257-2167
Museum covers Crockett's life. Video, replica frontier cabin.

6. FARRAGUT FOLKLIFE MUSEUM

Farragut, (865) 966-7057
Houses local historical artifacts and photographs, plus Adm. David Glasgow Farragut Collection (first commissioned U.S. Navy admiral) with uniform ornamentation, manuscripts, letters and scrimshaw.

Fort Donelson National Battlefield, Dover

7. FORT DONELSON NATIONAL BATTLEFIELD
Dover, (931) 232-5348
Site of Union's first major victory, February 1862. Confederate-built fort with river cannon batteries and earthen rifle pits, Dover Hotel, national cemetery and visitor center with museum. Walking tours of battlefield, 6-mile driving tour with 11 marked sites.

8. FORT LOUDOUN STATE HISTORIC PARK
Vonore, (423) 884-6217
Only planned British fort in "Overhill" country during French & Indian War. Cherokees forced surrender in 1760. Partially reconstructed fort, visitor center, museum, guided tours.

9. FORT NASHBOROUGH
Nashville, (615) 862-8400
1780 log fort was attacked by Indians in 1781. Raids continued until 1792. Self-guided tours of reconstructed fort.

10. FORT PILLOW STATE HISTORIC PARK
Henning, (731) 738-5581
1861 Confederate-built fort was site of April 1864 engagement. Visitor center with small museum, reconstruction of inner fort.

11. THE HERMITAGE
Hermitage, (615) 889-2941
Restored home of President Andrew Jackson. 28,000-sq.-ft. museum and visitor center with displays from his military career, including military portraits, medals and memorabilia.

CIVIL WAR GUIDE
The Tennessee Antebellum Trail is a 90-mile, self-guided driving loop tour from Spring Hill to Nashville that features more than 55 Civil War sites, battlefields, antebellum homes and plantations, many of which are open to the public. Call 1-800-381-1865 for a free brochure.

For information on 11 more Civil War history driving tours, contact the Tennessee Department of Environment & Conservation at (615) 532-0104 for the brochure *A Path Divided: Tennessee's Civil War Heritage Trail.*

Hazen Brigade Monument at Stones River National Battlefield, Murfreesboro

❄   ❄   ❄
Tennessee Native:
DAVY CROCKETT

Crockett served with the Tennessee Militia and the U.S. Army, September 1813–March 1815, during the Creek War. After the war, he became a militia officer. A spokesman for the common man, the Greeneville, Tenn., native fought for their rights during three terms in the House of Representatives. As a state and U.S. legislator, his crusading cause was land rights for the dispossessed.

12. NATHAN BEDFORD FORREST STATE PARK
Eva, (731) 584-6356
Site of November 1864 raid that destroyed federal supply and munitions depot. Monument, interpretive sign and map at **TENNESSEE RIVER FOLKLIFE MUSEUM.**

13. SALEM CEMETERY BATTLEFIELD
Jackson, (731) 424-1279
Site of December 1862 battle. Two monuments, flagpole, battle map inlay, historical marker, cemetery.

14. SGT. ALVIN C. YORK STATE HISTORIC PARK
Pall Mall, (931) 879-6456
Honors Medal of Honor recipient, one of the most-decorated soldiers of WWI. Welcome center, grist mill, York home and cemetery.

15. SHILOH NATIONAL MILITARY PARK
Shiloh, (731) 689-5696
Site of first western battle of the Civil War, April 1862. Visitor center contains relics, exhibits, maps and 25-minute film. More than 150 monuments, 600 troop position markers and 200 cannons dot the battlefield. National cemetery, 10-mile self-guided driving tour with 14 wayside exhibits.

16. STONES RIVER NATIONAL BATTLEFIELD
Murfreesboro, (615) 893-9501
Site of December 1862-January 1863 battle. Visitor center with small museum, orientation film. Earthen remains of Fortress Rosecrans, plus Hazen Brigade Monument, the oldest intact Civil War monument still standing in its original location. National cemetery, self-guided driving tour with trails and exhibits at each stop.

Sculpture at Corinth Civil War Interpretive Center, part of Shiloh National Military Park, Shiloh

Tennessee State Museum, Nashville

✳ ✳ ✳
DID YOU KNOW?
The greatest maritime disaster in American history occurred on the Mississippi River near Memphis in April 1865, when the steamer *Sultana*—overloaded with recently freed Union POWs—exploded, killing 1,800.

17. SYCAMORE SHOALS STATE PARK

Elizabethton, (423) 543-5808

First permanent American settlement outside original 13 colonies. Besieged by Indians in 1775. Muster point for militia that defeated British in Revolutionary War Battle of King's Mountain. Origin of the **OVERMOUNTAIN VICTORY NATIONAL HISTORIC TRAIL.** Visitor center, museum, film, reconstructed **FORT WATAUGA.**

18. TENNESSEE RIVER MUSEUM

Savannah, 1-800-552-3866

Exhibits include "The War on the River" with gunboat artifacts, "Army" with Shiloh artifacts, and "Johnsonville" with cavalry artifacts.

19. TENNESSEE STATE MUSEUM

Nashville, (615) 741-2692

An entire floor devoted to tracing state Civil War history. Exhibits include audiovisual presentations, firearms, uniforms, photographs and flags.

20. TENNESSEE STATE MUSEUM MILITARY BRANCH

Nashville, (615) 741-2692

Covers America's overseas conflicts from Spanish-American War through Vietnam. Exhibits include dioramas, weapons, uniforms, flags, photographs and fine art. Outdoor memorials to state soldiers killed in WWI, Korea and Vietnam.

21. WWII PT BOATS, BASES & TENDERS ARCHIVES

Germantown, (901) 755-8440

Features artifacts, memorabilia, film, boat blueprints, documentation and 10,000 photographs.

TEXAS

Say Lone Star State and you think Alamo. Texas is unique in having fought its own war of independence, and it is remembered well at Fannin Battleground and San Jacinto. Palo Alto Battlefield National Historic Site is the only National Park Service site covering the Mexican War (1846-48). In addition to Civil and Indian War battlefields, Texas also hosts many frontier forts, three U.S. Army museums, two Army division museums and several aviation museums.

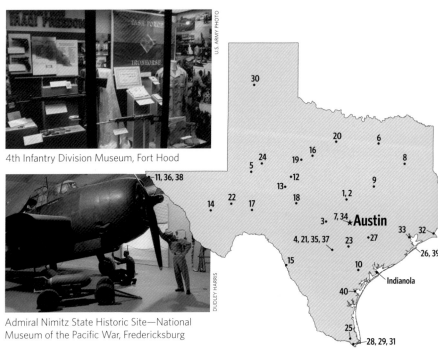

4th Infantry Division Museum, Fort Hood

Admiral Nimitz State Historic Site—National Museum of the Pacific War, Fredericksburg

1. 1ST CAVALRY DIVISION MUSEUM
Fort Hood (Killeen)
(254) 287-3626
   Covers history of horse soldier regiments in the Civil, Indian and Spanish-American wars to the division's formation in 1921. Includes galleries on WWII, Korea, Vietnam, Persian Gulf War, Bosnia and war on terrorism. Vehicles, aircraft, artillery and foreign equipment on outdoor display.

2. 4TH INFANTRY DIVISION MUSEUM
Fort Hood, (254) 287-8811
   Covers history of the division from 1917 to the present with artifacts, photos, personal stories and multi-media presentations. Building 419 includes WWI and WWII combat history. Building 418 covers WWII to the present, including a large section on Vietnam and the Iraq War. 68 vehicles and weapons systems on outdoor display. (Will eventually move to Colorado.)

3. ADMIRAL NIMITZ STATE HISTORIC SITE—NATIONAL MUSEUM OF THE PACIFIC WAR
Fredericksburg, (830) 997-4379
   Only continental-U.S. museum dedicated exclusively to WWII's Pacific Theater. Nearly 24,000 square feet include History Walk of the Pacific War, Surface Warfare Plaza, Memorial and Victory walls, Veterans Walk of Honor and **CENTER FOR PACIFIC WAR STUDIES.** Outdoor displays.

The Alamo, San Antonio

4. THE ALAMO

San Antonio, (210) 225-1391

Site of famous 1836 battle between Mexican Gen. Santa Anna and Texas volunteers. Old church building and Long Barrack remain, with exhibits on history, evolution and heroes of the Alamo. Also outdoor Wall of History.

5. AMERICAN AIRPOWER HERITAGE MUSEUM

Midland, (432) 563-1000

40,000 square feet of hands-on exhibits detailing the history of WWII and WWII aviation. Includes world's largest collection of original WWII nose art panels and 12-16 classic warbirds on display in hangar.

6. AUDIE MURPHY AMERICAN COTTON MUSEUM

Greenville, (903) 454-1990

Audie L. Murphy Memorial Hunt County Veterans Exhibit includes memorabilia from Murphy's military service and movie career, and items from other county veterans.

7. BOB BULLOCK TEXAS STATE HISTORY MUSEUM

Austin, 1-866-369-7108

Covers frontier military fort system, battles for Texas independence, Mexican War, Civil War, WWII. Artifacts dating back to early 1800s.

8. CAMP FORD HISTORIC PARK

Tyler, (903) 592-5993

Site of largest Confederate POW camp west of the Mississippi, 1863-1865. Features a kiosk with graphics detailing the camp's history, walking trail with interpretive signs and reconstruction of Lt. Col. J.B. Leake cabin.

9. CONFEDERATE REUNION GROUNDS HISTORIC SITE

Mexia, (254) 562-5751

Park where Texas Confederate veterans held annual reunions from 1889 to 1946. Features 1872 Heritage House, 1893 dance pavilion and a Civil War cannon.

✳ ✳ ✳ MILITARY GUIDE

From 1848 to 1900, the U.S. Army built 44 major posts and set up more than 100 temporary camps in Texas—the nation's largest military department.

Today, the Texas Forts Trail in West-Central Texas leads to 8 of the famous frontier forts, including one presidio from the Spanish colonial period. The 650-mile tour route begins in Abilene and highlights 40 attractions, though it may be started at any point and driven in either direction.

Also available for exploration is the Texas Independence Trail, which stretches more than 250 miles from San Antonio to Galveston and features 40 sites.

To obtain brochures for these trails, contact:
Texas Historical Commission
PO Box 12276
Austin, TX 78711-2276
(512) 463-6100
thc@thc.state.tx.us
www.thc.state.tx.us

Fort Davis National Historic Site, Fort Davis

10. FANNIN BATTLEGROUND STATE HISTORIC SITE

Fannin, (361) 645-3405

Site of March 20, 1836 Battle of Coleto and subsequent execution of Col. J.W. Fannin and more than 200 of his men (342 soldiers and prisoners total were killed) following their surrender. Monument.

11. FORT BLISS MUSEUM

Fort Bliss (El Paso)
(915) 568-6940

Four half-scale adobe buildings are replicas of 1854-68 fort buildings. Life-size dioramas, exhibits and photos document history of fort and Army's involvement in settlement of the Southwest.

12. FORT CHADBOURNE

Bronte, (325) 743-2555

Established 1852. Self-guided tours of ruins, reconstructed barracks and visitor center/museum with fort artifacts.

13. FORT CONCHO

San Angelo, (325) 481-2646

Active 1867-89. 23 original and restored structures include Barracks 1 with visitor center; Barracks 2 with reproduction artillery piece; Barracks 5 with 19th century squad room, orderly rooms and mess hall; Post Headquarters with original pecan wood flooring and Fort Concho Museum; reconstructed hospital; and Officers Quarters 3 furnished as period quarters.

❊   ❊   ❊
DID YOU KNOW?
The original Fort Davis, named after Secretary of War Jefferson Davis, was garrisoned from 1854 to 1861, when its primitive structures were abandoned by the federal government following Texas' secession from the Union.

After occupations by both Confederate and Union forces, it lay deserted until it was reoccupied in 1867. The new post was constructed just east of the original site. Foundations of several buildings from the first fort can still be seen behind the present-day Officers Row.

Fort Chadbourne, Bronte

Fort McKavett State Historic Site, Fort McKavett

Fort Phantom Hill, Abilene

14. FORT DAVIS NATIONAL HISTORIC SITE
Fort Davis, (432) 426-3224, ext. 20

Protected west Texas and travelers on San Antonio-El Paso Road from Comanches and Apaches from 1854 to 1891. One of best-preserved of Southwest forts. Fort, visitor center in restored barracks, exhibits.

15. FORT DUNCAN MUSEUM
Eagle Pass, (830) 758-1445

Fort active off and on from 1849 to 1920. 7 original buildings in use by the city include the Headquarters with a museum covering county history with emphasis on the fort.

16. FORT GRIFFIN STATE PARK & HISTORIC SITE
Albany, (325) 762-3592

Active 1867-81. Ruins include a mess hall, barracks, hospital, powder magazine, first sergeant's quarters, restored bakery and replicas of enlisted soldier huts. Visitor center, historic trails.

17. FORT LANCASTER STATE HISTORIC SITE
Sheffield, (432) 836-4391

Active 1855-61. Fort ruins and interpretive center with exhibits and fort artifacts.

18. FORT MCKAVETT STATE HISTORIC SITE
Fort McKavett, (325) 396-2358

Active 1852-59 and 1868-83. More than 25 restored buildings include 1870 hospital with interpretive center, officers quarters, barracks and post headquarters.

19. FORT PHANTOM HILL
Abilene, (325) 677-1309

Active 1851-54. Original stone powder magazine, guardhouse, commissary, more than a dozen stone chimneys and stone foundations. Interpretive signs, free brochures.

Palo Alto Battlefield National Historic Site, Brownsville

DID YOU KNOW?

Prior to the Civil War, in an effort to ease the burden on the Army's horses and mules, Secretary of War Jefferson Davis authorized the use of camels in the Southwest. They arrived in Indianola, Texas, in 1856 and were permanently quartered at Camp Verde.

Accustomed to the arid, rocky and sandy terrain, the camels were able to carry loads up to 4 times as heavy as a mule, for longer distances and with less food and water. They were used with some success, but with the onset of the Civil War they were forgotten, sold at public auction in 1865.

Rio Grande Valley Wing CAF Museum, Brownsville

20. FORT RICHARDSON STATE HISTORIC PARK

Jacksboro, (940) 567-3506

Base for U.S. soldiers from 1867 to 1878. Seven restored buildings, interpretive center.

21. FORT SAM HOUSTON MUSEUM

Fort Sam Houston (San Antonio), (210) 221-1886

Covers history of fort and Army in San Antonio from 1845 to present. Uniforms, photos, equipment, audiovisual presentation.

22. FORT STOCKTON

Fort Stockton, 1-877-336-8525, ext. 16

Active 1858-61 and 1867-86. Original and reconstructed buildings include officers row, guardhouse and enlisted barracks, with museum and visitor center in Barracks #1 and #2.

23. GONZALES MEMORIAL MUSEUM

Gonzales, (830) 672-6350

Includes frontier firearms, captured weapons from WWI and WWII, the "Come and Take It" cannon and a monument to the 32 men who answered Travis' call at the Alamo.

24. HANGAR 25 AIR MUSEUM

Big Spring, (432) 264-1999

Reconstructed Webb AFB hangar with 5 military aircraft, B-52 nose and several displays of artifacts and photos from Webb personnel.

25. IWO JIMA MEMORIAL & MUSEUM

Harlingen, (956) 421-2207

Original sculpture used in casting the famous Marine Corps Memorial in Arlington, Va. Museum features Marine Corps memorabilia, 30-minute film "The Battle of Iwo Jima" and a veterans hall of fame.

26. LONE STAR FLIGHT MUSEUM

Galveston, (409) 740-7722

Features more than 24 vintage aircraft, including a B-17 Flying Fortress and P-47 Thunderbolt. Conoco Hall of Power includes air combat memorabilia and wartime vehicles.

Monument Hill & Kreische Brewery State Historic Site, La Grange

27. Monument Hill & Kreische Brewery State Historic Site

La Grange, (979) 968-5658

Monument Hill is site of the tomb of 2 groups of Texans—36 volunteer militiamen killed by Mexicans Sept. 18, 1842 at Salado Creek, and 17 executed March 23, 1843 at Hacienda Salado in Mexico.

28. Palmito Ranch Battlefield

Brownsville, (956) 784-7500

Site of last land engagement of the Civil War, May 12, 1865—a month after Lee's surrender at Appomattox. Historical marker 12 miles east on Texas Highway 4.

29. Palo Alto Battlefield National Historic Site

Brownsville, (956) 541-2785

Site of first battle of the Mexican War, May 8, 1846. Only National Park Service unit with primary focus on this war, so it interprets the entire conflict. Visitor center with exhibits on the battle and the war, plus 15-minute video program "War on the Rio Grande." Half-mile trail to overlook of battlefield with interpretive panels. **Resaca de la Palma Battlefield** (May 9, 1846 battle) is nearby.

30. Palo Duro Canyon State Park

Canyon, (806) 488-2227

Site of last major Indian battle in Texas, September 1874. Battle site not accessible. Park visitor center has display, historical marker.

31. Rio Grande Valley Wing CAF Museum

Brownsville, (956) 541-8585

Commemorative Air Force museum features memorabilia, equipment and artifacts dating to the 1920s, including WWII exhibits, history of Brownsville airport, memorial and vintage aircraft.

32. SABINE PASS BATTLEGROUND STATE PARK & HISTORIC SITE

Sabine Pass, (409) 971-2559

Site of Sept. 8, 1863 Navy battle. Interpretive pavilion illustrating story of the battle, walking trail with historical markers and 4 WWII ammunition bunkers. Temporarily closed due to hurricane damage.

33. SAN JACINTO BATTLEGROUND STATE HISTORIC SITE

La Porte, (281) 479-2431

Site of April 1836 battle between Mexican Gen. Santa Anna and Gen. Sam Houston in which Texas independence was secured. Monument is world's tallest stone column memorial structure, features museum and observation floor. **BATTLESHIP TEXAS** also on site.

34. TEXAS MILITARY FORCES MUSEUM

Austin, (512) 782-6967

Presents history of Texas military from 1835 through the present. Includes dioramas, uniforms, weapons, vehicles. Library of more than 10,000 books. Four galleries plus outdoor exhibits.

35. U.S. AIR FORCE HISTORY & TRADITIONS MUSEUM

Lackland AFB (San Antonio) (210) 671-3055

Covers basic military training since 1947 and history of Lackland AFB, plus history of Air Force uniforms. 38 aircraft on outdoor display.

36. U.S. ARMY AIR DEFENSE ARTILLERY MUSEUM

Fort Bliss (El Paso) (915) 568-6009

Only U.S. museum dedicated to history of ground-based air-defense weaponry. Covers history of air defense from days of coast artillery to present. Outdoor displays.

San Jacinto Battleground State Historic Site, La Porte

37. U.S. ARMY MEDICAL DEPARTMENT MUSEUM

Fort Sam Houston (San Antonio), (210) 221-6358

Covers history of Army Medical Department from 1775 to the present with audiovisual presentation, 2 galleries and large medical equipment/vehicles. Collections include military medical equipment, artwork, insignia and artifacts from medical WWII POWs.

38. U.S. ARMY MUSEUM OF THE NCO

Fort Bliss (El Paso) (915) 568-8646

Covers history of the Army non-commissioned officer from 1775 to the present, with exhibits on the NCO role as a small unit leader, development of NCO symbols and insignia, and evolution of the NCO Corps.

Battleship *Texas* at San Jacinto Battleground State Historic Site, La Porte

USS Lexington Museum, Corpus Christi

39. USS Cavalla

Galveston, (409) 744-7854

Submarine sank 30,000-ton aircraft carrier Shokaku on maiden voyage. Now serves as memorial to lost sub *USS Seawolf* and is open for tours in Seawolf Park. Destroyer escort *USS Stewart* nearby.

40. USS Lexington Museum

Corpus Christi, (361) 888-4873

Aircraft carrier features 100,000 square feet and 11 decks for touring. Hangar deck includes exhibits and a theater.

✻ ✻ ✻

Texas Native: AUDIE MURPHY

The most-decorated U.S. combat soldier of WWII, this Greenville, Texas, native earned 33 awards during the war—every decoration for valor the U.S. offered, including the Medal of Honor, and five from France and Belgium. He is credited with killing at least 240 German soldiers while wounding and capturing many others. He fought in 9 major campaigns in North Africa and Europe and was wounded 3 times.

After the war, he became an actor and starred in 44 feature films. His successful autobiography *To Hell and Back* was made into an equally successful movie, in which Murphy starred as himself. He also was a rancher, racehorse owner and breeder and songwriter.

He spoke out candidly about what is now known as post-traumatic stress disorder, urging the U.S. government to study the emotional impact war has on veterans.

Murphy was killed in a plane crash in 1971 at the age of 46. His grave in Arlington National Cemetery is the second-most visited gravesite in the cemetery, behind only President John F. Kennedy.

UTAH

Museums are the prime destination in the Beehive State, from firearms to the world's only open atomic bomb loading pit at Wendover where the 509th trained.

Hill Aerospace Museum, Roy

1. BROWNING FIREARMS MUSEUM
Ogden (inside Union Station)
(801) 393-9886
   Collection of firearms invented by John M. Browning, including original Browning Automatic Rifle (BAR), mainstay of U.S. Army for 80 years. Displays include original and reproduced models of Browning rifles, shotguns, pistols, machine guns, cannons and re-creation of workshop.

2. CAMP FLOYD-STAGECOACH INN STATE PARK
Fairfield, (801) 768-8932
   Built in 1858 to house troops sent to stop perceived Mormon rebellion. Abandoned in 1861 with outbreak of Civil War. Only commissary building remains, houses museum.

3. FORT DOUGLAS MILITARY MUSEUM
Fort Douglas (Salt Lake City)
(801) 581-1710
   Housed in 1875 barracks, museum covers history of Fort Douglas and U.S. Army in Utah from 1858 to present. Indoor and outdoor exhibits include military uniforms from 1858 to Persian Gulf War, guns, ammunition, tanks and artillery pieces. 1,500-volume military history library, honor rolls and walls of honor, self-guided tours through fort.

> ✴ ✴ ✴
> **DID YOU KNOW?**
> During World War II, Alta ski area became involved in the war effort when ski troops from the 10th Mountain Division trained on its slopes.

4. HILL AEROSPACE MUSEUM
Hill Air Force Base (Roy)
(801) 777-6868
   Displays include more than 70 military aircraft, missiles and aerospace vehicles, plus ordnance, aerospace ground equipment, military vehicles, uniforms and other historical artifacts.

5. VETERANS MEMORIAL STATE PARK
Riverton, (801) 254-9036
   Thirty-acre park includes cemetery, memorial, chapel, wall of honor listing names of state's veterans and museum of military memorabilia.

6. WENDOVER AIR FIELD & MUSEUM
Wendover, (435) 665-2308
   Self-guided tours of training site of 509th Composite Group, which dropped atomic bombs on Japan to end WWII. Tours of buildings and world's only open atomic bomb loading pit available by appointment. Small museum housed in airport operations building includes photos and info detailing training, dioramas, model aircraft and short film. Memorial to 509th at city welcome center.

VERMONT

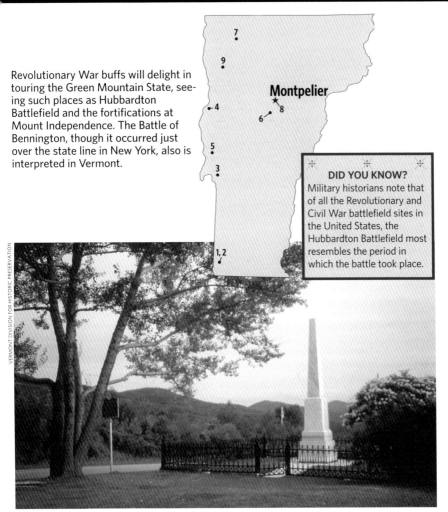

Revolutionary War buffs will delight in touring the Green Mountain State, seeing such places as Hubbardton Battlefield and the fortifications at Mount Independence. The Battle of Bennington, though it occurred just over the state line in New York, also is interpreted in Vermont.

Montpelier

* DID YOU KNOW? *
Military historians note that of all the Revolutionary and Civil War battlefield sites in the United States, the Hubbardton Battlefield most resembles the period in which the battle took place.

VERMONT DIVISION FOR HISTORIC PRESERVATION

Bennington Battle Monument State Historic Site, Bennington

1. BENNINGTON BATTLE MONUMENT STATE HISTORIC SITE
Bennington, (802) 447-1571
306-ft. stone obelisk commemorating Aug. 16, 1777, Battle of Bennington (in New York). Elevator ride to observation floor, plus diorama and interpretive exhibits on ground floor. Additional monuments on grounds.

2. BENNINGTON MUSEUM
Bennington, (802) 447-1571
Battle of Bennington gallery focuses on battle through maps, art and artifacts, plus exhibit of Vermont-made firearms.

3. HUBBARDTON BATTLEFIELD STATE HISTORIC SITE
Castleton, (802) 273-2282, 759-2412 off-season
Site of state's only Revolutionary War battle, July 7, 1777. Visitor center and museum with exhibit, artifacts, 3-D fiber-optic map and diorama of battle. Monument.

Lake Champlain Maritime Museum, Basin Harbor

4. LAKE CHAMPLAIN MARITIME MUSEUM

Basin Harbor, (802) 475-2022

Military exhibits cover the Revolution in the Champlain Valley, with replica 1776 gunboat Philadelphia II.

5. MOUNT INDEPENDENCE STATE HISTORIC SITE

Orwell, (802) 948-2000, 759-2412 off-season

Site of largest military fortifications of Revolution. Includes remains of blockhouses, barracks, gun batteries and hospital. Visitor center museum traces history of the site with archaeological artifacts and 12-minute video. Self-guided walking trails.

6. NORWICH UNIVERSITY MUSEUM

Northfield, (802) 485-2379

Country's first private military college and birthplace of ROTC. New 16,000-sq.-ft. museum features Civil War uniforms and weapons, WWI and WWII artifacts, and items from alumni.

Mount Independence State Historic Site, Orwell

7. ST. ALBANS HISTORICAL MUSEUM

St. Albans, (802) 527-7933

Includes Revolutionary War relics and Civil War exhibit on 1864 St. Albans raid by Confederate soldiers.

8. VERMONT HISTORICAL SOCIETY MUSEUM

Montpelier, (802) 828-2291

"Freedom and Unity" exhibit includes coverage of state residents' sacrifices from the Civil War and WWII.

9. VERMONT VETERANS MILITIA MUSEUM & LIBRARY

Colchester, (802) 338-3360

Covers state military history with displays from Revolution through Iraq. Includes WWI field kitchen, vehicles, helicopters, weapons, Vermont Air Guard and a naval display. Open Tuesdays only.

VIRGINIA

Virginia is America's quintessential military history destination. Dating back to 1607, it has been the scene of warfare ranging from Indian attacks on Jamestown to the surrender of Confederate troops during the Civil War. Besides at least 21 interpreted battlefields, it boasts a host of first-class military museums. No tour of the nation's martial past is complete without a trip to the Old Dominion.

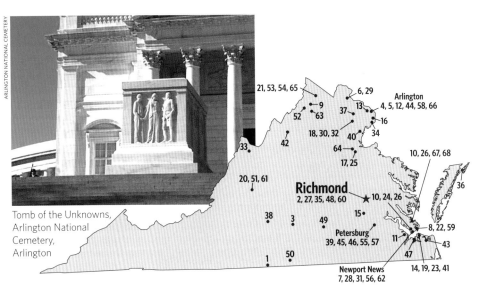

ARLINGTON NATIONAL CEMETERY

Tomb of the Unknowns, Arlington National Cemetery, Arlington

1. AAF (AMERICAN ARMOURED FOUNDATION) TANK MUSEUM
Danville, (434) 836-5323
More than 300,000 square feet of 15,000 international tank and cavalry artifacts from 1509 to the present.

2. AMERICAN CIVIL WAR CENTER AT HISTORIC TREDEGAR
Richmond, (804) 780-1865
Housed in 1861 gun foundry of historic Tredegar Iron Works. Covers Civil War from Union, Confederate and African-American perspectives with videos, music, touchscreens and displays.

3. APPOMATTOX COURT HOUSE NATIONAL HISTORICAL PARK
Appomattox, (434) 352-8987
Park's McLean house was site of Gen. Robert E. Lee's April 9, 1865, surrender to Gen. Ulysses S. Grant. Reconstructed courthouse serves as visitor center with museum and audiovisual programs. 27 restored 19th century structures, self-guided walking tours, 6-mile History Trail, summer living history programs.

4. ARLINGTON HOUSE, THE ROBERT E. LEE MEMORIAL
Arlington, (703) 235-1530
Residence (1831-61) of Robert E. Lee, restored to 1861 appearance, features self-guided tours and museum.

5. ARLINGTON NATIONAL CEMETERY
Arlington, (703) 607-8000
Established in 1864. Famous for the Tomb of the Unknowns. Features monuments and memorials from the Civil War through the Sept. 11 Pentagon memorial. Visitor center provides overview of entire cemetery.

6. BALL'S BLUFF BATTLEFIELD REGIONAL PARK
Leesburg, (703) 737-7800
Site of October 1861 battle. One-mile trail, interpretive signs, smallest national cemetery in the country.

143

CASEMATE MUSEUM

Casemate Museum, Fort Monroe

FORT C.F. SMITH PARK

Fort C.F. Smith Park, Arlington

7. BATTLE OF DAM NO. 1

Newport News, (757) 247-8523
Site of April 16, 1862, battle. Earthworks, trail and interpretive panels.

8. CASEMATE MUSEUM

Fort Monroe (Hampton)
(757) 788-3391
Chronicles history of Fort Monroe with restored casemates, Confederate President Jefferson Davis' prison cell, exhibits, audiovisual presentations and walking tours of fort.

9. CEDAR CREEK & BELLE GROVE NATIONAL HISTORICAL PARK

Middletown, (540) 868-9176
Newly designated park has no National Park Service-operated facilities yet, but includes privately run Cedar Creek Battlefield, site of October 1864 battle. Visitor center overlooks battlefield and includes interpretive displays, battle artifacts and video on Shenandoah Valley Campaign of 1864. Two battlefield monuments, self-guided tours. Park also includes 18th-century Belle Grove Plantation.

10. COLONIAL NATIONAL HISTORICAL PARK

Yorktown, (757) 898-2410
Includes **HISTORIC JAMESTOWNE** (see page 147) and **YORKTOWN BATTLE-FIELD** (see page 155). 23-mile Colonial Parkway connecting Yorktown to Jamestown features descriptive roadside markers.

11. FORT BOYKIN HISTORIC PARK

Smithfield, (757) 357-2291
Seven-pointed star fort built in 1623. Walking trail includes remainders of Civil War gun salients and magazines. Confederate artifacts from site on display in **ISLE OF WIGHT COUNTY MUSEUM** in town.

The Archaearium at Historic Jamestowne, Jamestown

12. FORT C. F. SMITH PARK

Arlington, (703) 243-7329

Well-preserved earthwork ruins include bomb-proof, well, north magazine and 11 of 22 gun emplacements. Restored 20th century Hendry House, ½ mile of trails and interpretive signage throughout grounds.

13. FORT MARCY

McLean, (703) 289-2500

Earthwork fort in wooded area features wayside exhibit with detailed brochure, 2 original cannons in position and trail. Considered one of best-preserved of the 68 defense of Washington fortifications.

14. FORT NORFOLK

Norfolk, (757) 640-1720

Last remaining of 19 harborfront forts authorized by George Washington in 1794. Active in War of 1812 and Civil War. Includes earthwork embankments, ramparts, dungeon, officers quarters, powder magazine, barracks and guardhouse, most dating to 1810.

15. FORT STEVENS

Chesterfield, (804) 777-9663

Involved in Second Battle of Drewry's Bluff, May 1864. Earthworks, interpretive signs and walking trail.

16. FORT WARD MUSEUM & HISTORIC SITE

Alexandria, (703) 838-4848

Best-preserved of forts built to protect Washington, D.C., during Civil War. Self-guided fort tours include reconstructed officers hut, bomb-proofs, northwest bastion with cannon, powder magazine and north bastion with rifle trench. Civil War exhibits, 12-minute video.

17. FREDERICKSBURG & SPOTSYLVANIA NATIONAL MILITARY PARK

Fredericksburg
(540) 373-4510

Commemorates 4 major Civil War actions: Battle of Fredericksburg, December 1862; Chancellorsville Campaign, April-May 1863; Battle of the Wilderness, May 1864; and Battle of Spotsylvania Court House, May 1864. Complete driving tour of battlefields covers 70 miles with 16 stops.

Fredericksburg battlefield features visitor center with 2-story museum and 22-minute slide film, walking tour with signs, monuments, pictures, historic house, audio program and national cemetery. Chancellorsville battlefield features visitor center with 12-minute slide presentation, museum with exhibits and dioramas, monument and walking trail to nearby earthworks. Wilderness and Spotsylvania battlefields feature exhibit shelters with maps and battle explanations, and self-guided tours.

All battlefields have driving tours with roadside markers, maps, exhibits and interpretive narratives. Park also includes 18th century Chatham manor, Salem Church and Stonewall Jackson Shrine. Written guides to several nearby battlefields, including Brandy Station (June 1863), Cedar Mountain (August 1862) and Kelly's Ford (May 1863) available at both visitor centers.

Fredericksburg & Spotsylvania National Military Park, Fredericksburg

18. FREEDOM MUSEUM

Manassas, (703) 393-0660

Located at Manassas Regional Airport and operated by a coalition of veterans organizations. Exhibits include photos, artifacts and models depicting 20th century military action, plus home front efforts and support organizations such as USO.

19. GENERAL DOUGLAS MACARTHUR MEMORIAL

Norfolk, (757) 441-2965

Nine permanent and two changing exhibit galleries in restored 1850 city hall portray MacArthur's life and military career. Includes 25-minute film, tomb, Japanese WWII surrender documents and his trademark corncob pipe.

20. GEORGE C. MARSHALL MUSEUM

Lexington, (540) 463-7103

Follows Marshall's career, including life as a cadet at Virginia Military Institute, in WWI and WWII, and as secretary of state when he proposed the Marshall Plan. Features 1942 Jeep, uniforms, 3 videos, 27-minute narrated WWII map, library and archives.

21. GEORGE WASHINGTON'S OFFICE MUSEUM

Winchester, (540) 662-4412

Small log building served as Washington's office 1755-56 while he built Fort Loudoun. Museum displays cover his surveying career, service in French & Indian War and election to House of Burgesses.

22. HAMPTON HISTORY MUSEUM

Hampton, (757) 727-1610

Eighteenth Century Gallery includes city's role in the Revolution. Civil War gallery covers Battle of Big Bethel, importance of Fort Monroe and the many military camps and hospitals in the area.

THE MacARTHUR MEMORIAL

General Douglas MacArthur Memorial, Norfolk

Library at George C. Marshall Museum, Lexington

✳   ✳   ✳

**Virginia Native:
GEORGE WASHINGTON**

As commander-in-chief of the Continental Army, Washington took the field at Cambridge, Mass., on July 3, 1775, leading the war effort until the very end in 1783. "His ability to stay calm in moments of crisis was the key to his ability to rule men, both soldiers and politicians," one historian wrote.

The Westmoreland County, Va., native took office as the first President April 30, 1789, two years after presiding over the Constitutional Convention. Establishing the President as pre-eminent in foreign policy, he steered a neutral course, thus allowing the fledgling Republic to grow strong and prosper.

English King George III called him the "greatest character of the age." By the time he left office in 1797, he had molded 13 disparate colonies into a united nation. Washington died of a throat infection at age 67 in Mount Vernon.

23. HAMPTON ROADS NAVAL MUSEUM (*See Nauticus, The National Maritime Center*)

24. HISTORIC JAMESTOWNE
Jamestown, (757) 229-1733
First permanent English settlement in North America. Site of the 1607 James Fort. Visitor center contains theater and exhibits. Archaearium museum features artifacts found on site. Guided tours, scenic drive with markers.

25. JAMES MONROE MUSEUM
Fredericksburg
(540) 654-1043
Covers his life and major achievements, including time in the Continental Army, presidency and strained relationship with George Washington.

26. JAMESTOWN SETTLEMENT & YORKTOWN VICTORY CENTER
Jamestown & Yorktown
(757) 253-4838
Re-created settlement includes 3 replica ships, Powhatan Indian village, palisaded colonial fort and museum with 15-minute film.

YORKTOWN VICTORY CENTER includes re-created outdoor Continental Army encampment and 1780s farm. Museum covers Revolutionary War with exhibits on experiences of ordinary soldiers, the siege at Yorktown and British ships lost during the war.

27. JOHN MARSHALL HOUSE
Richmond, (804) 648-7998
Revolutionary War soldier, secretary of state and 34-year Supreme Court chief justice's 1790 house contains largest collection of Marshall family furnishings and memorabilia in America.

National Air & Space Museum's Steven F. Udvar-Hazy Center, Chantilly

28. LEE'S MILL BATTLEFIELD

Newport News, (757) 247-8523
Site of April 5, 1862, Union attack. Earthworks, trail and interpretive signs.

29. LOUDON MUSEUM

Leesburg, (703) 777-7427
Covers county history with Civil War exhibits on Robert E. Lee's first invasion of the north, artifacts from Battle of Ball's Bluff and Dranesville, and 15-minute film.

30. MANASSAS NATIONAL BATTLEFIELD PARK

Manassas, (703) 361-1339
Site of First (July 1861) and Second (August 1862) Battle of Manassas (Bull Run). **HENRY HILL VISITOR CENTER** features museum, 45-minute film and 3-D map. **STUART'S HILL VISITOR CENTER** open summers only. Self-guided 1-mile walking trail of first battle with taped messages and interpretive signs. 16-mile self-guided driving tour of second battle covers 11 sites. Visitor center pamphlet details 5- and 6-mile hiking trails through battlefield.

31. MARINERS' MUSEUM

Newport News, (757) 596-2222
More than 60,000 square feet of exhibits include "Defending the Seas" gallery, which covers history of U.S. Navy using re-created sections of ships, and artifacts from the *USS Monitor,* the first ironclad, steam-powered warship, which sank December 1862.

32. MAYFIELD FORT

Manassas, (703) 368-1873
Site features earthwork ruins of fort, 8 interpretive markers and Confederate Quaker gun replicas.

33. McDOWELL BATTLEFIELD

McDowell, (540) 396-4478
Site of first Confederate victory of Stonewall Jackson's 1862 Valley Campaign. Hiking trail with interpretive signs. Highland County Museum & Heritage Center includes battle orientation center with artifacts, informational panels and documentary film.

Manassas National Battlefield Park, Manassas

34. MOUNT VERNON

Mount Vernon
(703) 780-2000
Home of George Washington from 1759-99 includes restored mansion, tomb, 12 outbuildings and distillery. Two underground museums with 25 theaters and galleries, 500 original artifacts, 11 History Channel videos, and immersion theater experiences.

Museum exhibit at Mount Vernon, home of George Washington

✳   ✳   ✳

**Virginia Native:
ROBERT E. LEE**

Robert E. Lee was a lieutenant colonel in command of the U.S. Army's 2nd Cavalry when the lower Southern states seceded from the Union. He loved the Union and the Army, had no sympathies with slavery and was averse to secession.

But loyalty to his home state of Virginia came first. He declined the field command of U.S. forces, and upon Virginia's secession, resigned from the Army on April 20, 1861.

Lee assumed command of Virginia's forces 3 days later and was soon made a Confed-

erate general. He saw victories in the Seven Days battles (June 26-July 2, 1862), the second battle of Bull Run (Aug. 29-30, 1862), Fredericksburg (Dec. 13, 1862) and Chancellorsville (May 2-4, 1863). His defeats included Antietam (Sept. 17, 1862, though the battle had no clear winner and Lee "lost" because he withdrew to Virginia) and Gettysburg (July 1-3, 1863).

Two months before he surrendered to Gen. Ulysses S. Grant at Appomattox Courthouse, Lee was appointed general-in-chief of all Confederate armies.

After the war, Lee became president of Washington College (now Washington and Lee University) in Lexington, Va. He died Oct. 12, 1870, from effects of pneumonia following a probable stroke.

To learn more about Robert E. Lee, visit Arlington House, The Robert E. Lee Memorial, located in Arlington National Cemetery.

35. MUSEUM OF THE CONFEDERACY
Richmond, (804) 649-1861

Houses the world's largest and most comprehensive Confederate collection. Features 3 floors of exhibits with some 15,000 artifacts, including personal belongings of generals and soldiers, 1,000 artifacts from postwar veterans reunions and monument dedications, 300 edged weapons, 250 firearms, 215 uniforms, 150 paintings, a photographic collection of some 6,000 original images and an extensive library. Restored **WHITE HOUSE OF THE CONFEDERACY** next door features 11 period rooms on exhibit and guided tours.

36. NASA VISITORS CENTER
Chincoteague, (757) 824-1344

Exhibits include NASA projects; scale models of space probes, satellites and aircraft; Project Apollo and moon rock displays; and interactive computer displays. Full-scale rockets and aircraft on outdoor display.

37. NATIONAL AIR & SPACE MUSEUM'S STEVEN F. UDVAR-HAZY CENTER
Chantilly, (202) 633-1000

Massive 760,000-sq.-ft. complex at Washington Dulles International Airport features 103 aircraft, 122 large space artifacts and more than 1,500 smaller items on display in a large aviation hangar, space hangar and observation tower. Two-thirds of aviation hangar devoted to military aircraft from WWII to the present, including B-29 Superfortress Enola Gay. Elevated walkways run parallel to 2 tiers of aircraft suspended from ceiling, with a third tier on floor level. Space hangar features space shuttle Enterprise and other space artifacts.

38. NATIONAL D-DAY MEMORIAL

Bedford, (540) 587-3619

88-acre memorial consists of 3 plazas, 10 life-sized sculptures, granite wall with inscribed names of Americans and Allies killed that encircles a pool, and 44-foot Overlord Arch.

39. NATIONAL MUSEUM OF THE CIVIL WAR SOLDIER

(See Pamplin Historical Park)

40. NATIONAL MUSEUM OF THE MARINE CORPS

Quantico, 1-800-397-7585

Opened November 2006. Current 118,000 square feet of exhibits include galleries on boot camp, WWII, Korea, Vietnam, war on terrorism and combat art. "Legacy Walk" connects galleries and provides introduction to each era of Marine Corps history through dramatic vignettes.

Future galleries will cover early Corps history from its creation up until WWII, with exhibits on the Civil War, War of 1812, Mexican War, Latin America, the USMC Band, WWI and development of Corps tactics, techniques and materials.

National Museum of the Marine Corps, Quantico

Old Guard Museum, Arlington

41. NAUTICUS, THE NATIONAL MARITIME CENTER

Norfolk, (757) 664-1000

Military points of interest include exhibit on modern Navy with computer simulation games, scale-model vessels and battle-simulation theater. **HAMPTON ROADS NAVAL MUSEUM** covers area naval history from Revolutionary War to the present. Battleship *Wisconsin* features self-guided tour of main deck with interactive exhibits. Two-hour cruises of **NAVAL STATION NORFOLK** depart from the site.

Pamplin Historical Park, Petersburg

Nauticus, the National Maritime Center, Norfolk

42. NEW MARKET BATTLEFIELD HISTORICAL PARK

New Market, (540) 740-3101

Site of May 1864 battle that included participation of 257 teenage cadets from Virginia Military Institute, which supports the park. Visitor center housed in **HALL OF VALOR MUSEUM,** which covers the war through dioramas, artifacts, 2 short films and the 45-minute award-winning film "Field of Lost Shoes." 1-mile walking tour of battlefield.

43. OLD COAST GUARD STATION MUSEUM

Virginia Beach, (757) 422-1587

1903 lifesaving station houses two floors of exhibits covering history of lifesaving, the Coast Guard, Virginia shipwrecks and the Battle of the Atlantic in WWII.

44. OLD GUARD MUSEUM

Arlington, (703) 696-6670

Covers history of 3rd Infantry Regiment, Army's oldest infantry unit, from 1784 to the present. Exhibits include War of 1812 through Vietnam, plus unit's part in recovery after Sept. 11 attack on the Pentagon, its current role as the Army's official ceremonial unit and escort to the President, and history of Ft. Myer.

✳   ✳   ✳
DID YOU KNOW?

Civil War battles were generally named after the closest river, stream or creek by the North, and after towns or railroad junctions by the South. Hence the Confederates named the Battle of Manassas after Manassas Junction while the Union named it the Battle of Bull Run for the stream Bull Run.

---

45. PAMPLIN HISTORICAL PARK & NATIONAL MUSEUM OF THE CIVIL WAR SOLDIER

Petersburg, (804) 861-2408

Site of April 1865 "breakthrough" battle that ended Petersburg campaign. Includes 4 museums, 4 antebellum homes, living history venues and guided tours. Centerpiece is 25,000-sq.-ft. **NATIONAL MUSEUM OF THE CIVIL WAR SOLDIER**, with interactive learning stations, videos, life-sized dioramas, more than 1,000 original objects and a multi-sensory battlefield simulation.

Battlefield Center features a fiber-optic battle map, exhibits, theater, interactive computer learning centers and guided tour of battlefield. Park also includes 3 miles of interpretive trails with wayside exhibits and well-preserved earthworks.

Malvern Hill at Richmond National Battlefield Park, Richmond

46. PETERSBURG NATIONAL BATTLEFIELD

Petersburg, (804) 732-3531

Site of June 1864 battle and subsequent 9½-month Union siege—the longest siege in American history. Visitor center features exhibits and map program explaining the battle. Extensive earthworks can be seen on 16-mile self-guided Siege Line Tour (with 6 stops) and 4-mile Battlefield Tour, whose 8 stops feature audio stations, wayside exhibits and short, interpretive walking trails.

Nearby **FIVE FORKS BATTLEFIELD** has seasonal information station and wayside exhibits. **GRANT'S HEADQUARTERS** at City Point in Hopewell features a video presentation, exhibits, Appomattox Manor house and Grant's original cabin.

47. PORTSMOUTH NAVAL SHIPYARD MUSEUM

Portsmouth, (757) 393-8591

Covers history of U.S. Navy in Portsmouth and Norfolk areas from colonial times to the present. Includes history and model of *CSS Virginia*, other ship models, weapons and documents.

48. RICHMOND NATIONAL BATTLEFIELD PARK

Richmond, (804) 226-1981

Park encompasses 10 sites of significance in 1862 Peninsula Campaign, 1862 Seven Days Battle and 1864 Overland Campaign, including Cold Harbor battlefield, Glendale/Malvern Hill battlefield and Fort Harrison. Complete driving tour of park covers 80 miles. Main visitor center at Tredegar Iron Works features 3 floors of exhibits and audiovisual presentations on Richmond's role in the war. **CHIMBORAZO MEDICAL MUSEUM** tells story of life in 1861 Chimborazo Hospital, which treated more than 76,000 Confederate patients.

Additional exhibits at visitor centers at Cold Harbor, Glendale (open seasonally) and Fort Harrison (open seasonally). Chickahominy Bluff, Malvern Hill, Fort Harrison and Drewry's Bluff have interpretive facilities with audio station and exhibits. Gaines' Mill, Malvern Hill, Cold Harbor, Fort Harrison, Fort Brady and Drewry's Bluff have short self-guided trails with historical features.

Portsmouth Naval Shipyard Museum, Portsmouth

152

Stonewall Jackson Museum at Hupp's Hill, Strasburg

Sailor's Creek Battlefield Historic State Park, Deatonville

✳   ✳   ✳
DID YOU KNOW?
Confederate Gen. Stonewall Jackson was shot by his own men during the battle of Chancellorsville in 1863. His left arm was amputated, but he died of pneumonia 8 days later. Jackson is buried in Lexington. But his arm is buried in Chancellorsville.

Visitors to the Chancellorsville Visitor Center inside Fredericksburg & Spotsylvania National Military Park can visit the grave, marked by a headstone simply inscribed with "Arm of Stonewall Jackson, May 3, 1863."

49. SAILOR'S CREEK BATTLEFIELD HISTORIC STATE PARK
Deatonville, (434) 392-3435
Site of last major Civil War battle in Virginia, April 1865. Overton-Hillsman House, used as field hospital during battle, open summers or by appointment. Interpretive signs.

50. STAUNTON RIVER BATTLEFIELD STATE PARK
South Boston, (434) 454-4312
Site of June 1864 battle of "old men and young boys." Visitor center includes Civil War exhibits on the battle, Wilson's raid and home life during the war. Extensive earthworks ranked among best-preserved in the state. Rebuilt bridge, artillery emplacement and self-guided walking trail.

51. STONEWALL JACKSON HOUSE
Lexington, (540) 463-2552
Jackson's home from 1859 to his death in 1863. Restored house and garden furnished with original pieces and personal effects. Changing exhibits and guided tours.

52. STONEWALL JACKSON MUSEUM AT HUPP'S HILL
Strasburg, (540) 465-5884
Site of October 1864 Battle of Hupp's Hill. Original Confederate entrenchments and Federal gun positions still visible. Exhibits cover Jackson's campaign through maps, photographs, original artifacts and hands-on reproductions.

53. STONEWALL JACKSON'S HEADQUARTERS MUSEUM
Winchester, (540) 667-3242
1854 Gothic Revival house served as Jackson's headquarters, November 1861 to March 1862. Interprets Jackson Campaign and includes personal items of Jackson, cavalry general Turner Ashby and topographer Jed Hotchkiss.

54. THIRD WINCHESTER BATTLEFIELD
Winchester, (202) 367-1861
Site of Sept. 19, 1864 battle (also called Opequon), the bloodiest fought in the Shenandoah Valley. 5 miles of hiking/biking trails with wayside exhibits open Summer 2007.

Women in Military Service for America Memorial, Arlington

55. U.S. ARMY QUARTERMASTER MUSEUM
Fort Lee (Petersburg)
(804) 734-4203

23,000 artifacts cover past and current missions of Quartermaster Corps, including transportation, food and rations, uniforms, airdrop of supplies, and search, identification and burial of the dead. Features dioramas, multimedia shows and visitor information kiosks. Artifacts include Gen. George Patton's jeep, Dwight Eisenhower's uniforms and Ulysses S. Grant's saddle.

56. U.S. ARMY TRANSPORTATION MUSEUM
Fort Eustis (Williamsburg, Newport News), (757) 878-1115

Covers history of military transportation from colonial times to the present through scale models, dioramas and films, with exhibit on history of Fort Eustis and Confederate earthwork Fort Crafford. Vehicles, boats, rail equipment, experimental craft and more than 20 historic aircraft on outdoor display.

57. U.S. ARMY WOMEN'S MUSEUM
Fort Lee (Petersburg)
(804) 734-4326

40 state-of-the-art exhibits cover history of women's role in the Army from Revolutionary War to the present through interactive maps, kiosks, dioramas, artifacts, photos and audiovisual presentations. Exhibits include Army nurses, WWII Women's Army Corps posters, women paratroopers, women in Operation Just Cause and women in Iraq.

58. U.S. MARINE CORPS WAR MEMORIAL
Arlington, (703) 289-2500

Bronze statue depicts WWII flag raising on Iwo Jima and is dedicated to all Marines killed in service since 1775.

59. VIRGINIA AIR & SPACE CENTER
Hampton, (757) 727-0900

More than 100 interactive exhibits include "Adventures in Flight Gallery" with military aircraft, and "Space Gallery" with Apollo 12 command module and NASA's history in the area.

60. VIRGINIA HISTORICAL SOCIETY MUSEUM
Richmond, (804) 358-4901

Two galleries in "The Story of Virginia" exhibit cover the Civil War and the Virginia WWII home front. Mural gallery features largest collection of Confederate-made weaponry in existence and 4 gigantic murals depicting Civil War scenes through the seasons.

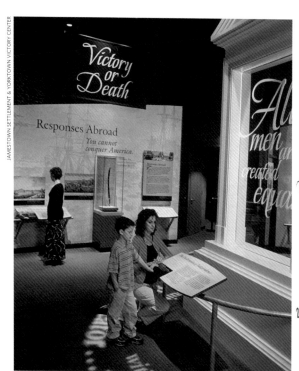

Yorktown Victory Center, Yorktown

61. VIRGINIA MILITARY INSTITUTE MUSEUM

Lexington, (540) 464-7232

Covers history of nation's first state military college, with exhibits on cadet uniforms and equipment, antique firearms, VMI's involvement in the Civil War, Stonewall Jackson and Vietnam experiences of 3 graduates. Exhibits on Stonewall Jackson and Gen. George Patton.

62. VIRGINIA WAR MUSEUM

Newport News, (757) 247-8523

Museum of American military history features more than 60,000 artifacts from 1775 to the present, focusing on Revolutionary War through Vietnam and including War of 1812, Mexican War and Indian wars. Exhibits include women at war, prisoners of war, arms and the evolution of weaponry.

63. WARREN RIFLES CONFEDERATE MUSEUM

Front Royal, (540) 636-6982

Includes documents, weapons, uniforms and equipment of Confederate soldiers, plus personal items of Confederate spy Belle Boyd and generals Stonewall Jackson, Robert E. Lee and Turner Ashby.

64. WHITE OAK CIVIL WAR MUSEUM

Falmouth, (540) 371-4234

Features Union and Confederate artifacts from battlefields around Fredericksburg area. Includes 90,000 bullets, 13-inch mortar shell, soldier relics such as bayonets and canteens, and soldier huts replicating a Union camp site.

65. WINCHESTER-FREDERICK COUNTY CONVENTION & VISITORS BUREAU

Winchester, (540) 542-1326

Photos, maps and brochures offer information on area Civil War attractions, museums and battlefields, including Kernstown, Winchester and Cedar Creek battles.

66. WOMEN IN MILITARY SERVICE FOR AMERICA MEMORIAL

Arlington, (703) 533-1155

Information center, exhibits, theater and interactive computer kiosk. Located at **ARLINGTON NATIONAL CEMETERY.**

67. YORKTOWN BATTLEFIELD

Yorktown, (757) 898-2410

Site of the last major battle of the Revolutionary War, August-October 1781. Visitor center features 15-minute film and exhibits. Two self-guided driving tours through battlefield include markers, field displays and other interpretive aids. Restored and reconstructed earthworks.

68. YORKTOWN VICTORY CENTER

(See Jamestown Settlement & Yorktown Victory Center)

✳   ✳   ✳
DID YOU KNOW?
The 9,000 American forces fighting in the Revolutionary War's Yorktown Campaign were in the minority. The French army and navy combined had more than 25,000 men, while the British army and navy participants numbered more than 21,000.

The 1781 siege of Yorktown was a decisive victory for the American and French troops, leading to the surrender of British general Lord Cornwallis' army and the eventual end of the war.

WASHINGTON

The Evergreen State's coast makes it the perfect place to showcase naval history and coastal fortifications, which it does through two naval museums and five forts. Naval artifacts can be found at the Bremerton Naval Museum, which also contains the oldest known cannon, a piece from Korea dating back to 1377.

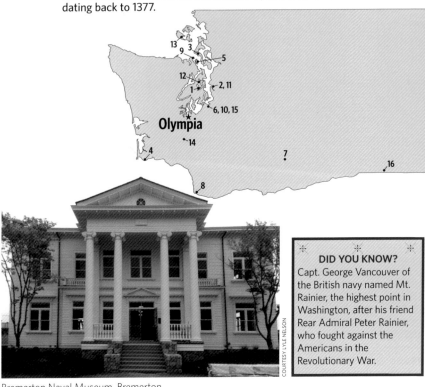

Bremerton Naval Museum, Bremerton

> ✳   ✳   ✳
> **DID YOU KNOW?**
> Capt. George Vancouver of the British navy named Mt. Rainier, the highest point in Washington, after his friend Rear Admiral Peter Rainier, who fought against the Americans in the Revolutionary War.

1. BREMERTON NAVAL MUSEUM (NAVAL MEMORIAL MUSEUM OF THE PACIFIC)
Bremerton, (360) 479-7447

Covers history of Puget Sound Naval Shipyard, plus historical and naval artifacts from 1377 (oldest known cannon, from Korea) to the present. Focuses primarily on WWII. Nearby, destroyer **USS TURNER JOY,** *(360) 792-2457,* is open for tours summers only.

2. COAST GUARD MUSEUM-NORTHWEST
Seattle, (206) 217-6993

Coast Guard and northwestern U.S. maritime history from War of 1812 to present. 10,000 photos, 2,000 documents and 1,000 books.

3. FORT CASEY STATE PARK
Coupeville, (360) 678-4519

Part of Puget Sound defense system, active from 1900 through WWII. Fortifications, interpretive center in 1890 lighthouse.

4. FORT COLUMBIA STATE PARK
Chinook, (360) 642-3078

Typical coastal artillery fort built during Spanish-American War, operational from 1896 to 1947. One of the few intact coastal defense sites in U.S. Original fort, interpretive center, museum.

Fort Worden State Park, Port Townsend

5. FORT FLAGLER STATE PARK
Marrowstone Island (Nordland), (360) 385-1259
1897 fort includes historical buildings, museum with interactive display, 5 batteries and interpretive trail.

6. FORT LEWIS MILITARY MUSEUM
Tacoma, (253) 967-7206
Focus on U.S. Army in Pacific Northwest from 1804 to 1917 and histories of 9th Division, I Corps and Fort Lewis from 1918 to present. Military equipment on outdoor display.

7. FORT SIMCOE STATE PARK
White Swan, (360) 902-8844
1850s-era installation built to keep peace between settlers and Indians. Tells story of mid-19th century Army life. Partially restored fort, interpretive center.

8. FORT VANCOUVER NATIONAL HISTORIC SITE
Vancouver, (360) 816-6230
Fur-trading post from 1824-46. First military post in Pacific Northwest, built in 1849. Reconstructed fort, visitor center, museum, tours.

9. FORT WORDEN STATE PARK
Port Townsend (360) 385-4730
Fort provided 20th century coastal defense in Puget Sound area. Park encompasses original fort batteries, buildings. **COAST ARTILLERY MUSEUM** features fort artifacts and model of Battery Kinzie.

10. MCCHORD AIR MUSEUM
McChord AFB (Tacoma) (253) 982-2485
Exhibits include history of the base, enlisted pilots from 1912-57, Doolittle's Tokyo raiders, Project Firewall, flight simulators and aircraft on outdoor display. Call for security restrictions.

Museum of Flight, Seattle

11. MUSEUM OF FLIGHT

Seattle, (206) 764-5720

Great Gallery features exhibits on M-21 Blackbird and military jet cockpits. The 3-story, 88,000-sq.-ft. Personal Courage Wing covers WWI and WWII fighter aviation through interactive exhibits, flight simulations, dioramas, multimedia presentations and a live theater program. Features 28 restored WWI and WWII fighter planes, including Champlin Fighter Collection.

12. NAVAL UNDERSEA MUSEUM

Keyport, (360) 396-4148

History of exploration and evolution of undersea technology. Largest collection of naval undersea history and scientific artifacts in U.S.

13. SAN JUAN ISLAND NATIONAL HISTORIC PARK

Friday Harbor, (360) 378-2240

American and British military fortifications date to 1859. English camp at Garrison Bay, with blockhouse, commissary and restored barracks. Remains of U.S. camp on southeastern tip of island.

San Juan Island National Historic Park, Friday Harbor

14. VETERANS MEMORIAL MUSEUM

Chehalis, (360) 740-8875

Covers Revolution to the present, with 85 display cases of military items. Research library and viewing room with veterans' stories from WWI to Iraq.

15. WASHINGTON NATIONAL GUARD STATE HISTORICAL SOCIETY MUSEUM

Camp Murray (Tacoma) (253) 512-8268

History of state units dating back to 1848. Open by appointment only.

16. WHITMAN MISSION NATIONAL HISTORIC SITE

Walla Walla, (509) 522-6357

Memorial to missionaries Marcus and Narcissa Whitman and others, killed by Cayuse Indians in 1847. Visitor center, monument, mass grave, restored section of Oregon Trail, millpond.

WASHINGTON, D.C.

Memorializing Americans who died serving our country is a central focus of the nation's capital. Veterans are honored with national memorials for the Korean War, Vietnam War, WWII and others. World-renowned museums, from the Smithsonian museums to the National Museum of Health & Medicine, are all harbored within this history-rich city.

National WWII Memorial

1. ANDERSON HOUSE
(202) 785-2040

Headquarters, library and museum of The Society of the Cincinnati, founded by officers of the Continental Army and Navy in 1783. Displays cover Revolutionary War.

2. INTERNATIONAL SPY MUSEUM
(202) 393-7798

Exhibits include "Spies Among Us," featuring intelligence, code-breaking and Navajo codetalkers in WWII; and "War of the Spies," focusing on spies and intelligence of the Cold War.

3. KOREAN WAR VETERANS MEMORIAL
(202) 426-6841

National memorial features statues of 19 poncho-clad servicemen on patrol. 164-foot granite wall with etched photographic images of support personnel, adjacent Pool of Remembrance.

159

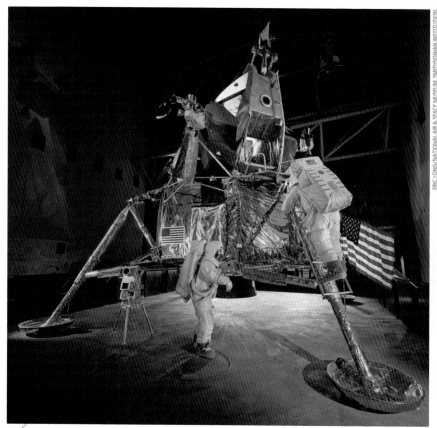

National Air & Space Museum

Credit along image edge: ERIC LONG/NATIONAL AIR & SPACE MUSEUM SMITHSONIAN INSTITUTION

4. NATIONAL AIR & SPACE MUSEUM

(202) 633-1000

Maintains largest collection of historic air and spacecraft in the world. More than 160,000 square feet include 22 exhibition galleries with 62 aircraft, 49 large space artifacts and some 2,000 smaller items; IMAX theater; planetarium; flight simulator gallery; and library and archives. Military exhibits include WWI, WWII and Apollo space program, plus displays with Cold War, Korean War and Vietnam aircraft. Free tours.

5. NATIONAL GUARD MEMORIAL MUSEUM

(202) 789-0031

Country's only national museum dedicated to the National Guard opened in 2003 and covers Guard history from first muster in 1636 through Iraq. 5,600 square feet with 6 core exhibit areas feature sound-and-light programs and object theaters with artifacts and equipment. Exhibits include militia era, WWII, Cold War, Korea, Vietnam, women in the Guard, terrorist attacks of Sept. 11, homeland security, Afghanistan and Iraq.

6. NATIONAL MUSEUM OF AMERICAN JEWISH MILITARY HISTORY

(202) 265-6280

Covers Revolutionary War to the Iraq War, including Jewish women in the military, WWII photographs, Gold Star mothers and Jewish Medal of Honor recipients.

7. NATIONAL MUSEUM OF HEALTH & MEDICINE

(202) 782-2200

Established during Civil War and still maintains emphasis on American military medicine. Exhibits include history of the museum, Civil War medicine, battlefield surgery from Civil War through Vietnam and combat medicine in the Korean War.

✳   ✳   ✳

Founding Father: PIERRE L'ENFANT

Paris, France, native Pierre-Charles L'Enfant was an officer in the Continental Army's engineers. He was severely wounded at the 1779 Siege of Savannah and was a POW for 18 months after being captured at Charleston. L'Enfant was commissioned by Washington in 1791 to design a new federal capital city, and he oversaw much of the planning and development of the 10-mile square federal territory. Washington, D.C., looks the way it does today largely because of his design.

International Spy Museum

Anderson House

8. NATIONAL WWII MEMORIAL

1-800-639-4992

Consists of a memorial plaza and reflecting pool, 24 bronze bas-relief panels, 2 43-ft. pavilions, 56 17-ft. granite pillars and a field of 4,000 gold stars commemorating those who died.

✳   ✳   ✳

DID YOU KNOW?

Washington, D.C., has been attacked 3 times in its history. First it was burned by the British in 1814. Then Confederate troops attacked the Union-held Fort Stevens in July 1864. The third time was on Sept. 11, 2001, when terrorists crashed a plane into the Pentagon.

9. ROCK CREEK PARK

(202) 895-6070

Park includes three Civil War forts maintained by the National Park Service. Each features earthworks, plaque and wayside exhibit.

FORT DERUSSY. 1861. Helped defend Ft. Stevens, July 1864. Parapet, dry moat and rifle trenches still visible.

FORT STEVENS. Site of only battle fought in District of Columbia, July 1864. Parapet remains where President Lincoln stood, the only sitting president to come under enemy fire. One-acre national cemetery, monuments.

FORT TOTTEN. 1863 fort's 100-lb. Parrott rifle supported defense of Ft. Stevens. Powder magazines, rifle trenches and parapet gun-openings remain.

10. SMITHSONIAN NATIONAL MUSEUM OF AMERICAN HISTORY

(202) 633-1000

18,000-sq.-ft. exhibition "The Price of Freedom" covers history of U.S. military conflicts from 1750s to the present. 850 objects and 16 conflicts presented chronologically, with emphasis on Revolutionary War, Civil War, WWII and Vietnam. Displays include rare Revolutionary War uniform, WWII Jeep, restored UH-1H Huey helicopter, Hanoi Hilton cell re-creation, Medal of Honor recipients, interactive stations with first-person narratives and 9 videos. Closed for renovation until summer 2008.

Vietnam Veterans Memorial

U.S. Navy Memorial & Heritage Center

11. U.S. NAVY MEMORIAL & HERITAGE CENTER
(202) 737-2300

Ground-level 100-ft.-diameter granite map of the world surrounded by fountains, pools, flag masts and 26 bronze relief sculptures depicting naval history, including famous Lone Sailor statue. Adjacent Heritage Center includes theater, rotating exhibits and electronic memorial "Navy Log" listing more than 600,000 Navy veterans.

12. U.S. NAVY MUSEUM
(202) 433-4882

Covers history of the Navy from 1775 to the present. Exhibits include all major wars and lesser-known engagements such as the Barbary Wars. Highlights include simulated submarine combat center, replica gun deck of *USS Constitution* and video presentations. Call one day prior to visit to make reservation.

13. USS BARRY
(202) 433-3377

Destroyer operated off Korea, Vietnam and during Cuban Missile Crisis. Open for self-guided tours with explanations posted at numbered locations. Active-duty sailors provide additional interpretive information.

14. VIETNAM VETERANS MEMORIAL
(202) 619-7222

National memorial consists of "the Wall"—a V-shaped polished black granite wall with inscribed names of more than 58,000 KIAs and MIAs—life-size statue of 3 servicemen and statue of 3 nurses attending a wounded soldier. Underground Vietnam Veterans Memorial Center scheduled to open in 2012. Exhibits will include photos of fallen service members, artifacts left at the Wall, a chronology of the war's key actions and the history of the memorial.

WEST VIRGINIA

French & Indian War, as well as Revolutionary War, battles took place in West Virginia. Civil War battlefields such as Carnifex Ferry and Droop Mountain are preserved in state parks. Visitors will enjoy the four forts in the Mountain State, particularly Fort Mulligan, considered one of the best-preserved forts in the state.

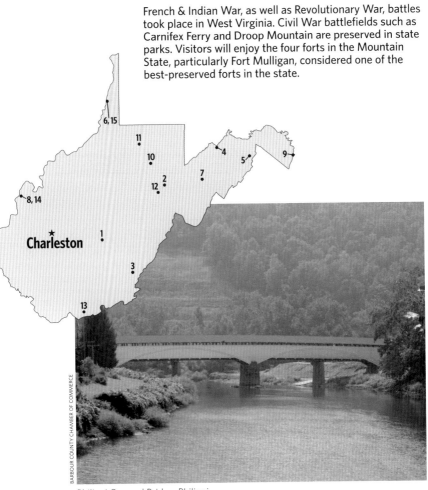

BARBOUR COUNTY CHAMBER OF COMMERCE

Philippi Covered Bridge, Philippi

1. CARNIFEX FERRY BATTLEFIELD STATE PARK
Summersville, (304) 872-0825
Site of Sept. 10, 1861 battle. Small **PATTERSON HOUSE MUSEUM** features artifacts from the battle and is open summer weekends only. Interpretive signs.

2. CHEAT SUMMIT FORT (FORT MILROY)
Elkins, (304) 636-1800
Located in **MONONGAHELA NATIONAL FOREST,** the Civil War site features interpretive signs, pit and parapet earthworks, and cabin sites. Nearby **CAMP ALLEGHENY** includes shallow trench and surface depressions from 35 cabins.

3. DROOP MOUNTAIN BATTLEFIELD STATE PARK
Droop, (304) 653-4254
Site of state's largest and last significant Civil War battle, Nov. 6, 1863. Log cabin museum with memorabilia, trenches, observation tower, monuments, walking trails.

Harpers Ferry National Historical Park, Harpers Ferry

NATIONAL PARK SERVICE

4. FORT ASHBY

Keyser, (304) 298-3319

1755 fort is only one remaining of the 69 George Washington built during French & Indian War. Barracks houses museum with fort and era artifacts. Open by appointment.

5. FORT EDWARDS

Capon Bridge, (304) 822-4655

Nearby battle of April 18, 1756, was largest of French & Indian War in the state. Visitor center with exhibits on fort and war. Partial fort reconstruction in progress. Open June-October.

6. FORT HENRY

Wheeling, (304) 242-7272

Site of last major battle of the Revolutionary War, Sept. 11-13, 1782. Site marked by memorial stone and marker on Main St. Displays in Mansion Museum in Oglebay Park.

7. FORT MULLIGAN

Petersburg, (304) 257-2637

1863 fort considered one of the best-preserved forts in the state. Earthworks, walking trail with 9 stops, monument.

8. FORT RANDOLPH

Point Pleasant, (304) 675-6788

Reconstruction of 18th century fort in Krodel Park. Open April-October with some weekend interpreters.

9. HARPERS FERRY NATIONAL HISTORICAL PARK

Harpers Ferry, (304) 535-6223

Military attractions include a Civil War museum and remnants of Civil War fortifications and campsites. Visitor center at Cavalier Heights area.

10. PHILIPPI COVERED BRIDGE

Philippi, (304) 457-1958

Town was site of first land battle of Civil War, June 3, 1861. Built in 1852, covered bridge was used by both sides during battle. Historical marker.

DID YOU KNOW?
The first land battle of the Civil War happened in Philippi on June 3, 1861. But it has another claim to fame: It's the town where the first limb was lost in the Civil War. Confederate J.E. Hanger was hit by a cannonball, had his leg amputated by a Union doctor, later invented an artificial limb, and started a company that became one of the largest manufacturers of wooden legs in the world. There's a plaque in Philippi that commemorates the fateful cannon blast.

West Virginia Independence Hall Museum, Wheeling

11. PRICKETT'S FORT STATE PARK

Fairmont, (304) 363-3030

Built 1774. Re-created fort, visitor center, museum. Open April-October.

12. RICH MOUNTAIN BATTLEFIELD

Beverly, (304) 637-7424

Site of July 11, 1861 battle. Confederate earthworks, historical marker, monument, interpretive sign, rocks with inscriptions carved by veterans. Visitor center located in Bushrod Crawford Building in town. Nearby **CAMP GARNETT** has extensive entrenchments, with trail and sign.

13. THOSE WHO SERVED WAR MUSEUM

Princeton, (304) 487-8397

800 items on display include war relics and personal effects from Civil War through Iraq, with emphasis on WWII.

14. TU-ENDIE-WEI STATE PARK (POINT PLEASANT BATTLE MONUMENT)

Point Pleasant
(304) 675-0869

Site of Battle of Point Pleasant, Oct. 10, 1774, between militia and Shawnee Indians. **MANSION HOUSE** (open May-Oct.) has relics from battle. 84-ft. granite obelisk honors 75 militiamen KIA.

15. WEST VIRGINIA INDEPENDENCE HALL MUSEUM

Wheeling, (304) 238-1300

Former Custom House considered the Civil War birthplace of West Virginia. Restored rooms, film. Civil War exhibit includes 3-D maps, artifacts and audiovisual displays.

> **DID YOU KNOW?**
> A naval battle was fought in West Virginia waters during the Civil War. U.S. Navy armored steamers were actively engaged in the Battle of Buffington Island near Ravenswood on July 19, 1863.

WISCONSIN

Aircraft aficionados will enjoy the aviation history the Badger State has to offer, particularly the six sites that include military aircraft on display. WWII history exhibits cover submarine-building during the war at the Wisconsin Maritime Museum and the five WWII-era buildings displayed at the Fort McCoy Commemorative Area, History Center & Equipment Park.

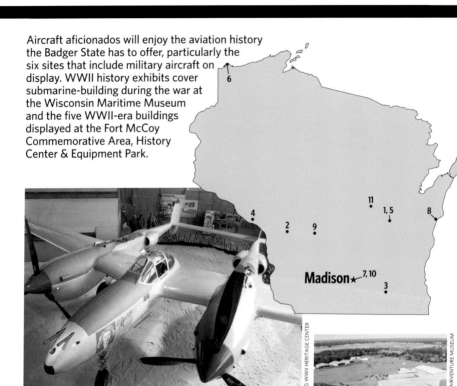

Richard I. Bong WWII Heritage Center, Superior

EAA AirVenture Museum, Oshkosh

1. EAA AIRVENTURE MUSEUM
Oshkosh, (920) 426-4818

Eagle Hangar features Warbirds Gallery, covering WWII with 8 aircraft, including Allied fighters and bombers, Army and Navy aircraft, and enemy planes. Temporary exhibit gallery, immersion theater and scale model of aircraft carrier *USS Enterprise* with 58 aircraft and 500 handmade figures.

2. FORT MCCOY COMMEMORATIVE AREA, HISTORY CENTER & EQUIPMENT PARK
Fort McCoy (Sparta) (608) 388-2407

Commemorative Area features 5 WWII-era buildings, 3 furnished to depict soldier life and 2 with displays on the history of the fort and WWII. History Center details the role of the fort in WWI, WWII, Korea, the Persian Gulf War and more. Both open by appointment only to groups of 20 or more. Outdoor Equipment Park includes more than 50 pieces—such as helicopters, howitzers and tanks—and is open to the public.

3. HOARD HISTORICAL MUSEUM
Fort Atkinson, (920) 563-7769

Includes displays on the Black Hawk War (1832) and the Civil War.

4. MEMORIAL PARK
Arcadia, (608) 323-2319

Park includes Soldiers Walk, featuring 6 war memorials, at least 12 war-related memorials and statues, a tank, howitzer and F-16 fighter jet.

Wisconsin Veterans Museum I, Madison

5. MILITARY VETERANS MUSEUM

Oshkosh, (920) 426-8615

Covers all branches of service and wars from Revolutionary War through the present. Exhibits include jeeps, weapons and uniforms.

6. RICHARD I. BONG WWII HERITAGE CENTER

Superior, (715) 392-7151

Features restored P-38 Lightning; displays, sounds and interactive exhibits on bombing of Pearl Harbor and war's impact on the home front; information maps, timelines and interactive exhibits on both WWII theaters; theater; and library.

7. WISCONSIN HISTORICAL MUSEUM

Madison, (608) 264-6555

Military artifacts include firearms, swords, equipment and accessories dating back to pre-Civil War militia units.

8. WISCONSIN MARITIME MUSEUM

Manitowoc, (920) 684-0218

Exhibit on submarine-building during WWII. Adjacent is *USS Cobia*, a WWII submarine open for tours.

9. WISCONSIN NATIONAL GUARD MEMORIAL LIBRARY AND MUSEUM

Camp Douglas, (608) 427-1280

Exhibits trace state military history from early 19th century to present. Special emphasis on 32nd Infantry Division. Two rooms profile Wisconsin Air National Guard. Vietnam, deployments to Germany and Persian Gulf War also are covered. Aircraft, artillery and tanks on static display.

10. WISCONSIN VETERANS MUSEUM I

Madison, (608) 267-1799

Covers state units from Civil War through Persian Gulf War with battle dioramas. Three aircraft suspended from ceiling over other displays, scale models of military ships and 17 bronze figures of Wisconsin veterans.

11. WISCONSIN VETERANS MUSEUM II

King (King Veterans Home) (608) 267-1799

Artifacts from WWI through Vietnam. Emphasizes 32nd Division.

WYOMING

Army forts and Indian battlefields tie many of the frontier sites in Wyoming together. Fort Phil Kearny State Historic Site has a fascinating past, with the bloodiest history of any Western fort. The Equality State also features the Museum of the Mountain Man covering the fur trade, and the Buffalo Bill Historical Center with a vast collection of firearms.

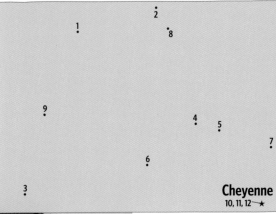

Cheyenne
10, 11, 12 →★

Ruins at Fort Fred Steele State Historic Site, Rawlins

1. BUFFALO BILL HISTORICAL CENTER
Cody, (307) 587-4771

Five-museum complex covers more than 300,000 square feet and three levels. Features Whitney Gallery of Western Art, Draper Museum of Natural History, Buffalo Bill Museum (life of Bill Cody and pioneer culture of western frontier), Plains Indian Museum (cultural history and artistry) and Cody Firearms Museum (more than 6,000 firearms, with world's largest collection of American West firearms).

2. CONNOR BATTLEFIELD STATE HISTORIC SITE
Ranchester, (307) 684-7629

Site of 1865 Powder River Expedition. Monument, interpretive signs.

3. FORT BRIDGER STATE HISTORIC SITE
Fort Bridger, (307) 782-3842

Established in 1843 as emigrant supply stop along Oregon Trail, later occupied by Mormons. Served as military post from 1858 to 1890. Partially restored fort, reconstructed trading post, museum in 1888 stone barracks building.

4. FORT CASPAR MUSEUM
Casper, (307) 235-8462

Now-reconstructed fort housed Army troops intermittently, 1858-67. Museum covers social and natural history of fort, city of Casper and central Wyoming, including military history of area. Markers on Battle of Red Buttes.

5. FORT FETTERMAN STATE HISTORIC SITE
Douglas, (307) 684-7629

Served as major supply point for Army operations against Indians, 1867-82. Partially restored fort, ruins, interpretive exhibits, interpretive trail with signage. Historical guided tours by appointment.

> ✳ ✳ ✳
> **DID YOU KNOW?**
> In the 40 years Fort Laramie was garrisoned, it was "attacked" only once. In the summer of 1864, 30 mounted Indians rode onto the parade ground and drove off the horses of a small cavalry patrol that had just returned. The horses were never recovered.

FORT FRED STEELE STATE HISTORIC SITE

Fort Laramie National Historic Site, Fort Laramie

Cody Firearms Museum at Buffalo Bill Historical Center, Cody

Fort Fetterman State Historic Site, Douglas

6. Fort Fred Steele State Historic Site

Rawlins, (307) 320-3013

Guarded transcontinental Union Pacific Railroad against Indian attack, 1868-86. Fort ruins.

7. Fort Laramie National Historic Site

Fort Laramie, (307) 837-2221

One of America's most important locations in the history of westward expansion and Indian resistance. Established in 1834 as fur-trading post; fort used by U.S. Army to protect emigrants along Oregon Trail, 1849-90. Staging area for Indian campaigns. Extensively restored fort, including 21 buildings and visitor center/museum.

8. Fort Phil Kearny State Historic Site

Story, (307) 684-7629

Established in 1866 to protect travelers on Bozeman Trail. Bloodiest history of any Western fort—attacked by Indians repeatedly and burned down. Interpretive center, self-guided tours of fort with building locations, archeological remains and interpretive signage. Includes battlefields:

Fetterman Fight Battlefield

Site of December 1866 battle in which all 81 soldiers were killed. Interpretation at Fort Phil Kearny visitor center. Interpretive trail through battlefield.

Wagon Box Fight Battlefield

Site of August 1867 battle with Sioux Indians. Interpretation at Fort Phil Kearny visitor center. Interpretive trail through battlefield, monument and plaque.

9. Museum of the Mountain Man

Pinedale, (307) 367-4101

Museum's 15,000 square feet cover history of Rocky Mountain fur-trade era with exhibits on fur trade, western exploration and early settlement of western Wyoming. Research library. Excellent coverage of "mountain men."

10. Warren ICBM & Heritage Museum

F.E. Warren AFB (Cheyenne) (307) 773-2980

Covers history of missiles and 90th Space Wing, and life of people stationed at the post/base from 1867 to present. Accessible only with military ID.

11. Wyoming State Museum

Cheyenne, (307) 777-7022

Permanent exhibit tells story of military in Wyoming, especially early Army forts along historic trails. Some traveling exhibits on Wyoming during WWII. Also, history of F.E. Warren Air Force Base and items from Persian Gulf War.

12. Wyoming Veterans Memorial Museum

Cheyenne, (307) 265-7372

Established 2002. Includes artifacts and memorabilia from all conflicts in which Wyoming residents participated, frontier times through present. Housed in 1942 servicemen's club.

CANADA

Eastern Canada was the scene of numerous American military actions beginning in 1613 and ending in 1870. Most were an extension of colonial wars with the French and national wars against the British. But added to the mix were a bizarre batch of private martial enterprises.

As British citizens, American colonists waged war in French Canada up through 1762. During the Revolutionary War and the War of 1812, U.S. armies invaded Canada to strike at the British. Then there were the "freelance" campaigns conducted by American pirates in the 1620s, American privateers during the

Revolution, "Patriots" (private U.S. citizens who favored annexation and illegally crossed into Ontario) in 1838 and members of the Fenian Brotherhood (the U.S. arm of the Irish Republican Brotherhood) in 1866 and 1870. All these later efforts were directed at unseating British authority in Canada.

Parks Canada, the national park system, preserves many sites of interest relevant to U.S. military history. Only historical markers remember other battle sites. Naturally, the Canadian/British perspective is emphasized. Nevertheless, a venture north of the border is well worth the time.

NHSC = National Historic Site of Canada

Carleton Martello Tower NHSC, Saint John

Fort Beausejour NHSC, Sackville

Fort Howe Lookout, Saint John

NEW BRUNSWICK

1. CARLETON MARTELLO TOWER NHSC
Saint John, (506) 636-4011
Involved in Fenian incursions (1866 & 1870) and Maine border dispute (Aroostook "War," 1838-39). Restored powder magazine and barracks room, plus exhibits.

2. FORT BEAUSEJOUR NHSC
Sackville, (506) 364-5080
Captured by 2,000 New England troops in 1755 during French & Indian War. Called Fort Cumberland under British, with minor fighting in 1776. Restored ruins and museum in visitor center.

3. FORT GASPAREAUX NHSC
Port Elgin, (506) 364-5080
Capitulated without a shot in 1755 during French & Indian War. Ruins of fort, cairn (memorial) and cemetery.

4. FORT HOWE LOOKOUT
Saint John, (506) 658-2855
American privateers burned Fort Frederick (circa 1758) in 1775 and raided town in 1777. Reconstructed 1778 Fort Howe blockhouse.

5. ST. ANDREWS BLOCKHOUSE NHSC
St. Andrews, (506) 529-4270 or 636-4011
Involved in War of 1812, Fenian incursions (1866 & 1870) and Maine border dispute (1838-39). Restored blockhouse, cannons.

Signal Hill NHSC, St. John's

Castle Hill NHSC, Placentia

Silent Witness Memorial, Gander

NEWFOUNDLAND/ LABRADOR

6. CASTLE HILL NHSC
Placentia, (709) 227-2401

British attacked town in 1692 during King William's War (1689-97). British garrisoned from 1713-1811. Restored Fort Royal, visitor center.

✳   ✳   ✳
DID YOU KNOW?
Signal Hill is where Guglielmo Marconi, one of the inventors of radio, received the first transatlantic wireless signal on Dec. 12, 1901. Cabot Tower at Signal Hill NHSC features a Marconi exhibit.

---

7. SIGNAL HILL NHSC
St. John's, (709) 772-5367

Site of the last battle of the French & Indian War, Sept. 18, 1762, at **FORT WILLIAM:** Massachusetts troops and Royal American Regiment participated. Fort William also was attacked by the French in 1696 in King William's War (1689-97), 1708 in Queen Anne's War (1702-13) and earlier in 1762. It was garrisoned between 1618-1779.

In WWII, the U.S. Army maintained an anti-aircraft battery on the hill. Includes interpretation center, Queen's Battery, powder magazine and Soldiers' Canteen. A spectacular view of the city.

8. SILENT WITNESS MEMORIAL
Gander, (709) 651-5928 or 5927

Dedicated June 24, 1990, in Peacekeepers Park to the memory of 248 soldiers of the 101st Airborne Division and 8 civilian crew members killed in a 1985 aircraft crash returning from peacekeeping duties in the Sinai Desert.

9. QUIDI VIDI BATTERY PROVINCIAL HISTORIC SITE
St. John's, (709) 729-2977

Constructed to ward off possible U.S. attack during War of 1812. Reconstructed coastal battery.

N. TILESTON/PARKS CANADA

Fort Anne NHSC, Annapolis Royal

PARKS CANADA

Fortress of Louisbourg NHSC, Louisbourg

NOVA SCOTIA

10. Canso Islands NHSC
Canso, (902) 295-2069
Fortified New England fishing station. Raided by pirates in 1684, attacked by Micmac Indians several times in the early 1720s and 1744 (King George's War), and raided by John Paul Jones in 1776. Visitor center with artifacts, dioramas and audiovisual presentation.
Grassy Island Fort NHSC was a French fort destroyed by British in 1744. Two New England companies garrisoned temporarily in 1745. Panel on island.

11. Deadman's Island Historic Park
Halifax Harbor (Northwest Arm), (902) 490-5946
Maintained by Halifax Regional Municipality. A 6x8-ft. bronze memorial plaque on a granite base (courtesy of VA) was dedicated June 23, 2005, to the 195 American POWs who died in the military prison on nearby Melville Island during the War of 1812. Their names and hometowns appear on the plaque.

12. Fort Anne NHSC
Annapolis Royal
(902) 532-2397
Canada's oldest national historic site. Fort includes earthworks and officers barracks with museum (2 rooms devoted to sieges). Captured by English in 1710 during Queen Anne's War.
At Carleton Corner, near Bridgeton, a historical marker designates the first and second battles of Bloody Creek in 1711 (50 New England/British soldiers KIA) and 1757 (18 British KIA) by Indians and Acadians.

13. Fort Edward NHSC
Windsor, (902) 532-2321 or 798-4706
Canada's oldest surviving blockhouse, 1750. Involved in French & Indian War but never besieged.

14. Fortress of Louisbourg NHSC
Louisbourg, (902) 733-2280
Scene of major fighting in 1745 (4,000 New England troops in King George's War) and 1758 (including 500 Rangers in French & Indian War). At 30 square miles, it is the largest reconstructed 18th century French fortified town in North America. Visitor center (diorama on fort).
"Ruins Walk" includes 2 panels that mention the sieges, and a memorial to the 1,200 Americans who died during the 1745-46 occupation and were buried at Rochefort Point.
Remains of battlefield encampments, trenches, hospitals and store houses.
Interpretive panels at Kennington Cove, The Royal Battery and Lighthouse Point. These locations are well beyond the grounds of the fortress.

15. GRAND PRÉ NHSC
Grand Pré (outside Wolfville)
(902) 542-3631

Site of 1755 deportation of Acadians. Attacked by British in 1704 (Queen Anne's War) and 1747 (King George's War). French killed 71 New England troops here in 1747: historical marker. Visitor center has exhibit on battle with narrative.

16. HALIFAX CITADEL NHSC
Halifax, (902) 426-5080

British military base, circa 1856. Army museum. Fortress Halifax-Warden of the North (a 6-room exhibit) includes display cases relevant to U.S.

17. POINT PLEASANT PARK
Halifax, (902) 426-5080

185-acre coastal park harbors the **PRINCE OF WALES TOWER NHSC** (1796), plus several artillery battery remains. Several memorials located along Sailors Memorial Way. Plaque to the War of 1812 naval battle between the *HMS Shannon* and *USS Chesapeake* (74 U.S. KIA).

18. PORT ROYAL NHSC
Annapolis Royal
(902) 532-2898 or 2321

Reconstruction of first French settlement in Canada (1605). Burned by Virginians in 1613.

Prince of Wales Tower NHSC at Point Pleasant Park, Halifax

Port Royal NHSC, Annapolis Royal

✳   ✳   ✳
DID YOU KNOW?
Queen Anne's War (1702-1713) and King George's War (1744-1748), which both figured prominently in Nova Scotia history, were part of a series of four French and Indian wars fought between France and Great Britain for control of the North American continent. The first in the series was King William's War (1689-1697), and the last was the French & Indian War (1754-1763).

Halifax Citadel NHSC, Halifax

Canadian War Museum, Ottawa

ONTARIO

19. BATTLE OF THE WINDMILL NHSC
Prescott, (418) 648-7016
Site of a 5-day battle in November 1838 involving private American citizens who crossed the border during the French-Canadian Rebellion (1837-38). Restored windmill in which the rebels held out, historical markers.

20. BATTLEFIELD HOUSE MUSEUM AND PARK
Stoney Creek (Hamilton) (905) 662-8458
Site of 1813 Battle of Stoney Creek in War of 1812. Battlefield Park of 32 acres with museum, monument, Gage House and cemetery. Maintained by Niagara Parks Commission.

21. CANADIAN WAR MUSEUM
Ottawa, (819) 776-8600
Gallery 1: "Battleground: Wars on Our Soil—Earliest Times to 1885" covers French & Indian War with audiovisual presentation and 3-D model of the Battle of the Plains of Abraham, Revolutionary War invasions, War of 1812 battles, 1837 rebellions and Fenian raids.

22. CHIPPAWA BATTLEFIELD PARK
Niagara Parkway (905) 356-8554
Site of decisive 1814 U.S. victory during War of 1812. Monument and preserved 300-acre battleground. Pathway with interpretive signs. Operated by Niagara Parks Commission.

23. CRYSLER'S FARM BATTLEFIELD MEMORIAL
Near Morrisburg at Upper Canada Village 1-800-437-2233
Site of 1813 British victory. Granite memorial, cannons and Battlefield Memorial Building (mural, audiovisual presentation, artifacts). Maintained by St. Lawrence Parks Commission.

24. DIEFENBUNKER, CANADA'S COLD WAR MUSEUM
Carp, (613) 839-0007
Former Canadian Central Emergency Government Headquarters in a secret nuclear bunker. 100,000-sq.-ft., 4-story building includes the War Cabinet Room and communications facilities.

Fort Wellington NHSC, Prescott

25. OLD FORT ERIE

Fort Erie, (905) 871-0540

Site of 1813-14 battles during War of 1812: a key battlefield in Canada. U.S. occupied in 1814. Fenians occupied ruins in 1866. Completely restored, with war relics, battle re-enactments and monument. Maintained by Niagara Parks Commission.

26. FORT GEORGE NHSC

Niagara-on-the-Lake (905) 468-4257

Continually involved in battles during War of 1812. U.S. captured in 1813. Fully restored to the 1796-1813 period of British army occupation with visitor center.

27. FORT HENRY

Kingston, (613) 542-7388

Original fort built during War of 1812. The later fort was active during the 1838 French-Canadian Rebellion. Restored as a museum of military living history (circa 1867) in 1936. Maintained by St. Lawrence Parks Commission and Parks Canada.

28. FORT MALDEN NHSC

Amherstburg, (519) 736-5416

U.S. occupied site of burned fort ruins in 1813. 1840-era earthworks, 1819 restored brick barracks, exhibition buildings and interpretation center. Focuses on 1837-38 rebellion.

29. FORT ST. JOSEPH NHSC

Richards Landing (705) 246-2664

Burned in 1814 by U.S. troops during War of 1812. Ruins and visitor center.

30. FORT WELLINGTON NHSC

Prescott, (613) 925-2896

Never besieged during the War of 1812. Active in 1838 during French-Canadian Rebellion. Original 1813 fortifications and 1839 blockhouse, officers quarters and other structures. Refurnished to 1846 era of the Royal Canadian Rifle Regiment.

✢　　✢　　✢
Ontario Native: JOHN McCRAE

Lt. Col. John McCrae, a field surgeon during the 2nd Battle of Ypres in WWI, wrote the famous poem *In Flanders Fields* after the burial of a friend killed in the 1915 battle.

The Guelph, Ontario, native also served in the Second Boer War. He died Jan. 28, 1918, after catching pneumonia and meningitis in France while commanding a Canadian army hospital.

McCrae House, Guelph

Fort George NHSC, Niagara-on-the-Lake

31. HISTORIC FORT YORK
Toronto, (416) 392-6907
Captured by U.S. troops on April 27, 1813. Constitutes the largest collection of War of 1812 buildings (8) in Canada, including barracks, blockhouses, powder magazines and officers quarters. Military displays, demonstrations, costumed interpreters and tours.

32. LUNDY'S LANE HISTORICAL MUSEUM
Niagara Falls, (905) 358-5082
On the site of the 1814 Battle of Lundy's Lane, which ended in a draw. Holds a significant collection of War of 1812 artifacts. Drummond Hill Cemetery includes American graves.

33. McCRAE HOUSE
Guelph, (519) 836-1221
Birthplace of WWI Lt. Col. John McCrae, author of the poem *In Flanders Fields*. Exhibits depict his military and medical careers.

34. NANCY ISLAND PROVINCIAL HISTORIC SITE
Wasaga Beach, (705) 429-2728
Final naval battle of the War of 1812 in North America, Aug. 14, 1814. Involved *USS Niagara, Tigress* and *Scorpion*. Preserved hull of *HMS Nancy* and museum on Nancy Island within Wasaga Beach Provincial Park.

35. POINT PELEE NATIONAL PARK
Leamington, (519) 322-2365
Site of May 28, 1763 ambush during Pontiac's Rebellion in which 50 British/colonial (Royal American Regiment) soldiers were killed by Indians. Historical marker only.

36. QUEENSTON HEIGHTS NHSC
Niagara-on-the-Lake (905) 468-4257
Site of October 1812 battle. Brock's Monument and surrounding park. Fort Drummond was a redoubt and battery. Battlefield walking tour with self-guiding brochure and interpretive markers.

37. TECUMSEH PARK
Thamesville, 1-888-773-8888
Site of 1813 Battle of the Thames (Moraviantown) during War of 1812. Monument to Shawnee Indian chief only. There is no mention of the decisive U.S. victory here.

Fort Chambly NHSC, Chambly

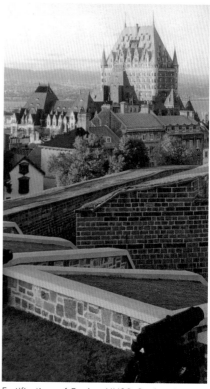

QUEBEC CITY AND AREA TOURISM AND CONVENTION BUREAU

P. ST. JACQUES/PARKS CANADA

The Citadel of Quebec, Quebec City

Fortifications of Quebec NHSC, Quebec City

QUEBEC

38. ARTILLERY PARK HERITAGE SITE

Quebec City, (418) 648-4205

Central to French defense network during Queen Anne's War (1702-13) and French & Indian War. Restored Arsenal Foundry with interpretation center, 4-story Dauphine Redoubt with barracks and exhibits, and officers quarters.

39. BATTLE OF THE CHATEAUGUAY NHSC

Howick, (450) 829-2003

Site of 1813 battle with mixed force in War of 1812. Canadian monument and interpretation center with documentary film, dioramas and exhibits.

40. BATTLE OF THE RESTIGOUCHE NHSC

Pointe-a-la-Croix
(418) 788-5676

Site of French & Indian War's last naval battle, on the Restigouche River, on July 8, 1760. Royal Navy defeated a French relief fleet. Parts of French frigate *Machault* are on display in the Interpretation Center. Documentary film.

41. THE CITADEL OF QUEBEC

Quebec City, (418) 694-2815

Battles in 1629 (Anglo-French War), 1690 (King William's War) and 1775 (Revolutionary War). Old French powder magazine houses Museum of the French-speaking Royal 22nd Regiment. Encompasses Cap Diamont Redoubt (1693), Chapel, Officers Mess, Armory Room and King's Bastion.

42. FORT CHAMBLY NHSC

Chambly, (450) 658-1585

Captured by British in 1760 during French & Indian War. Americans attacked in 1775 and again in War of 1812. Restored to era of 1750 French soldiers. Nearby cemetery contains American remains.

43. FORT LENNOX NHSC

Saint-Paul-de-l'Île-aux-Noix
(450) 291-5700

Captured by British in 1760 during French & Indian War (200 Rogers Rangers attacked island earlier); Americans occupied 1775-76. Naval shipyard during War of 1812. Actual fort ruins date from 1819-29 period with officers quarters, guardhouse, powder magazine, barracks and commissary. Only a small, silver memorial marker on the north end of the island mentions Americans.

Diorama at Musée du Fort, Quebec City

44. FORTIFICATIONS OF QUEBEC NHSC
Quebec City, (418) 648-7016
Involved in French & Indian War. Includes interpretive center, powder magazine, redoubt, battery, ramparts, Artillery Park and The Citadel (see **THE CITADEL OF QUEBEC**).

45. LACOLLE RIVER BLOCKHOUSE PROVINCIAL HISTORIC SITE
Saint-Paul-de-l'Île-aux-Noix (450) 246-3227
Site of the 1814 Battle of LaColle Mill and 1838 Battle of Odelltown (the last of the French-Canadian Rebellion). Restored blockhouse with displays.

46. LEVIS FORTS NHSC
Levis, (418) 835-5182
Fort No. 1 was built between 1865 and 1872 to protect against a potential U.S. invasion, but was never garrisoned. Restored fort with casemates, barracks and underground passageways. Multimedia exhibit on fort history. Guided tours.

Montmorency Falls Park, Beauport

47. MONTMORENCY FALLS PARK
Beauport, (418) 663-3330
Site of 1759 Battle of Montmorency Gorge during French & Indian War. 200 Royal American Regiment (3rd Battalion) members participated. Redoubt, trail marked with 5 plaques erected by Quebec Provincial Parks. Magnificent view of waterfalls.

48. MUSÉE DU FORT
Quebec City, (418) 692-2175
Sight-and-sound diorama depicts the city's 6 sieges (1629-1775).

49. MUSÉE DU FORT SAINT-JEAN
St. Jean, (450) 358-6777
In former Protestant chapel on campus of closed College Royal Militaire de St. Jean. Site of 1775 battles. Includes artifacts from old Fort St. Jean, plus displays on American Revolution.

National Battlefields Park, Quebec City

50. NATIONAL BATTLEFIELDS PARK

Quebec City, (418) 648-4071

250 acres encompass the site of the French & Indian War's 1759 Battle of the Plains of Abraham and the 1760 Battle of Sainte Foy (**DES BRAVES PARK**). 400 Rogers Rangers (6 companies) participated in the Quebec campaign; the 2nd Battalion (New York) of the Royal American Regiment fought on the Plains and at Ste. Foy.

THE DISCOVERY PAVILION, *(418) 649-6157*, includes exhibits on the 1759-60 battles, displays on Revolutionary War invasion and multimedia show.

QUEBEC MARTELLO TOWERS are British sandstone fortifications, circa 1808-12. No. 1 Tower has exhibits on battles of 1759, 1760 and 1775.

51. NAVAL MUSEUM

Quebec City, (418) 694-5387

Focuses mostly on Canadian naval operations against German submarines prowling near the Gulf of St. Lawrence during WWII.

© MINISTÈRE DU TOURISME DU QUÉBEC / PIERRE LAMBERT

Place Royale/Royale Battery, Quebec City

52. THE STEWART MUSEUM AT THE FORT

Montreal, (514) 861-6701

Erected between 1820-24 to defend against possible U.S. aggression. Barracks, armory, arsenal, blockhouse, powder magazine. Museum contains military artifacts. There was no fighting during the French & Indian War near here, but fighting occurred in Montreal in 1775. A Fenian blockhouse from 1866 is on site.

53. PLACE ROYALE/ROYALE BATTERY

Quebec City, (418) 646-3167

Built to counter New England troops in 1690 in King William's War. 10 cannons with plaques on display in the small park.

> **DID YOU KNOW?**
> Surrounded by a defense system of stone walls, Quebec City is the only remaining fortified city in North America.

LEARN MORE

Barbour, R.L. *South Carolina's Revolutionary War Battlefields*. Gretna, La.: Pelican Publishing Company, Inc., 2002.

Barefoot, Daniel W. *Touring North Carolina's Revolutionary War Sites*. Winston-Salem, N.C.: John F. Blair, Publisher, 1998.

———. *Touring South Carolina's Revolutionary War Sites*. Winston-Salem, N.C.: John F. Blair, Publisher, 1999.

Bell, Fred L. *Army Museums West of the Mississippi*. Grants Pass, Ore.: Hellgate Press, 1997.

Butcher, Russell D. *Exploring Our National Historic Parks and Sites*. Lanham, Md.: Roberts Rinehart Publishers, 1997.

Civil War Preservation Trust. *Civil War Sites: The Official Guide to Battlefields, Monuments, and More*. Ed. Sarah Richards. Guilford, Conn.: The Globe Pequot Press, 2003.

The Civil War Trust. *Frommer's The Civil War Trust's Official Guide to the Civil War Discovery Trail*. Ed. Susan Collier Braselton. N.Y.: Macmillan Publishing Company, 1996.

Coffin, Howard, et al. *Guns Over the Champlain Valley: A Guide to Historic Military Sites and Battlefields*. Woodstock, Vt.: The Countryman Press, 2005.

Collins, Gilbert. *Guidebook to the Historic Sites of the War of 1812*. Toronto, Ontario: Dundurn Press, 1998.

The Conservation Fund. *The Civil War Battlefield Guide*. Boston: Houghton Mifflin Co., 1998.

Di Ionno, Mark. *A Guide to New Jersey's Revolutionary War Trail*. New Brunswick, N.J.: Rutgers University Press, 2001.

Eicher, David J. *Civil War Battlefields: A Touring Guide*. Lanham, Md.: Taylor Trade Pub., 1995.

Ferris, Robert G. *Soldier and Brave: Historic Places Associated with Indian Affairs and Indian Wars in the Trans-Mississippi West*. Washington: U.S. Department of the Interior, 1971.

Gelbert, Doug. *American Revolutionary War Sites, Memorials, Museums and Library Collections: A State-by-State Guidebook to Places Open to the Public*. Jefferson, N.C.: McFarland & Co., Inc., 1998.

———. *Civil War Sites, Memorials, Museums and Library Collections: A State-by-State Guidebook to Places Open to the Public*. Jefferson, N.C.: McFarland & Co., Inc., 1997.

Gleason, Michael P. *The Insiders' Guide to Civil War Sites in the Eastern Theater*. Manteo, N.C.: Insiders' Publishing Inc., 1997.

Groneman, Bill. *Battlefields of Texas*. Plano: Republic of Texas Press, 1998.

Hedren, Paul L. *Traveler's Guide to the Great Sioux War: The Battlefields, Forts, and Related Sites of America's Greatest Indian War*. Helena, Mont.: Montana State Historical Society Press, 1996.

Hoig, Stan. *A Travel Guide to the Plains Indian Wars*. Albuquerque: University of New Mexico Press, 2006.

Johnson, Clint. *In the Footsteps of J.E.B. Stuart*. Winston-Salem, N.C.: John F. Blair, Publisher, 2003.

———. *In the Footsteps of Robert E. Lee*. Winston-Salem, N.C.: John F. Blair, Publisher, 2001.

———. *In the Footsteps of Stonewall Jackson*. Winston-Salem, N.C.: John F. Blair, Publisher, 2002.

———. *Touring the Carolinas' Civil War Sites*. Winston-Salem, N.C.: John F. Blair, Publisher, 1996.

———. *Touring Virginia's and West Virginia's Civil War Sites.* Winston-Salem, N.C.: John F. Blair, Publisher, 1999.

Jones, Charles A. *Hawaii's World War II Military Sites: A Comprehensive Guide Focusing on O'ahu.* Honolulu: Mutual Publishing, 2002.

Kramb, Edwin A. *Buckeye Battlefields.* Springboro, Ohio: Valhalla Press, 1999.

McDermott, John D. *A Guide to the Indian Wars of the West—Over 100 Historic Sites in 17 States.* Lincoln: University of Nebraska Press, 1998.

McKay, John. *Civil War Sites in the Southern States.* 3rd ed. Guilford, Conn.: The Globe Pequot Press, 2005.

Miller, Arthur & Marjorie. *Pennsylvania Battlefields & Military Landmarks.* Mechanicsburg, Pa.: Stackpole Books, 2000.

The National Parks: Index 2005-2007. Washington: U.S. Department of the Interior, 2005.

Newark, Tim. *In Heroes' Footsteps: A Walker's Guide to the Battlefields of the World.* Hauppauge, N.Y.: Barron's, 2001.

Newark, Tim. *Where They Fell: A Walker's Guide to the Battlefields of the World.* Hauppauge, N.Y.: Barron's, 2000.

Nishiura, Elizabeth. *American Battle Monuments: A Guide to Battlefields & Cemeteries of the U.S. Armed Forces.* Detroit: Omnigraphics, Inc., 1989.

Phillips, R. Cody. *A Guide to U.S. Army Museums.* Washington: Center of Military History, 2005.

Rajtar, Steve. *Indian War Sites: A Guidebook to Battlefields, Monuments and Memorials— State by State with Canada and Mexico.* Jefferson, N.C.: McFarland, 1999.

Rajtar, Steve and Frances Elizabeth Franks. *War Monuments, Museums, and Library Collections of 20th Century Conflicts: A Directory of United States Sites.* Jefferson, N.C.: McFarland & Company, Inc., Publishers, 2002.

The Reader's Digest Association, Inc. *Explore America: Forts and Battlefields.* Pleasantville, N.Y.: Reader's Digest, 1997.

Robinson, Charles M. III. *Texas and the Mexican War.* Austin: Texas State Historical Association, 2004.

Sarles, Frank B. Jr. & Charles E. Shedd. *Colonials and Patriots: Historic Places Commemorating Our Forebears, 1700-1783.* Washington: U.S. Department of the Interior, 1964.

Shively, Julie. *The Ideals Guide to American Civil War Places.* Nashville, Tenn.: Ideals Publications, 1999.

———. *The Ideals Guide to Places of the American Revolution.* Nashville, Tenn.: Ideals Publications, 2001.

Silber, Nina. *Landmarks of the Civil War.* N.Y.: Oxford University Press, 2003.

Stevens, Joseph E. *America's National Battlefield Parks: A Guide.* Oklahoma City: University of Oklahoma Press, 1991.

Swift, Robert B. *The Mid-Appalachian Frontier: A Guide to Historic Sites of the French and Indian War.* Gettysburg, Pa.: Thomas Publications, 2001.

Thompson, Bryce D. *U.S. Military Museums, Historic Sites & Exhibits.* Falls Church, Va.: Military Living Publications, 1992.

Thompson, Chuck. *The 25 Best World War II Sites: Pacific Theater—The Ultimate Traveler's Guide to Battlefields, Monuments and Museums.* San Francisco: Greenline Publications, 2002.

Thum, Marcella and Gladys Thum. *Exploring Military America.* N.Y.: Atheneum, 1982.

Unrau, Harlan D. *Here Was the Revolution: Historic Sites of the War for American Independence.* Washington: U.S. Department of the Interior, 1976.

FIND SITES

Fort Dix Museum: 82
Fort Dobbs State Historic Site: 100
Fort Dodge Museum & Frontier Village: 41
Fort Donelson National Battlefield: 128
Fort Dorchester: 173
Fort Douglas Military Museum: 140
Fort Drum Historical Holding: 91
Fort Duffield: 46
Fort Duncan Museum: 135
Fort Dupont State Park: 21
Fort Duquesne: 118
Fort Edgecomb State Historic Site: 52
Fort Edward NHSC: 173
Fort Edwards: 164
Fort Erie NHSC: 176
Fort Fetterman State Historic Site: 168
Fort Fisher State Historic Site: 100
Fort Flagler State Park: 157
Fort Foote Park: 56
Fort Foster Park: 52
Fort Foster State Historic Site: 24
Fort Fred Steele State Historic Site: 169
Fort Frederica National Monument: 29
Fort Frederick State Park: 56
Fort Gadsden Historic Site: 24
Fort Gaines Historic Site: 6
Fort Garland Museum: 17
Fort Gaspareaux NHSC: 171
Fort George G. Meade Museum: 56
Fort George NHSC: 176
Fort George: 52
Fort Gibson Historic Site: 109
Fort Griffin State Park & Historic Site: 135
Fort Griswold Battlefield State Park: 19
Fort Halifax State Historic Site: 52
Fort Hancock: 83
Fort Harker Museum: 42
Fort Harrison: 152
Fort Hartsuff State Historical Park: 78
Fort Hays State Historic Site: 42
Fort Henry: 164
Fort Henry: 176
Fort Howe Lookout: 171
Fort Huachuca Historical Museum: 10
Fort Humboldt State Historic Park: 14
Fort Independence: 61
Fort Jackson Museum: 123
Fort Jackson: 49
Fort Jefferson National Monument: 24
Fort Jesup State Historic Site: 49
Fort Kaskaskia State Historic Site: 36
Fort Kearny State Historical Park: 78
Fort Kent State Historic Site: 52
Fort King George State Historic Site: 29
Fort Klamath Museum: 111
Fort Knox State Historic Site: 52
Fort Lancaster State Historic Site: 135
Fort Laramie National Historic Site: 169

Fort Larned National Historic Site: 43
Fort Laurens State Memorial: 106
Fort LeBoeuf Museum: 115
Fort Lee Historic Park: 83
Fort Lennox NHSC: 179
Fort Lewis Military Museum: 157
Fort Ligonier: 115
Fort Lincoln: 59
Fort Loudon: 115
Fort Loudoun State Historic Park: 129
Fort Lowell Museum: 10
Fort Mackinac: 65
Fort Macon State Park: 100
Fort Madison: 52
Fort Malden NHSC: 176
Fort Marcy: 145
Fort Massac State Park: 37
Fort Massachusetts: 69
Fort Matanzas National Monument: 24
Fort McAllister State Historic Park: 29
Fort McClary State Historic Site: 52
Fort McCoy Commemorative Area, History Center & Equipment Park: 166
Fort McHenry National Monument & Historic Shrine: 56
Fort McKavett State Historic Site: 135
Fort McKinley: 52
Fort Meigs State Memorial: 106
Fort Mifflin: 115
Fort Miles Historical Area: 21
Fort Milroy: 163
Fort Mims: 6
Fort Monroe: 144
Fort Montgomery State Historic Site: 91
Fort Morgan State Historic Site: 6
Fort Morris State Historic Site: 29
Fort Mott State Park: 83
Fort Moultrie National Monument: 123
Fort Mulligan: 164
Fort Nashborough: 129
Fort Nathan Hale: 19
Fort Necessity National Battlefield: 115
Fort Nonsense: 84
Fort Norfolk: 145
Fort O'Brien State Historic Site: 52
Fort Ontario State Historic Site: 91
Fort Osage: 72
Fort Pentagoet: 52
Fort Phantom Hill: 135
Fort Phil Kearny State Historic Site: 169
Fort Phoenix: 62
Fort Pickens: 25
Fort Pickering: 62
Fort Pike State Historic Site: 49
Fort Pillow State Historic Park: 129
Fort Pitt Blockhouse: 118
Fort Pitt Museum: 118
Fort Point National Historic Site: 14
Fort Point State Park: 52

Fort Polk Military Museum: 49
Fort Popham State Historic Site: 53
Fort Pownall: 52
Fort Preble: 53
Fort Pulaski National Monument: 29
Fort Putnam: 96
Fort Raleigh National Historic Site: 101
Fort Randall: 126
Fort Randolph: 164
Fort Recovery State Memorial: 107
Fort Richardson State Historic Park: 136
Fort Ridgely State Historic Site: 67
Fort Riley Regimental Museum: 43
Fort Roberdeau Historic Site: 115
Fort Robinson State Park: 78
Fort Rodman: 62
Fort Royal: 172
Fort Sam Houston Museum: 136
Fort Scammel: 53
Fort Scott National Historic Site: 43
Fort Sedgwick Museum: 17
Fort Selden State Monument: 86
Fort Sewall: 62
Fort Sherman Museum: 34
Fort Sidney Complex: 78
Fort Simcoe State Park: 157
Fort Sisseton State Park: 126
Fort Smith National Historic Site: 11
Fort St. Clair Park: 107
Fort St. Frederic: 90
Fort St. Jean Baptiste State Historic Site: 49
Fort St. Joseph Museum: 65
Fort St. Joseph NHSC: 176
Fort Standish: 62
Fort Stanwix National Monument: 92
Fort Stark Historic Site: 81
Fort Stevens State Park: 112
Fort Stevens: 145
Fort Stevens: 161
Fort Stewart Museum: 30
Fort Stockton: 136
Fort Sullivan: 51
Fort Sumner State Monument: 87
Fort Sumter National Monument: 123
Fort Supply Historic Site: 109
Fort Taber Park: 62
Fort Tejon State Historic Park: 14
Fort Ticonderoga: 92
Fort Totten State Historic Site: 104
Fort Totten: 161
Fort Towson Historic Site: 110
Fort Trumbull State Park: 19
Fort Tyler: 30
Fort Union National Monument: 87
Fort Union Trading Post National Historic Site: 104
Fort Vancouver National Historic Site: 157
Fort Verde State Historic Park: 10

Lundy's Lane Historical Museum: 177

MacArthur Museum of Arkansas Military History: 12

Maine Military Historical Society Museum: 53

Maine State Museum: 53

Major General Frederick Funston Boyhood Home & Museum: 44

Malmstrom Air Force Base Museum: 77

Manassas National Battlefield Park: 148

Mansfield State Historic Site: 50

Marais des Cygnes Massacre State Historic Site: 44

Marcellus Post 4054 Military Museum: 65

March Field Air Museum: 15

Marine Corps Amphibious Vehicle Museum: 15

Marine Corps Museum: 100

Marine Corps Recruit Depot (MCRD) Command Museum: 15

Mariners' Museum: 148

Maritime Museum of San Diego: 15

Marks' Mills State Park: 12

Maryland Historical Society Museum: 58

Maryland National Guard Museum: 58

Massachusetts National Guard Museum: 63

Mayfield Fort: 148

McChord Air Museum: 157

McCrae House: 177

McDowell Battlefield: 148

Memorial Hall Museum: 63

Memorial Park (Wisconsin): 166

Michigan Historical Museum: 65

Michigan's Own, Inc., Military & Space Museum: 65

Mid-America Air Museum: 44

Mid-Atlantic Air Museum: 117

Middle Creek National Battlefield: 46

Mighty Eighth Air Force Museum: 30

Military Historians Museum: 19

Military Museum of Southern New England: 19

Military Veterans Museum (Wisconsin): 167

Mill Creek Battlefield: 18

Mill Springs Battlefield: 46

Millville Army Air Field Museum: 83

Mine Creek Battlefield State Historic Site: 44

Minisink Battleground Park: 94

Minnesota Air Guard Museum: 67

Minnesota Military Museum: 67

Minute Man National Historical Park: 63

Minuteman Missile National Historic Site: 126

Mississippi Armed Forces Museum: 70

Missouri State Museum: 73

Monmouth Battlefield State Park: 83

Monocacy National Battlefield: 58

Montana Historical Society Museum: 77

Montana's Military History Museum: 77

Montmorency Falls Park: 179

Monument Hill & Kreische Brewery State Historic Site: 137

Moores Creek National Battlefield: 102

Morristown National Historical Park: 84

Motts Military Museum: 107

Mount Gulian: 94

Mount Independence State Historic Site: 142

Mount Vernon: 148

Musée du Fort: 179

Musée du Fort Saint-Jean: 180

Museum of Aviation: 30

Museum of Connecticut History: 20

Museum of Flight: 158

Museum of Florida History: 25

Museum of Florida's Military: 25

Museum of Mississippi History 2012: 70

Museum of Missouri Military History: 73

Museum of Nebraska History: 79

Museum of New Hampshire History: 81

Museum of the Confederacy: 149

Museum of the Fur Trade: 79

Museum of the Kansas National Guard: 44

Museum of the Mountain Man: 169

Museum of the Tuskegee Airmen: 65

Museum of Westward Expansion: 73

Nancy Island Provincial Historic Site: 177

NASA Visitors Center: 149

Nathan Bedford Forrest State Park: 130

National Air & Space Museum: 160

National Air & Space Museum's Steven F. Udvar-Hazy Center: 149

National Atomic Museum: 88

National Battlefields Park: 180

National Civil War Museum: 117

National Cryptologic Museum: 58

National D-Day Memorial: 150

National Guard Memorial Museum: 160

National Guard Militia Museum of New Jersey: 84

National Infantry Museum: 30

National McKinley Birthplace Memorial: 107

National Medal of Honor Memorial: 40

National Memorial Cemetery of the Pacific (Punchbowl): 32

National Memorial Day Museum: 94

National Museum of American Jewish Military History: 160

National Museum of Civil War Medicine: 58

National Museum of Health & Medicine: 160

National Museum of Naval Aviation: 25

National Museum of Nuclear Science & History: 88

National Museum of the Civil War Soldier: 151

National Museum of the Marine Corps: 150

National Museum of the Pacific War: 132

National Prisoner of War Museum: 27

National Purple Heart Hall of Honor: 95

National Vigilance Park and Aerial Reconnaissance Memorial: 58

National WWI Museum at Liberty Memorial: 73

National WWII Memorial: 161

National WWII Museum: 50

Natural Bridge Battlefield Historic State Park: 26

Nauticus, the National Maritime Center: 150

Naval Air Station Wildwood Aviation Museum: 84

Naval Memorial Museum of the Pacific: 156

Naval Museum: 180

Naval Museum of Armament & Technology: 15

Naval Station Norfolk: 150

Naval Undersea Museum: 158

Naval War College Museum: 121

Navy Lakehurst Historical Society Information Center: 84

Nevada State Museum: 80

New England Air Museum: 20

New Hall Military Museum: 117

New Jersey Naval Museum: 85

New Jersey Vietnam Veterans Memorial & Vietnam Era Education Center: 85

New Market Battlefield Historical Park: 151

New Windsor Cantonment State Historic Site: 95

New York State Military Museum: 95

Newtown Battlefield State Park: 94

Nez Perce National Historical Park: 35

Ninety Six National Historic Site: 124

North Carolina Aviation Museum: 102

North Carolina Military History Museum: 102

North Carolina Museum of History: 102

North Dakota Heritage Center: 104

Norwich University Museum: 142

Nu'uanu Pali State Wayside: 32

Octave Chanute Aerospace Museum: 37

Ohio Society of Military History Museum: 107

Oklahoma History Center: 110

Old Barracks Museum: 85

Old Capitol Museum: 70

Old Coast Guard Station Museum: 151
Old Ford Niagara State Historic Site: 95
Old Fort Harrod State Park: 47
Old Fort Jackson: 31
Old Fort Madison: 41
Old Fort Meade Museum: 127
Old Fort Western: 53
Old Guard Museum: 151
Old Idaho Penitentiary State Historic Site: 35
Old State House Museum: 12
Old State House: 63
Old Stone House: 95
Olustee Battlefield Historic State Park: 26
Omar N. Bradley Museum: 118
Oregon Coast History Center: 112
Oregon Historical Society Museum: 112
Oregon Military Museum: 112
Oriskany Battlefield State Historic Site: 95
Pacific Aviation Museum: 33
Pacific Submarine Museum & USS Bowfin Memorial: 33
Palmito Ranch Battlefield: 137
Palo Alto Battlefield National Historic Site: 137
Palo Duro Canyon State Park: 137
Pamplin Historical Park & National Museum of the Civil War Soldier: 151
Pancho Villa State Park: 88
Paoli Massacre Site: 118
Parris Island Museum: 124
Patriot's Point Naval & Maritime Museum: 125
Patton Museum of Cavalry & Armor: 47
Patuxent River Naval Air Museum: 59
Pea Ridge National Military Park: 12
Pecos National Historical Park: 88
Pennsylvania Military Museum: 118
Pennsylvania National Guard Military Museum: 118
Perry's Victory & International Peace Memorial: 107
Perryville Battlefield State Historic Site: 47
Petersburg National Battlefield: 152
Peterson Air & Space Museum: 18
Philippi Covered Bridge: 164
Picacho Peak State Park: 10
Pickett's Mill Battlefield Historic Site: 31
Pigeon Roost State Historic Site: 40
Pima Air & Space Museum: 10
Place Royale/Royale Battery: 180
Planes of Fame Air Museum: 15
Plum Creek Massacre: 78
Point Lookout State Park: 59
Point Pelee National Park: 177
Point Pleasant Battle Monument: 165
Point Pleasant Park: 174

Point State Park: 118
Poison Spring State Park: 12
Port Columbus National Civil War Naval Museum: 31
Port Hudson State Historic Site: 50
Port Royal NHSC: 174
Portland Harbor Museum: 53
Portsmouth Naval Shipyard Museum: 152
Prairie Grove Battlefield State Park: 12
Presidio: 16
Prickett's Fort State Park: 165
Prince of Wales Tower NHSC: 174
Princeton Battlefield State Park: 85
Pueblo Weisbrod Aircraft Museum: 18
Putnam Memorial State Park: 20
Quebec Martello Towers: 180
Queenston Heights NHSC: 177
Quidi Vidi Battery Provincial Historic Site: 172
Red Bank Battlefield Park: 85
Reed Museum: 48
Resaca de la Palma Battlefield: 137
Rich Mountain Battlefield: 165
Richard I. Bong WWII Heritage Center: 167
Richmond National Battlefield Park: 152
Rio Grande Valley Wing CAF Museum: 137
River Raisin Battlefield Visitor Center: 65
Rivers Bridge State Historic Site: 125
Rochefort Point Cemetery: 174
Rock Creek Park: 161
Rock Island Arsenal Museum: 37
Rocky Mountain Museum of Military History: 77
Rosebud Battlefield State Park: 77
Rosie the Riveter/WWII Home Front National Historic Park: 16
Russell Military Museum: 37
Russian Sub Museum: 121
Rutherford B. Hayes Presidential Center: 108
Sabine Pass Battleground State Park & Historic Site: 138
Sackets Harbor Battlefield State Historic Site: 95
Sagamore Hill National Historic Site: 96
Sailor's Creek Battlefield Historic State Park: 153
Salem Cemetery Battlefield: 130
Sampson WWII Naval Museum: 96
San Diego Air & Space Museum: 16
San Jacinto Battleground State Historic Site: 138
San Juan Island National Historic Park: 158
San Marcos de Apalache Historic State Park: 26

San Pasqual Battlefield State Historic Park: 16
Sand Creek Massacre National Historic Site: 18
Saratoga Monument: 96
Saratoga National Historic Park: 96
Savannah History Museum: 31
Selfridge Military Air Museum: 65
Sgt. Alvin C. York State Historic Park: 130
Shiloh National Military Park: 130
Signal Hill NHSC: 172
Silent Witness Memorial: 172
Skenesborough Museum: 96
Slim Buttes Battlefield: 127
Smithsonian National Museum of American History: 161
Soldiers & Sailors National Military Museum & Memorial: 119
Soldiers National Museum: 118
Soldiers' & Sailors' Monument: 40
Soldiers' Memorial Military Museum: 74
South Carolina Confederate Relic Room & Museum: 125
South Carolina Military Museum: 125
South Carolina State Museum: 125
South Dakota Air & Space Museum: 127
South Dakota National Guard Museum: 127
South Dakota State Historical Society Museum: 127
South Mountain State Battlefield: 59
Southern Museum of Civil War & Locomotive History: 31
Southern Museum of Flight: 7
Special Operations Memorial: 26
Springfield Armory National Historic Site: 63
SS Jeremiah O'Brien: 16
SS Red Oak Victory: 16
St. Albans Historical Museum: 142
St. Andrews Blockhouse NHSC: 171
St. Clair's Defeat Memorial: 108
St. Mary's Submarine Museum: 31
Stars & Stripes Museum & Library: 74
State Arsenal Museum: 79
State Historical Society of Iowa Museum: 41
State Museum of Pennsylvania: 119
State National Historic Park: 8
Staunton River Battlefield State Park: 153
Steuben Memorial State Historic Site: 96
Stockdale Soldier Citizen Museum: 37
Stones River National Battlefield: 130
Stonewall Jackson House: 153
Stonewall Jackson Museum at Hupp's Hall: 153
Stonewall Jackson's Headquarters Museum: 153